REACHING PEOPLE

The Structure of Neighborhood Services

SOCIAL SERVICE DELIVERY SYSTEMS

An International Annual

Series Editors

DANIEL THURSZ
School of Social Work and Community Planning
University of Maryland at Baltimore

JOSEPH L. VIGILANTE
School of Social Work
Adelphi University

Editorial Advisory Board

SOCIAL SERVICE DELIVERY SYSTEMS
An International Annual
Volume 3

REACHING PEOPLE

The Structure of Neighborhood Services

Editors
DANIEL THURSZ
and
JOSEPH L. VIGILANTE

SAGE Publications   Beverly Hills / London

For information address:

SAGE PUBLICATIONS, INC.
275 South Beverly Drive
Beverly Hills, California 90212

SAGE PUBLICATIONS LTD
28 Banner Street
London EC1Y 8QE

Printed in the United States of America

International Standard Book Number 0-8039-0817-2 (cloth)
International Standard Book Number 0-8039-0818-0 (paper)

Library of Congress Catalog Card No. 77-79869

FIRST PRINTING

CONTENTS

FOREWORD

This third volume of *Social Service Delivery Systems: An International Annual,* is directed at two major themes: Methods of delivering social services at the neighborhood and the local level; and the conceptual work which is available to help planners in organizing, analyzing, and rationalizing neighborhood service systems. Chapters by Michael Austin and Brian Segal; Alfred Kahn and Sheila Kamerman; Arthur Naparstek and Chester D. Haskell; by Donald Fandetti; Eugene Litwak; and Daniel Thursz and Joseph L. Vigilante deal with issues about and rationale for neighborhood delivery systems. Naparstek and Haskell are concerned with ethnicity and linkages between neighborhood systems and higher levels of government. Kahn and Kamerman's comparisons between European systems and Litwak's balanced theory and linkages at the neighborhood level are conceptual ingredients helpful to teachers and planners in understanding some of the dynamics of neighborhood delivery. The remaining chapters are primarily descriptive of local or neighborhood delivery systems in France, India, Israel, Switzerland, the United Kingdom, and Zambia.

This volume should prove helpful to students of international social welfare, to professionals interested in administration and delivery of public and social welfare systems, to social planners, to those who are interested in problems of design and structure in public service delivery systems at the local level, and to neighborhood activists interested in service architecture. This third volume brings the total number of countries of the world reported in the series to 27. Volume III, therefore, becomes the only resource available in which the social welfare programs of most of the countries of the world are described.

A good deal of this volume grew out of an exciting conference held in October 1974 at the Community Service Society of New York, under the leadership of the General Director, Dr. Alvin Schorr. The Community Service Society celebrated its 125th Anniversary by sponsoring an international conference on neighborhoods. Among the participants at the conference were several authors of this volume including: Jacqueline Ancelin; Alfred Kahn; Sheila

Kamerman; Eugene Litwak; Arthur Naparstek; Peter Westland; and Joseph L. Vigilante. Versions of some of the chapters included here were first read at the conference. The editors of the volume are greatly indebted to Alvin Schorr and the Community Service Society for its help and for stimulating international interest in neighborhood social service delivery systems.

Daniel Thursz
Executive Vice President
B'nai B'rith
Joseph L. Vigilante
Adelphi University
School of Social Work

October, 1977

PREFACE

Perhaps the most surprising finding of the editors, as they prepared Volumes 1 and 2 of this series, was the concern for decentralization in the organization and structure of social service delivery systems throughout the world. We sensed a growing disenchantment with what had become traditional moves toward administrative centralization of services, and we found many social welfare experts throughout the world puzzled as to how to obtain the efficiency and equitability advantages of centralized services, while preserving the "caring quality" in service delivery. From Chicago to Cairo, there was a growing interest in neighborhoods, variously defined. We found, moreover, that social workers and other social welfare experts were doing considerable theoretical work on the meaning of neighborhoods as a structure for service delivery. This volume, therefore, combines conceptual and theoretical treatment of the issues, with descriptive chapters dealing with how neighborhoods are used in several countries.

With regard to the use of the neighborhood and concern with the neighborhood, we suggest that some of the theoretical and organizational shortcomings which we noted in Volumes 1 and 2 are being addressed. Our views have become somewhat more optimistic as a result.

Once again we acknowledge the help of people who have worked closely with use in this enterprise. Daniel Thursz has relocated his professional base of operations from the University of Maryland to the National B'nai B'rith Organization, of which he is now Executive Vice-President. His secretary, Mrs. Nancy Steele, remains involved in support of this project as well as the many new projects Thursz has undertaken in his new role. At Adelphi University, the secretaries to the Dean, Maria Georgiou and Marjorie Bradley, along with Graduate Assistants, Norma Berman and Joan Kleinerman, have been, again, of invaluable help. This volume, of course, could not have been possible without their able assistance.

Each year as a new volume goes to press, we relax in relief—all of us—but we wish to assure readers that by this time we are deep into the combined drudgery, excitement, and stimulation of preparing Volume 4. With a preliminary recognition of our professional colleagues who are now assisting us with the fourth volume, and a sense of gratitude for those who have assisted us with the first three, we acquit all of any errors, and we assume responsibility for all errors.

Daniel Thursz
Joseph L. Vigilante
Adelphi University
Oak Street Campus
December, 1977

1

NEIGHBORHOODS:
A WORLDWIDE PHENOMENON

DANIEL THURSZ
JOSEPH L. VIGILANTE

From Hannibal, Missouri, to London's Limehouse, there are and have been neighborhoods. Since pre-industrial days until the post-technological days, which we are now experiencing in many parts of the world, the grouping of families and people with mutual identifications, related to where they live, has been a characteristic of almost all societies. As concepts of mutual help were born and have grown, the "neighborhood" has been an important geographic component of service delivery networks. And although societies have flirted with ideas of organizing human service systems through centralized bureaucracies (from the early 1930s to the early 1970s), the "neighborhood" as an instrument for service delivery systems remains in almost all parts of the world.

The United Kingdom is a good example. From the time of the Bevridge Report (1939) there developed continuing efforts toward centralization of services along government lines. But with the implementation of the Seebohm report in the early 1970s, a new emphasis on neighborhood has arisen in that country, which has been, perhaps, the leader in the design of human service delivery systems. To be sure, the Seebohm system does not abandon the involvement of central government in service delivery, while it does stress the value of neighborhood involvement and participation at the front line of social service delivery.

In many countries the village or town has achieved new recognition as an active, dynamic instrument of human service delivery. The editors of this volume view these "neighborhood" dynamics with respect to service delivery operations, as applicable to village and town as it is to the city; specific instrumentalities and techniques may vary.

As Alvin Schorr (1974) has pointed out, the centralizing process seems not to have met expectations for better care or even for more equitable distribution of services (which is not to say that some redistribution of opportunities for service has not taken place). There is, also, the counterculture phenomenon (a reaction to the postindustrialized, cybernetic age) which demands more direct human contact in services and resents the bureaucratic procedures which attenuate social services. Added to this is the assumption that relatively intimate, face-to-face contact between the deliverer and receiver is necessary to individualize human services.

The neighborhood as a locus for delivery systems gains interest as greater value is placed on principles of participant democracy and maximum feasible participation, by recipients of service. Further, we are beginning to learn much more about the importance of community life-styles and their implications for delivery of social services. The culture (or subculture) of the client group (often defined by the neighborhood or village) demands consideration in planning for service delivery.

WHAT NEIGHBORHOOD SERVICE IS

Alfred J. Kahn (1976), in tracing the development of a new concern with "community," identifies the practice of reaching out to "hard-core" families in the late 1950s as a benchmark in social work's move back to the neighborhood. "Reaching out" had evolved into urban community development. The service goal changed from "residual" for maladjusted individuals, as in the early 20th or late 19th century, to "institutionalized" normal social utilities especially designed for disadvantaged groups. Neighborhood service today goes beyond that in many parts of the world. A model for neighborhood social services has many more characteristics than "localness." It demands a variety of components integrated with one another and, perhaps most important, with the ambience of the neighborhood. Eugene Litwak's chapter in this volume addresses this issue.

Neighborhood service has potential for discouraging an "anti-alienation" quality. That is to say, it can address a major problem of contemporary living: human alienation—one individual from another, individuals from the group, and groups from other groups. Neighborhood service often respects and uses race and ethnicity as instruments for delivery. It need not select among social classes, although it should recognize the distinctive character of the various social classes in their styles of service consumption, and it can be universal rather than selective. This is possible because there is increasing evidence today of a clear mixture between classes in neighborhoods and villages.

Characteristics and Desiderata

"Neighborhood" has a geographic connotation and it means a small geographic area. To borrow a phrase from the British, neighborhood services are those located within "pram-pushing distance." In large cities this may mean a service center for approximately every 200,000 population. For the suburbs of technologically advanced societies, we need another rule of thumb. In the suburbs and the rural localities of technologically advanced societies, we suggest that "neighborhood" may be defined by distances requiring the consumption of not more than a half gallon of gasoline.

Neighborhood definitions must be "sociological" in the sense that the neighborhood is defined by the meanings which social institutions within it have for the residents. It has been suggested that some neighborhoods have more or less "affective" meaning to residents as a function of social class. Basing her work on that of Herbert Gans and Mark Fried, Florence Vigilante (1975) suggests a theoretical continuum of communities: from the "geographic-affective" communities of the poor and working classes to the "cognitive-functional" communities of the middle and upper-middle classes. She emphasizes that lower working-class people experience the community in a dependent manner (as an extension of self and family) while the upper classes experience the community more remotely and cognitively. To disrupt (through neighborhood renewal, for example) a lower-class community is more emotionally taxing to its residents than it would be for upper-class communities. It may be that the tendency to cling to the village and reject central government services in nonindustrialized countries is related to this phenomenon.

Most important in the definition of the neighborhood service system is that it serve *all* citizens in the neighborhood. It should not isolate particular target groups as defined by their age or the nature of the problems they are experiencing. Another dimension of this "universal" as opposed to "selective" characteristic is that its program should be "not for the poor alone" (Kahn and Kamerman, 1975).

If the principle of universalism is followed, social services can become true social utilities at the neighborhood level. We have long recognized that organizing services by categorizing groups is shortsighted and results in the development of professional specialization to an extent which cannot be comfortably tolerated in a "functionally organized" profession. Moreover, too many people fall between the cracks of categories, thus aggravating their problems and creating new ones. And there is always the danger of discriminating against the rich, who often experience great social need, however reluctant they may be to admit it.

Problems of selectivity are easier to overcome at the neighborhood level primarily because of size, but also because of the action imperatives which result from the proximity of different social classes within and around some neighborhoods. This is particularly evident in New York City, where, for example, a welfare client (with a strong arm) can stand on the corner of 97th Street and Madison Avenue in front of his tenement building and, by throwing a rock south, hit the window of one of several apartments (or perhaps a Rolls

Royce windshield) occupied by millionaires. Millionaires and welfare clinets in New York City literally live within a stone's throw of each other. There are mixed neighborhoods in many cities of the world, where the poor live close to the working class, to the middle class, and to the rich. Services can be made available to all of these populations once the barrier of selectivity of target group is overcome.

From the experiences of trying to deliver social services during the period of unprecedented social unrest of the sixties, Americans developed a new phrase: "maximum feasible participation." Associated with this term were the concepts of "indigenous personnel," "social action," "direct services," and the linkages among them. These three concepts are characteristic of neighborhood delivery systems, but they are quite different and should not be viewed as the same. The term "maximum feasible participation" refers to the policymaking role of residents of the community being serviced. In its most simple form, maximum feasible participation means inclusion of these citizens on the boards of directors of social agencies. "Indigenous personnel" refers to individuals from the community who are employed in the service systems, often as paraprofessionals, often as aides, and less often as professionals in management positions.

Joining social action to direct service creates a different order of things. This concept has the connotation of obtaining services through social action. It also often refers to the use of the service for organizing clients for social action. And it has at least one other implication: that there will be a standing social action structure to improve any and all services in the community. Whatever the case, if these are desired characteristics, they are possible at the neighborhood level. This requirement, of course, mitigates against unilateral decisions made by government offices at higher levels of government. At the same time it has created serious social and political conflict.

Neighborhood centers appear to have two major functions: "access" and "direct service" functions. The former provides the means to link the client with the array of services, and the latter provides the specialized service required. Access services include, for example, information, advice, referral, community and group education, follow-up and escort services, case advocacy, policy advocacy, institutional and individual linkage, and social brokerage. Direct services include the provision of housing, employment, day care, legal services, child placement services, personal and family counseling, and other services well known to social workers and often identified with specific "practice settings" or, to use the British term, "specialisms."

A greater emphasis on the access function in service delivery, as related to the concept of nonuniform services developed by Litwak, presents opportunities for new forms of volunteer services at the neighborhood level. Volunteers have been used in the information and referral process, as a part of advocacy programs involving legal rights of the poor and the like. The potential for large voluntary input in a broader range of activities, including direct service, is great at the neighborhood level.

The above characteristics are generally dependent upon *integrated* services at the neighborhood level. Most writers use the terms "neighborhood service center" and "multi-service center" interchangeably. The integration of services, that is, providing linkage and easy accessibility to a variety of services, in all probability works best in neighborhood settings. But services may also be integrated at other levels.

Integrated services are usually typified by efforts to put all the social services under one roof. Thus, family counseling services, day-care services, public assistance services, public health services, probation services, information and referral services, community organization programs, case advocacy services, and the like are housed in one center—the so-called *multiservice agency*. This "umbrella" model is based on the assumption that clients should not travel all over the neighborhood, community, city, or village to get help. Efforts to provide services under one roof have been extremely complicated and have quite often resulted in only slight improvement in coordination.

Professional, Institutional, and Client Autonomy

Another concept which seems to characterize the work of neighborhood delivery systems is "autonomy." We see frequent references to the autonomy of the client. The idea of autonomy is also applied to the neighborhood service center itself. An example is the Local Authority in the United Kingdom, as discussed by Peter Westland in this volume. The Local Authority is under the jurisdiction of the national government. Its principal charge is to "integrate services at the local level." How this integration takes place differs from one authority to another and is generally left to the discretion of local leadership (autonomy). Conscious efforts are made to keep administrative and policy guidelines at a minimal level. In the United States, autonomy along similar lines would seem to be a sine qua non for neighborhood service centers. The Community Service Society of New York is wrestling with the problem of supporting local neighborhood services and is testing a concept of "shared power." Client autonomy in the United States has been greatly reinforced by the administrative separation of income payments from social services in the public welfare agency. The popularity of the new autonomous life-styles and new forms of communal and family living have also contributed. The client closely participates in a contract agreement with the agency and/or worker carrying out services. He participates in the assessment of his social situation and in making decisions as to which service options are available to him and which he will use. Clients who have a sense of linkage with the agency through representation on its governing body may indeed feel a greater sense of autonomy.

A third example is the autonomy of the worker at the direct service line, where there is more emphasis on independent decision making, compared to traditional agency intervention in the professional decision-making process. The professional is encouraged to see himself as making decisions without having to turn to a supervisor repeatedly for advice and counsel. The freedom of the professional to make a contract with the client or client group is encouraged. There is less mutual dependency among staff members, although there is a great deal of evidence of an emphasis on teamwork. The British experiment reveals close identity of the staff and the area team with the population in the neighborhood. This has also been noted in the United States by evaluators of the Community Action Programs under the Economic Opportunity Act of 1964. Staff and area teams tend to see themselves as a part of the community. Communities appear to accept them in this sense. This contributes to a sense of caring on a "human scale," perhaps one of the most important reasons for increased interest in neighborhood service.

ISSUES AND PROBLEMS

All the characteristics and desiderata of neighborhood service centers discussed above exist together nowhere to our knowledge. The many reviews and evaluations of these programs suggest that they have achieved only minimally some of the goals which have been suggested. While the development of neighborhood services demands autonomy as we have suggested, these programs probably cannot exist without government support. Aside from funding the programs, higher levels of government must provide minimum standards for service, as well as checks and balances among the variety of political and administrative inputs and relationships affecting services. But as Alfred Kahn (1976) has indicated, although front-line service can and should be integrated, it cannot be if the funding and guidance source is fragmented in regard to the responsibility for program supervision or monitoring.

Evaluation and monitoring are tasks which create knotty problems. A solution may be to set up neighborhood delivery systems on a general systems model. The systems model provides for information stations and feedback, and assumes a readiness to change policies and procedures in response to feedback data. But the feedback system is only as good as the standards and criteria for consumer evaluation are accurate and comparable. How do we set standards? How do we enable consumers to articulate their concerns about the services received?

Another potential problem, rarely noted, is that of contamination of community styles by professional service. One of the advantages of neighborhood service models, as suggested, is their ability to use neighborhood life-styles in patterning services. But, unfortunately, the placement of professionals in the neighborhood at times appears to encourage communities to emulate the professional style, often not compatible with that of the community. This may prove to be dysfunctional to the community in the long run.

Much has been made of the importance of universalism as compared to selectivity with respect to the groups which are served by neighborhood programs. Universalism is a desideratum. But how does one avoid the fear of the stigma of social services among middle-class and blue-collar groups? What does one do about the inevitability of expanding services as one expands the consumer population? If services are universalized, will the most powerful people (perhaps the least needy in the neighborhood) monopolize the service as is evident in some American suburban communities? How does one obtain balance between access services and direct services?

A SUGGESTED MODEL

We suggest the following model for a neighborhood system:

Component I: Social Ambience. The structure of a neighborhood service system must be such as to fit the social ambience of the neighborhood it serves. A large part of neighborhood ambience is determined by group and ethnic life-style, family structure, social communication variables, and variables relating to how the community perceives itself.

Component II: Mapping. A community development component is necessary to keep the program connected with community life. The community development service should also be responsible for mapping needs, resources, and their relationships. Where are the services located? In what quantities? How are services distributed in the community? How do they compare with needs as these are identified? How are they used? The mapping process, linked with life-style and ethnicity factors, associated with physical distance factors, and related to other service systems, will help to define the geographic perimeters of the service community.

Component III: Social Policy Liaison. Linkage with decision makers—government and private—aside from getting feedback information and having some direct influence in the policy decision making that affect human services, can provide consultation services and feedback to decision makers regarding the impact of public policy on services.

Component IV: Linkages to Financial Aid Programs. Although the process of offering social services must be separated from financial aid, there ought to be a linkage with financial aid services to provide support to clients as they negotiate public assistance and to inform the providers of the impact of public assistance systems on the lives of recipients.

Component V: Information and Referral. Information and referral service is fundamental and basic to all neighborhood services. It can provide the net under the cracks between services. It has the potential for eliminating many problems quickly, since individuals can be helped if they become informed and are given guides to finding service.

Component VI: Emergency Services. These should include access services (information and referral, escort services, case advocacy, policy advocacy, institutional and individual linkage, and social brokerage) as well as direct services, such as services for alcoholics; services for potential suicides, depressives, and abandoned children; immediate, temporary housing; legal services; homemaker services; and crisis counseling services.

Component VII: Direct Services. These should reflect the needs identified through outreach, community education, information and referral, and publicity services.

Component VIII: Medical Facility Linkage. There need not be a centralized medical facility for each neighborhood, but there should be a planned distribution of medical services to each neighborhood.

Component IX: A Management System. This would provide input stations at every phase of service and a systems feedback for monitoring policy.

Our observations, derived to a large extent from the reports represented in the chapters in this volume and our own independent work in the fields of ethnicity and neighborhood development, reveal a dilemma. Although there seems to be a growing enthusiasm among professionals, as well as receivers of social services throughout the world, regarding the advantages of decentralizing services to the neighborhood level, reports from the United States, the United Kingdom, as well as other parts of the world (including both Egypt and Israel) reveal that decentralization toward the neighborhood meets with high resistance among political forces. Political people (elected officials, as well as public administrators), who ultimately must be involved in plans for implementing the neighborhood, seem threatened by the aspect of dissembling power. There is a general conservative mood regarding organizing and financing social services that seems to be extant throughout the world. Whatever the reasons, although the neighborhood idea is well accepted among sophisticated welfare planners and academicians, they appear to be far from general implementation by social policy decision makers, except in those few instances which we have cited.

REFERENCES

KAHN, A.J. (1976). "Service delivery at the neighborhood level: Experience theory, and fads." Social Service Review, 50(March):13-14.

KAHN, A.J., and KAMERMAN, S.B. (1975). Not for the poor alone. Philadelphia: Temple University Press.

SCHORR, A.L. (1974). "Social services after Eden, or who promised us a rose garden." Memorial lecture for Richard M. Titmuss, November 7, Conventry, England.

VIGILANTE, F. (1975). "Two communities: Two concepts." New York: Wurzweiler School of Social Work, Yeshiva University. (Unpublished paper.)

2

COMPARING SOCIAL WELFARE SYSTEMS: A SCHEMA FOR ANALYSIS

MICHAEL J. AUSTIN
BRIAN SEGAL
MEYER SCHWARTZ

The teaching of comparative social welfare can be seen as a process of examining the social welfare programs and policies of foreign countries to expand our knowledge and assist in examining our own system. The heightened interest in comparative social welfare at all levels of undergraduate and graduate education comes at a time when our world is shrinking and telecommunications allow us to gain detailed information about other lands on our evening TV news programs. Students want to learn more about other countries. Interest in the history and arts of other countries is now expanding into curiosity about the health, education, and welfare systems of both developing and industrialized countries.

What can we learn from the British system of health care? How does Israel work to prevent juvenile delinquency? How does Russia care for its mentally ill? And how does the children's allowance work in New Zealand? These and other questions lead to many more questions about the social order and customs of various countries. How, then, can one gain a perspective on the social welfare system of a foreign country in the context of its social, economic, and political structure? The approach taken in this paper is the development of an analytic schema as a tool for increasing student understanding of the complex nature of social welfare in foreign countries. The obvious goal is to make our neighbors across the seas less foreign to the students of social welfare. A byproduct of such an analysis should lead to a better understanding of our own social welfare system.

In an effort to get students quickly involved in analyzing the social welfare system of another country, it is helpful to encourage them to imagine a situation in which they had a short time period to prepare for assuming a mission as a social welfare consultant to a foreign country about which they know very little. Hence, they are under pressure, not unknown to international consultants, to prepare themselves with enough knowledge and understanding to gain a "fix" or an orientation to the foreign social system. In the parlance of the time, they need to prepare themselves to give an in-class "briefing" on a particular country.

The educational value of this approach resides in gaining quickly the capacity to identify, describe, and understand those factors that explain particular foreign welfare systems which appear salient. Moreover, this approach requires early decision making in choosing whether or not to understand all the components of welfare programs and services or select for understanding those which appear to be more salient than others and/or select those for which there is relatively more information. Again, this is a situation not unknown to international consultants. And indeed, it may be argued, a circumstance endemic to all who assume the consultant role in whatever tasks.

A perusal of governmental documents and the limited literature in international social welfare revealed that, more often than not, a dull static description was presented by describing various components of welfare services and programs of a particular foreign welfare system. Seldom was an effort made to make understandable *why* the welfare system was fashioned and developing in a particular way, let alone comparing different systems.

THE SCHEMA FOR SOCIAL WELFARE SYSTEMS ANALYSIS

The proposed schema (see Figure 1) is designed as a tentative conceptualization derived from the analysis of the social welfare systems in both developing and industrialized countries. It evolved from several stages of analysis as follows:

(1) questions one might ask about the social welfare system of the country;

(2) development of a framework for a search of the literature;

(3) a process of comparing the features of one country with another; and

(4) synthesizing of facts about the country with the use of analytic linkages.

The synthesizing of multiple and disparate facts into a framework of understanding is based on several goals. The first objective is to gain an understanding of the social welfare system as it exists in particular developed and developing countries.[1] The second aim is to gain, indirectly, further insights into the American social welfare system in the light of the experiences of other nations. And the third objective is to attempt the development of an instrument useful for the comparative analysis of any given social problem (e.g., child welfare, community development, population control, etc.) in two or more nations.[2] Inherent in the search for a relevant schema is the explication of

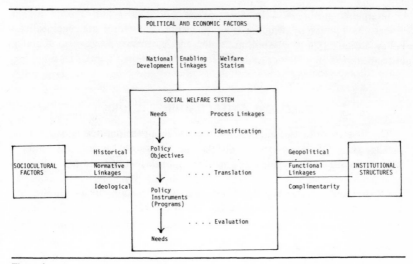

Figure 1:

commonalities and differences found in both the conditions of a country and the adaptations to the conditions as reflected in the social welfare policies and programs.

Linkages—From Where to Where?

Before moving into a discussion of the schema, it is important to define the usage of the term "linkage" and to caution that the logic of the usage is exploratory. The term linkage is borrowed from the conceptual work of Esman and Blaise (1966) developed as part of the University of Pittsburgh Institution Building Project.

First of all, the term "linkage" is used conceptually to denote external links and internal links. External linkages refer to the interdependence which exists *between* the social welfare system and other relevant parts of the society. Internal linkages refer to the interdependence which exists within the social welfare system among its component parts.

The following schema which attempts to relate three categories of facts (political and economic factors, sociocultural factors, and institutional structures) the the welfare system reflects both types of linkages. External to the social welfare system are three types of linkages:

(1) enabling linkages

(2) normative linkages

(3) functional linkages.

Internal to the social welfare system are *process* linkages or linkages which reflect the process by which needs are identified to form policy objectives. Policy objectives are translated into policy instruments or programs, and policy instruments are evaluated in terms of recurring needs.

POLITICAL AND ECONOMIC FACTORS

The first set of factors includes information about the political and economic characteristics of a country. The following questions suggest the kind of information necessary to gain some insights about this set of factors:

(1) Is there an articulated *economic* and social policy which embodies the concept of a basic minimum standard of living?

(2) How does national and local political power *transfer* in the country?

(3) Who owns and/or operates the channels of mass communication (press, radio, television), and are social welfare policies and programs debatable by the citizenry?[3]

In an effort to link answers to these questions to the social welfare system it becomes apparent that the concepts of "sanctions" and "resources" are important. However, political sanctions and economic resources are not specific enough to highlight the enabling linkages between the economics and politics of a country and its social welfare system. Therefore, two variables have been selected which cut across the concepts of political sanctions and economic resources. They are welfare statism and national development which serve to facilitate an understanding of the unique impact that economic resources and political sanctions have on a social welfare system.

The degree to which a country can be characterized as a welfare state provides variables of welfare statism that can be operationalized in five major ways, reflecting the nature and extent to which a nation:

(1) maximizes the use of the machinery of state, particularly in market mechanisms;

(2) insures its citizens against the common burdens of existence;

(3) maintains a high standard of living as reflected, in part, through low unemployment rates;

(4) seeks to narrow the gap between the classes;

(5) maintains an honest, efficient, and influential civil service. [Schottland, 1967; Samuel, 1970]

When the political and economic aspects of a country provide a significant enabling linkage to the social welfare system, one can assume a strong societal support for a welfare state.

The second variable concerns national development. This variable is more difficult to operationalize but serves as a rough measure of the economic intentions (plans) and realities of a country. In this situation, national development refers primarily to the nature and extent of economic development. Of particular interest is the relationship between economic development and social development. This variable attempts to determine the nature of the blend, from strictly economic development concerns to a highly mixed economic and social development emphasis. To gain a perspective of this variable, it is suggested that a nation be assessed according to the nature and extent of:

(1) intervening government policies in which economic considerations take precedence over social considerations;

(2) time lags in planned national development;

(3) the relationship between the growth of gross national product and population growth.

In this section, then, the variables of welfare statism and national development can be viewed in the context of enabling linkages between a country's economy and politics and its social welfare system.

INSTITUTIONAL STRUCTURES

A second set of factors has been labeled institutional structures. The following list of questions reflect the kind of information needed to make an assessment of the institutions (e.g., the army, civil service, etc.) which exist alongside the social welfare system as well as the institutional features of the social welfare system itself. In addition, it seems appropriate to include in this set of factors information about the rather fixed characteristics of the country, namely geography, demography, and natural resources. In developing questions about the civil service, the military, and the actual welfare institutions, one might ask:

(1) If there is a coalition government, which political party controls the social welfare ministry or department?

(2) To what extent do the armed forces hold political power, if at all?

(3) Is there a central state organization for economic and/or social planning?

(4) Is there a significant private voluntary welfare sector?

(5) Is there a specified way of producing trained manpower for social welfare practice?

The connection between the country's institutional structures and social welfare system is made through functional linkages. These linkages have been operationalized in terms of variables labeled complementarity and geopolitical.

As a variable, complementarity refers to the degree to which another institution in the society complements the social welfare system. For example, if the trade unions are particularly active in promoting social benefits for their members, such efforts can be viewed as complementary to the social welfare system by serving the needs of a segment of the population. The opposite, or lack of complementarity, might exist in the case of industrial institutions who fail to serve the social needs of their employees (e.g., lack of disability benefits, inadequate pensions, etc.) and, in turn, add to the burdens of the social welfare system.

Implied in the complementarity dimension is the adequate cataloging of significant institutional structures in a society. This task, as with the other sets of factors, requires an extensive literature search and greatly benefits from actual on-the-spot experience. In this connection, the overseas field placement provides an ideal exposure for students to gain insights into significant institutional structures.

The second variable used to elaborate a functional linkage is concerned with the geopolitical status of a country. The number of factors and their variablity is immense and range, for example, from good climate to poor soil, from disputed borders to a highly dependent populace, and from skilled manpower shortages to inadequate land reform. In operationalizing this variable it becomes apparent that the very resources of a country in the form of men, land, and machinery are functionally related to the social welfare system. Such a system must, by the very nature of geopolitical factors, respond in some ways to the needs of a population based on the adequacy of existing tangible and intangible resources.

SOCIOCULTURAL FACTORS

The intensity and degree of nationalism and the population structure of the society are but two of a multitude of social factors affecting the welfare system of any country. These two sets of factors have been selected for analysis as they provide a major input into the social welfare system. A sampling of questions provides a sense of direction for obtaining more information about these factors:

(1) Is it a country with a well developed sense of being a distinctive nation or is it struggling for a sense of national identity?

(2) Is the population homogeneous or heterogeneous and, if heterogeneous, what are the gaps in the standard of living between different social groups?

The magnitude of the number of factors within any given society is extensive. The operationalization of a notion such as cultural style is exceedingly complex. An analysis of sociocultural factors should focus, for example, on the structure and function of the nuclear and extended *families* and on the nature of both functional and geographic *communities* within the society. With regard to the family it is important to assess child-rearing patterns, matriarchal versus patriarchal leadership, and various forms of cultural transmission. For the communities it is important to highlight the functional aspects (e.g., power structures, secular and nonsecular community organizations, etc.).

Normative Linkages: Ideology

Sociocultural factors in the form of national identity and the population structure can influence the social welfare system through the normative linkages of ideology and critical historical processes. *Ideology* can be operationalized in at least five ways which identify the nature and degree to which the nation:

(1) has consensus within the population concerning the governments' political doctrine (e.g., factionalism, underground movements, etc.);

(2) has consensus with the populace in identifying with government symbols (e.g., constitution, laws, treaties, flag, etc.);

(3) shares common values and beliefs about the internal processes of the society and societal goals (e.g., profit motive, legal and judiciary system, federalism versus statism, etc.);

(4) shares a permeating pattern of attitudes toward life (e.g., fatalism, commitarianism, individualism, determinism, etc.);

(5) senses the right and duty of citizen participation in the political sphere (e.g., role of voluntary organizations, voter registration, freedom of the press, etc.).

A nation with a strong ideological orientation will generally provide a more stable and standardized influence (positive or negative) on the welfare system. The sanctions and legitimation for the social welfare system will tend to be more consistent and provide clues as to the direction of social welfare programming. With a weak ideological component, the social welfare system will symbolically resemble the ideological mix which, in turn, may give evidence of the instability in the social structure of the country.

An examination of two distinct types of welfare policies—universal and selective—may provide further insight for the effects of the ideological variable on the social welfare system. Universal refers to a system of social welfare services which is provided for everyone. These services are available to the total population in such ways as would not involve users in any humiliating loss of status, dignity, or self-respect. There exists no sense of shame, pauperism, or stigma in the use of a publicly provided service. Universal services are associated with concepts of social rights, prevention, and remedial services. A selective policy refers to a system of social welfare services which discriminates on a territorial, group, or rights basis in favor of the poor, the handicapped, minority groups, the homeless and deprived.

Hence in a country with a strong ideology (egalitarian or dictatorship), the welfare system will most likely reflect the values and beliefs of the larger society. In such a system the welfare programs tend to be unidirectional in the sense that there does not exist universal and selective policies acting at cross purposes with each other. In a country with a weak ideology, the welfare system might represent the lack of ideological consensus in the country possibly resulting in a mix of universal and selective policies sometimes functioning at cross purposes with each other.

Normative Linkages: Critical Historical Processes

The second dimension of the normative linkage, *critical historical processes,* consists of at least three dimensions:

(1) burdens of the relevant past,

(2) critical political changes, and

(3) recent unsettling trends.

The burdens of the relevant past is another mechanism through which the sociocultural factors are linked to the social welfare system. In Kenya, for example, burdens of the past within the sociocultural factors, such as racial separation, illiteracy, lack of a common national language, malnutrition, and tribal customs, strongly affect the identification of needs and the formulation of welfare programs. When the burdens of the past are so overpowering, the development of the welfare programs must relate to the basic core needs of the population in terms of subsistence. Thus more familiar Western welfare programs may be alien to a country whose burdens of the past mitigate more advanced welfare policies such as income maintenance and redistribution.

In Kenya, critical political changes such as the Mau Mau rebellion, decolonization, and intertribal conflict link the state of nationalism to the social welfare system. These critical political changes create movements toward African Socialism and Africanization policies which reverberate through the leadership, control, and direction of a welfare system. Thus the sociocultural factors, which provide the normative linkage to the welfare system, become operational when the characteristics of ideology and critical historical processes are identified.

SOCIAL WELFARE SYSTEM

Until now, the social welfare system has been analyzed by looking at its external linkages to relevant societal systems. As mentioned previously, the social welfare system has internal linkages which reflect the process by which needs are identified to form policy objectives. Policy objectives are translated into policy instruments or programs, and policy instruments are evaluated in terms of recurring needs. The questions below reflect the type of information needed to gain insight into the needs, policies, and programs as interrelated by process linkages:

(1) Can the inadequacies of social resources be identified (lack of broad range welfare, educational and health services; lack of skilled personnel; segmentation of minority, ethnic, racial, tribal, and religious groups; boundary disputes and hostilities)?

(2) Can needs be identified through an analysis of urban and rural population distribution?

(3) If severe problem areas exist, what are the stated social and economic policies of the government and voluntary agencies regarding these needs?

(4) To what extent can the social needs of the country be translated into social policies and programs with regard to the aged, the young, the retarded, etc.?

Process Linkages: Identification, Translation, and Evaluation

The process linkages attempt to reflect the dynamism of the social welfare system. The identification linkage can be used to assess the extent to which the social welfare needs of the population are sufficiently identified and the extent to which such needs are reflected in policies.

With the translation linkage, it is possible to assess the manner in which needs and policies are accounted for in actual programs. It is this transition or lack thereof which provides significant clues about the functioning of the social welfare system.

Finally, evaluation proves to be a vital linkage between existing programs and unmet needs, providing major input into the processes of social planning. The assessment of whether or not a program is accomplishing its objectives will point out whether the needs are being met and what further planning is required to further program goals. Evaluation is a major feedback translation that linkages are functioning effectively.

All three process linkages rely ultimately upon a certain explication of programs in the social welfare system by analyzing the following factors:

auspice, source of financing, eligibility, service and goods delivered, accessibility of services and goods, program accountability, and the skill of the staff.

SUMMARY

It is important to stress again the tentative nature of our thinking. The schema represents an attempt to conceptualize a framework for understanding social welfare systems from the multitude of disparate facts available for any given country. Further analysis is necessary in order to develop a more precise understanding of the unique impact of sociocultural, political, economic, and institutional factors upon the primary comments of a social welfare system. Such analysis should serve to extend our knowledge about the internal workings of a social welfare system with reference to health, education, welfare, and housing.

NOTES

1. The term is used to refer "both to a state of individual or social well-being and to the action programs and services designed to bring about this state of well-being or alleviate impediments to its existence" (Council on Social Work Education, 1969).

2. "In only a few countries social welfare is an all-inclusive term including child care, education, public health, housing, social insurance, delinquency control, cultural and recreational programs, and a host of other activities. In others it is sharply limited to social security, that is, social insurance supplemented by certain public assistance mechanisms. In still others it falls between these two extremes, being considered an independent sector embracing specific programs, social assistance, family and child welfare, community development (both urban and rural), and a variety of remedial and specialized services for vulnerable groups" (Council on Social Work Education, 1969:3).

3. These are samples of the questions developed by Professor Meyer Schwartz, United Nations Social Welfare Consultant to Israel and Taiwan.

REFERENCES

AUSTIN, D.M. (1970). "Social work's relation to national development in developing countries." Social Work, (January).

Council on Social Work Education (1969). The essential task: Training social welfare manpower. Paper from proceedings of the International Conference of Ministers Responsible for Social Welfare, United Nations (ST/SOA/89E Conf. 55/12), New York.

ESMAN, M., and BLAISE, H. (1966). Institutional building research: The guilding concepts. Pittsburgh: Inter-University Research in Institution Building, University of Pittsburgh.

MACAROV, D. et al. (1967). "Consultants and consultees: The view from within." Social Service Review, (September).

MENCHER, S. (1961). "The changing balance of status and contrast in assistance policy." Social Service Review, (March).

SAMUEL, E. (1970). "Lectures on the welfare state." Pittsburgh: Graduate School of Public and International Affairs, University of Pittsburgh.

SCHOTTLAND, C. (ed., 1967). The welfare state. New York: Harper and Row.

TITMUS, R. (1968). Commitment to welfare. London: Allen and Unwin.

3

URBAN POLICIES AND
NEIGHBORHOOD SERVICES

ARTHUR J. NAPARSTEK
CHESTER D. HASKELL

In recent years mental health professionals in the United States have earnestly sought to bring services into the community arena. A result of this effort is the community mental health movement which, we believe, has had a profound impact on service delivery.[1] However, in spite of such significant reforms and the many important research efforts carried out, providers and consumers have not been satisfied during the past decade. There are those who still claim that services are delivered in a fragmented manner, that services are often offered in an inefficient, duplicative, and bureaucratically confusing fashion to those who have the need, that services are lacking in accountability, and that service delivery systems do not provide for attention to prolonged needs or for comprehensive analysis of the patients' problems.

In part, such judgments are due to the fact that we do not know very much about how groups of people who differ ethnically, racially, and socially solve problems and cope with crises. Service delivery systems are often developed without regard to the unique elements of community and neighborhood life.

It is our premise that the efficacy of a mental health system depends on recognizing the proper context or stage for delivery. Although important work has been carried out with regard to linking service delivery to poor neighborhoods, the results have been disappointing. Despite the rhetoric supporting community involvement, mental health professionals have shown little real understanding of the dynamics of urban life.

During the past two decades human problems were defined in the context of macrosocial and economic forces. A result was the belief that poverty was the central issue and that innovations were needed to reform social institutions and provide mobility opportunities for poor people and, more particularly, blacks.

[31]

By the late 1960s, however, there was widespread disillusionment with the effectiveness of this approach. Under the guise of administrative reform, the first Nixon administration began to dismantle the service change initiatives taken during the early part of the decade. The justification for dismantling was based on the alleged inefficient administration and organization of Great Society programs.

The assumptions and beliefs underlying the service initiatives and theoretical systems of the sixties and early seventies have not been directed toward the micro aspects of problem solving in a neighborhood context. Nor were these past efforts explicitly directed to the universal problems of inequality, social injustice, and exclusion. In the sixties, these issues were given attention, but only within the context of poverty; in the seventies, they are not even discussed.

A recurring theme in mental health has been the search for new models for the delivery of services. It is not our intention to put forth new models; instead, we believe a new analysis is needed. Central to this analysis is the notion that a neighborhood approach cannot be cast only in policy and program terms. First and foremost, it is a process requiring involvement from all concerned sectors in a city. Second, if it is to be successful, it must be a pluralistic process which can meet the diverse needs of different groups of people. Third, if there is one particular lesson to be learned from both the successes and failures of neighborhood level approaches, it is the need for "approachable scale." This is not a question of absolute size, but rather, what scale is appropriate for what we are trying to do. Small is not necessarily better than large, nor is neighborhood necessarily better than city. Some activities are best carried out at a larger scale than the neighborhood where the conventional notions of "economies of scale" come into play. In Schumacher's (1973) words, "for his different purposes man needs many different structures, both small ones and large ones, some exclusive and some comprehensive."

Money, or cost saving, is not and should not be the prime rationale for alterations in the ways in which services are delivered. The discomfort of America's urban populace is not solely related to quantifiable issues such as the cost of services or fee for service rates. For there is a profound alienation operating in cities which encompasses feelings of powerlessness, meaninglessness, isolation, and self-estrangement. Thus, an underlying problem is whether the roots of alienation can be found in the neighborhood, and whether human services can make a difference in reversing or negating those elements of community life which are alienating.

Alienation and community are two concepts that have been central to sociological work. However, each concept is extremely broad, laden with value implications, and has been used in an extraordinary variety of ways. Such social theorists as Toennies, Marx, Weber, Durkheim, and Simmel are perhaps most responsible for providing the "content" of the 20th century use of the word "alienation" (Nesbit, 1966). Each of these social theorists conceptualizes community so as to make it possible to identify on a theoretical level the processes which lead toward the depersonalization of human relations and intensification of the alienation process in community.

Although it is not the purpose of this paper to discuss the theoretical constructs put forth by each of the aforementioned writers, if we are to analyze current programs from a neighborhood dimension, it is important to identify central themes which flow through their work. Two major themes appear dominant: (1) when a person is unable to participate in, control, or understand the processes that are shaping his social being, he will feel a sense of deprivation, dependency, and manipulation; and (2) alienating conditions arise when the community or the institutions in that community are unresponsive to the needs of the individual. Thus, it can be assumed that the failure of many community mental health efforts results from two interrelated problems: first, in most cases these efforts do not deal directly with the issues of devolving power to citizens on a neighborhood level; and, second, the administrative arrangements of the formal mental health system are not supportive of a process which is consistently responsive to the needs of different groups of people. We must, therefore, learn more about the devolution of power and identify options for linking services to neighborhoods.

PRINCIPLES GUIDING THE DEVOLUTION OF POWER

Resource allocation must be a fundamental component of any strategy to devolve power. Policies which do not consider the ways in which citizens can control the allocation of resources are inadequate. There is not a public or private agency in the country that does not in some way or other follow a strategy of resource allocation to neighborhoods. Monies and services are usually distributed to different neighborhood service districts on the basis of need as perceived by a small number of decision makers. Often the criteria for defining need is predicated by a complex convergence of administrative, political, and economic forces, which often have little to do with the true citizen needs of a particular neighborhood. On the other hand, citizens determine their resource needs quite subjectively, utilizing criteria that are different from the professional. In assessing needs, citizens appear to be guided by two interrelated principles: equity and sufficiency.

Equity

The principle of equity is usually defined by citizens at the neighborhood level in two ways: whether their investment (objective or subjective) is equal to their return; and whether their neighborhood is getting its fair share of resources as compared to other parts of the city. Thus, when citizens invest through the tax system, they expect a return in services and amenities. However, the problem is complicated because the return is hardly ever within the control of the citizens or even local decision makers. Often, even well-intentioned policies developed on a national level can be extremely disruptive on a local level. An example of this is the impact of the U.S. Community Mental Health Centers Act of 1963 (CMCH). The act was a part of the federal government's commitment to end poverty and racial discrimination. This legislation, together with the 1964 Economic Opportunity Act, could be considered a unique form of race and class legislation: it designated a special group in the population (the poverty group) as eligible for the benefits of the law.

A working alliance between mental health professionals, social and political scientists, federal bureaucrats, and others attempted to forge together a national effort that would serve local communities through mental health centers. But, by 1970, these alliances broke down, and public support for the War on Poverty and the CMHC act dramatically abated.

The social policies of the 1960s drew lines: the policy makers in effect said, "whites don't have problems—racial minorities do." The anger and hostility that is felt by whites is not a result of their lack of sympathy for needs of the poor and nonwhites. Rather, it stems from a perception of inequity and a sense of being left out and ignored.

S.M. Miller contends that efforts to improve the circumstances of the poor will inevitably affect those groups that can be considered to be economically and socially contiguous to the poor. He explained that, in 1968, the group of people who had incomes between $3,450 (the 1968 poverty line for a family of four) and approximately $10,000 ($9750 was the income figure set by the United States Bureau of Labor Statistics as an "adequate but modest standard") felt ignored and neglected. Miller claimed that the responsibility for those feelings lay with the War on Poverty and a sense that "working class" populations with marginal incomes in this income range were "picking up the tab" for the poor. Consider the following:

> Indeed, many feel that they are "put upon" by these efforts at change, bearing the burdens with little support and aid from the society at large. The likelihood is that these non-affluent, but non-poor groups will be calling for social services and other aids for themselves. Not only will they be seeking social services as mobility aids (for they too feel that their and their children's economic mobility is limited) but they will call for social services as basic amenities to which they have a claim. [Miller and Altschuler, 1968]

Neither the Great Society programs or the CMHC Act could have possibly fulfilled the expectations of their various constituencies. Rather than introducing "neighborhood programs" through successive stages of accomplishment and functional expansion, the reverse occurred: full dosage of decentralization was introduced to an unorganized, and often overwhelmed, neighborhood populace. When neighborhood residents were unable to fulfill the mandate of these programs, the delivery system retrenched into greater centralization by reducing the devolution of control.

The mental health and poverty programs of the 1960s tended to be defined in the context of race and an absolute definition of poverty. Thus, programs originally intended to serve the poor were quickly perceived (with even greater selectivity) as programs designed primarily for poor blacks. Though in most cities, these categorical programs began on a small scale, they grew in time, and attained a high visibility. For example, the mandate of Great Society policies related to neighborhood control and service decentralization. Thus, neighborhood residents became actively involved and anxiously waited for their neighborhood conditions to improve. By 1968, subjective judgments evaluating the policies' impact in program terms were harsh. Tom Wicker commented that the War on Poverty "somehow managed to wind up alienating many of the black and poor, as well as white conservatives . . . and members of Congress" (New York Times, 1968). Lee Rainwater (1970) notes that "though the E.O.A. made promises to the black community through its psuedo-radical rhetoric, it angered and insulted the working class and at the same time delivered no more than symbolic resources to black people."

There are important lessons to be learned from these community oriented policies. Robert Wood's analysis of the policies of the sixties links the past to the present and provides a framework for discussing current efforts. Wood notes that a criticial policy issue raised in the sixties involved the complications inherent in the majoritarian system working on a minority problem. He points out that policies which fail to take into account the economic and social needs of a majority are likely to stimulate fears which, in turn, override the minority needs:

> The critical factor is how minority needs are presented to a majority and coupled with them, not the impossibility of gaining majority approval. This requires skill and leadership of special proportions. [Wood, 1972:67]

Implicit in Wood's analysis are the skills needed to generate a process which will confront conditions of inequity as perceived by different groups of people.

We know that on a local level, actual or perceived states of inequity have significant consequences. For example:

(1) If residents have sufficient resources, they will leave the neighborhood and refuse to invest socially, physically, and economically;

(2) Residents will feel threatened by those they regard as below them in social and economic status, a consequence of which is increased hostility toward those who are considered to be different;

(3) If a local agency projects an appearance of responsiveness, but does not fully permit power to be shared, people feel cheated and manipulated. A result of this is an apartheid system of service delivery. Minorities receive inadequate care, and poor and working-class whites are caught in between—too poor to afford their own physicians, but unwilling to attend a public supported center.

Sufficiency

This principle is defined in terms of people being able to participate in processes of service delivery, so as to exercise some degree of control over these services, and so they have the ability to deal successfully with the problems confronting their community. When these conditions do not exist, one can expect levels of alienation which, in turn, negatively influence the self-perceptions of one's neighborhood.

The degree to which people feel sufficient is often determined by how the neighborhood defines itself and how others define it. Those neighborhoods which have strong ethnic, racial, or class identities often tend to have the greatest ability to deal with their problems. Such neighborhoods have a unique sense of pride which, in turn, affects the ways in which difficulties are resolved. Yet public officials and scholars often cast these communities in perjorative terms. Because of this, policymakers do not build on the strengths of the neighborhood and do not understand neighborhood social and cultural dynamics.

If we are to discuss the linkages between service delivery systems and neighborhoods, we need to understand the importance of the infrastructure within the neighborhood. The infrastructure, as we define it, is made up of those neighborhood-based networks (organizational and cultural) which can increase accountability between the "system" and the citizens. When such networks are not operating effectively, one can expect a low level of citizen involvement in areas of service delivery and a high level of mistrust between consumers and providers.

Although important work has been carried out with regard to linking service delivery to neighborhoods, little consideration has been given to neighborhoods which reflect a multiethnic population. We have not yet developed a full understanding of the intercultural dimensions of neighborhood life, particularly as it relates to service delivery. Too often delivery systems bypass those neighborhood-based cultural and organizational networks which may have the potential for support of services. More specifically, the impact different ethnic groups and subcultures have on issues related to prevention and treatment is not fully understood. Finally, the problem is made more complex as we do not yet have an understanding of the interdependencies existing between race, ethnicity, social class, and well-being.

Ethnicity, Social Class, and Well-Being

Human service delivery systems are usually organized according to the perceptions of "what is needed" by the providers. These people for the most part do not live in the neighborhoods where the service centers are located, nor are they likely to reflect the same socioeconomic or cultural make-up as their "consumers." Therefore, it seems logical to assume that there is a difference in the professional and client perceptions of need. This difference does not lend itself to developing the sensitivity necessary to understand not only the relationship of utilization patterns of human services to social, religious, and ethnic factors, but also to what degree and in what ways they are linked.

The relationship between well-being and ethnicity builds on the work of Mead, Benedict, Kluckholm, as well as Sullivan, Horney, Ferenczi, and Kardiner, all of whom stressed the influence of social and cultural environment in normal and deviant behavior. The works of Kolodny (1969), Spiegal (1965:576), Barrabe and Von Mering (1953:4950), and Zborowski (1964) suggest that various ethnic groups differ in their responses to health, illness and treatment. However, there is a lack of empirical evidence which links utilization patterns to ethnic variation (Kolm, 1973). Only recently has there been an understanding of the interrelationships between social class and mental health. The classic work of Hollingshead and Redlich (1958:95) bridged the gap between mental health and class by raising two fundamental questions: (1) Is mental health related to class? (2) Does a patient's position in the status system affect the treatment she or he receives? One conclusion drawn from the Yale study was that occupation is a potent force in determining a person's general life adjustments and ways of coping with problems. This conclusion is also supported by the Midtown Manhattan Study (Srole et al., 1962) and the Gurin, Veroff, and Field (1960) nationwide survey of 2,400 adults. Further, Gurin and Srole's work along with Leighton (1959) and Phillips (1966) has shown that as many as 50% of those who have emotional problems never seek and receive any kind of help.

Finally, it can be concluded from these investigations that the world of semi-skilled and unskilled blue-collar workers produces a life situation of deprivation, insecurity, and powerlessness resulting in fear, frustration, and a sense of helplessness and low self-esteem. The work of Kornhauser (1962), Mills (1960), and Fromm (1955) supports the aforementioned conclusion and strongly implies the work people do has important consequences for mental health.

In summary, the literature provides some empirical evidence that various ethnic groups differ in their responses to health, illness, and treatment, and that, by utilizing occupation as a principal indicator of social class, we move closer to establishing a causal relationship between work and behavior. However, the relationships between ethnic variation, occupation, and utilization rates are not clear. For example, can it be assumed that a large majority of workers identify themselves as ethnic? If so, which variable (ethnicity or occupational) has the more powerful impact on prevention and treatment? Giordano's (1973) review of the literature responds to the latter question and suggests that ethnicity has at least as powerful an impact on mental health and mental illness as social class. He points out that the influence of ethnicity becomes particularly significant in those studies where social class is held constant. However, he notes that, while professionals have already accepted class differentials, ethnic variation is still often ignored or, worse, denied outright.

Cultural and Organizational-Based Networks

Another body of literature shows the importance of neighborhood-based networks and suggests that it is imperative to know how people solve their problems and cope with crises when they are outside the system of professional agencies. Myers and Bean (1968), in their study of social class and mental illness, point out that, even for those in the professional system, the effectiveness of help received will depend on the social supports or lack of support in a person's neighborhood. The importance of neighborhood-based cultural or organizational networks on assisting professionals to deal with the physically and mentally ill has been noted by several scholars. Slater (1970), Glazer (1971), Warren (1971), Litwak (1961), and Breton (1964:193-205) present the issue in a similar way. For example, Glazer notes that a significant contribution to the present crisis in public social policy and service delivery is due to the breakdown of "traditional" organizations and ways of dealing with problems. Breton, analyzing the issue from the ethnic dimension, points out that greater attention should be given to the social organization (fraternal organizations, ethnic clubs, etc.) of ethnic communities and particularly to the wide variation which exists among them.

We argue that by avoiding existing neighborhood-based networks we are making it more difficult for people to utilize professional expertise in effective and differentiated ways. The important questions for service delivery have to do with how people who are not a part of the service delivery systems cope with their problems. What neighborhood-based formal and informal networks of service delivery are being used? What rearrangements of the formal delivery systems are necessary so that the social organization within the neighborhood is strengthened? Will a delivery system which is culturally compatible with the neighborhood increase utilization and reach people earlier in their illness?

POLICY IMPLICATION FOR THE FUTURE

David Musto (1975) pointed out that the future of the mental health service delivery system in the United States will be determined by the form of national health insurance that emerges in the next few years. In any event, service delivery in a neighborhood context is a prevalent and recurring issue today. Often it is cast in terms of breaking up a centralized service delivery system and moving toward decentralization. This concept has arisen in response to a number of overlapping and ill-defined pressures and forces, a major example being the sharp rise in demand for human services. Kahn (1974) and others have pointed to this phenomenon, finding some of its origins in the multi-ethnic characters of our larger cities. For example, postwar emigration resulted in the juxtaposition of numerous ethnic groups in relatively narrow physical spaces, with each having its own needs and methods of coping with crises. A companion factor has been the differing, problematic, and complex ways in which diverse classes and age groups are affected by the realities of modern urban life.

An additional force toward dencentralization is the recognition by the public officials that there are real inequities in the distribution of public services and resources among the city's neighborhoods. The result of this is a competitive climate where alienation is further encouraged when the residents of one neighborhood feel that their community is getting less than a "fair deal" relative to others. They articulate the problem in terms of political power or the lack of it. Of course, the perception of its absence does little to enhance their faith in local government concern or capabilities.

Finally, the tendency toward decentralization has received impetus from the federal government. The CMHC act and poverty programs, with their common emphasis on citizen involvement, set the foundation for legitimate client involvement in program planning. In addition to providing a strong impetus for such participation, these requirements legitimized citizen activity and even created a revolution of rising expectations among those citizens who believed they really should be involved in the processes by which their lives are affected.

The experience of the sixties suggests that decentralization of services and a straight resource approach to neighborhood, by themselves, will not support a viable neighborhood climate. Although the community mental health movement was predicated on the notion that its programs could improve the overall quality of community life, little attention has been given by mental health professionals to the complex set of legal, administrative, and fiscal policies which independently and/or collectively make it difficult or impossible to bring about change. These are obstacles to change which are structured into the urban system and act to create a set of disincentives for neighborhood viability. For example, neighborhoods cannot maintain a viable infrastructure (network) if local and state policies, ordinances, regulations, and judicial decisions negatively impact on a community. Further, such public actions often serve as legal obstacles which inhibit participation and foster a sense of insufficiency among residents. Another example is the relationship between general municipal services and neighborhood approaches to the human services. The interdependence among the delivery of various types of services is essential to a healthy community environment. The inequitable distribution of city services stimulates conditions in which people will not stay in a given neighborhood. Such disincentives serve to break down neighborhood-based networks and thus permit and engender conditions of inequity and insufficiency. Thus, a primary precondition for change must be the identification of such disincentives, their removal, and the concomitant creation of incentives for the maintenance and enhancement of neighborhood-based networks.

The decisions facing local mental health professionals on neighborhood-related issues are complex and politically hazardous. Often practitioners are confronted with a dwindling tax base, aging housing stock, increased numbers of aged and dependent people, underemployment, and a breakdown in social service delivery systems. All of the aforementioned lead to varied conditions of alienation and make it difficult to decentralize services in any meaningful way.

Further, these conditions foster the practice of social "triage": having to choose between services to white middle-class families, who are threatening to leave the city, and services to the poor and minorities.

Current thought now focuses on the integration of mental health and health policies and programs. However, there is a prior issue: the development of policies on the local, state, and federal levels which can support the viability of neighborhoods. Only within the context of a comprehensive neighborhood policy can we hope for the successful implementation of a community mental health strategy and only if neighborhoods are strong can they serve as the proper context for service delivery.

NOTE

1. The terms neighborhood and community are used interchangeably. Although there have been many studies using the two terms as the field of focus, it is still possible to raise fundamental questions of definition: What is a neighborhood? What is a community? The literature on neighborhoods and communities contains a multiplicity of definitions, none of which appear to have universal acceptance. The concepts are defined from a host of different perspectives and ideological frames of reference, with the result that the definitions are often useful in a theoretical context, but difficult to operationalize in administrative or policy terms.

REFERENCES

BARRABE, P., and Von MERING, O. (1953). "Ethnic variation in mental stress in families with psychotic children." Social Problems, 1(October):4950.

BRETON, R. (1964). "Institutional completeness of ethnic communities and the personal relations of immigrants." American Journal of Sociology, 70:193-205.

FROMM, E. (1955). The sane society. New York: Holt, Rinehart & Winston.

GIORDANO, J. (1973). Ethnicity and mental health. New York: American Jewish Committee.

GLAZER, N. (1971). "The limits of social policy." Commentary, (September):52:3.

GURIN, G., VEROFF, J. and FIELD, S. (1960). Americans view their mental health. New York: Basic Books.

HOLLINGSHEAD, A., and REDLICH, F. (1958). Social class and mental illness. New York: John Wiley.

KAHN, A. (1974). "Service delivery at the neighborhood level: Experience, theory and fads." Paper presented at the Symposium on Neighborhood Service Delivery, Community Service Society of New York (October).

KOLM, R. (ed., 1973). Annotated bibliography on ethnicity and ethnic groups. Rockville, Md.: NIMH.

KOLODNY, R. (1969). "Ethnic cleavages in the United States." Social Work, 14(January).

KORNHAUSER, A. (1962). "The mental health of factory workers: A Detroit study." Human Organization, 21.

LEIGHTON, A. (1959). My name is legion. New York: Basic Books.

LITWAK, E. (1961). "Voluntary associations and neighborhood cohesion." American Sociological Review, (April):26:2.

MILLER, S.M., and ALTSCHULER, J. (1968). "Services for people." Report of the Task Force on Organization of Social Services. U.S. Department of Health, Education and Welfare.

MILLS, C.W. (1951). White collar, the American middle classes. New York: Oxford University Press.

——— (1959). The power elite. New York: Oxford University Press.

——— (1960). The causes of World War II. New York.

MUSTO, D. (1975). "Whatever happened to community mental health." Public Interest, 39 (spring).

MYERS, J., and BEAN, L. (1968). A decade later: A follow-up of social class and mental illness. New York: John Wiley.

NESBIT, R. (1966). The sociological tradition. New York: Basic Books.

New York Times (1968). July 28.

PHILLIPS, D. (1966). "The true prevalence of mental illness in a New England state." Community Mental Health Journal, (spring):2:1.

RAINWATER, L. (1970). "Making the good life: Working class family and life style." (Unpublished manuscript).

SCHUMACHER, E.F. (1973). Small is beautiful; Economics as if people mattered. New York: Perennial.

SLATER, P. (1970). The pursuit of loneliness: American culture at the breaking point. Boston: Beacon.

SPIEGAL, J. (1965). "Some cultural aspects of transference and counter-transference." In M.W. Zold (ed.), Social welfare institutions. New York: John Wiley.

SROLE, L., et al. (1962). Mental health in the metropolis: The midtown Manhattan study. New York: McGraw-Hill.

WARREN, D. (1971). "Neighborhood in urban areas." Encyclopedia of Social Work. New York: NASW.

WOOD, R. (1972). The necessary majority: Middle America and the urban crisis. New York: Columbia University Press.

ZBOROWSKI, M. (1964). People in pain. San Francisco: Jossey-Bass.

4

ETHNICITY AND
NEIGHBORHOOD SERVICES

DONALD V. FANDETTI

An increasing number of individuals are engaged in the planning and organization of services in white ethnic central city neighborhoods. In many of these formerly dormant areas, ethnic interest groups and coalitions are also increasingly evident in bargaining with city and state agencies for their share of resources and service programs. The growing interest in European ethnicity, as a social phenomena, appears to have generated many active efforts to introduce a variety of human services in neglected, working-class, southern and eastern European ethnic neighborhoods around the nation.

These activities have stimulated considerable interest in accounting for class and European ethnic factors in service strategies aimed at reaching white ethnic neighborhoods. Interest in these issues is developing among individuals directly involved with ethnic neighborhoods and among practitioners who encounter clientele from ethnic neighborhoods in hospitals, mental health clinics, and sectarian-voluntary agencies. There is growing apprehension that excessive standardization and uniformity can deter access to public services in our complex and pluralistic local communities. Social, cultural as well as psychological variables shape the unique social identities of individuals, families, and communities in our society. Child-rearing patterns, for example, in the Anglo-Saxon, middle-class family are likely to be different from those found in working-class families of southern European heritage. Even to the most casual observer, a stroll through Little Italy should reveal social patterns and local institutional arrangements different from those found in other neighborhoods in the central city and suburbia.

Human service professionals, seeking to improve strategies aimed at reaching working-class ethnic neighborhoods, find that their efforts are hampered by the absence of adequate conceptual tools. The social sciences do not provide us with an adequate picture of distinctive patterns and life-styles in the ethnic neighborhood. Available knowledge has limited application toward improving the quality of human service intervention and planning. Despite these limitations it is possible to raise several issues related to reaching ethnic neighborhoods through an examination of the three key concepts: ethnicity, social class, and localism. These concepts assist in organizing information which gives the human service professional some idea of life-styles and institutional arrangements in the working-class, southern and eastern European ethnic neighborhood. The social identity of the ethnic neighborhood comes into focus as the overlapping influences of ethnic culture, social class, and local neighborhood are understood. Each of these influences needs to be better understood to determine whether ethnic neighborhoods require individualized systems for the structure and delivery of social services. The discovery of what should be done differently in ethnic neighborhoods is the crucial question from the social service perspective.

CURRENT STATUS

Some elaboration on the current status and socioeconomic characteristics will be presented as background to the discussion of class, ethnicity, and localism in the context of the ethnic neighborhood. Though data are limited and incomplete, two recent studies help to shed some light on the current status of ethnic neighborhoods in the United States. Surprisingly, there has been a great deal of persistence in white ethnic residential segregation in the urban areas of our northeastern and midwestern cities. For example, 51% of New York City's southern European, foreign born population and their children would have to be redistributed to achieve full residential integration with the city's northern European population (Kantrowitz, 1969:693). These residential patterns, however, do not reflect those of third and fourth generation ethnics in the New York City area.

A more recent survey of 54 ethnic neighborhoods also reveals persistence in ethnic residential clustering in central city areas (Baroni and Green, 1976). This study defines ethnic neighborhoods as those with predominately one ethnic group background or those with populations of predominantly two or more primary ethnic groups. Socioeconomic data for the 54 neighborhoods show that less than one-third of the residents of ethnic neighborhoods graduated from high school and only 9% attended college. While median income is roughly $8,000, it is significant that half of the residents have incomes between $7,000 and

$15,000. A significant number also have incomes over $15,000, suggesting that the ethnic neighborhoods continue to be blue collar in occupational identity with only a small number of the residents (13%) employed as professionals and managers.

Age distributions show that 18% of the residents are over 60 years of age. This is higher than the average for the metropolitan area as a whole, suggesting that ethnic neighborhoods have a disproportionate number of aged residents. Significantly, during the 1960s, ethnic neighborhoods also experienced some decline in pre-school age children and a loss in residents between the ages of 25 and 44, the primary child-rearing age. A comparison of age groups in the 54 ethnic neighborhoods with the metropolitan averages as a whole can be seen in Table 1.

The disproportionate number of aged residents and the loss of young families has resulted in debate as to the future and long term viability of central city ethnic neighborhoods. While criteria and data need to be established for determining which neighborhoods might maintain stability, age distributions in the neighborhoods seem to suggest that it would be premature to conclude that all ethnic neighborhoods have become simply enclaves for the aged. Ethnic neighborhoods with a strong political power base and adequate housing are likely to be viable for some time. It is likely that some, but not all, ethnic neighborhoods are facing decline or redevelopment. Recent changes in the economy may also curtail the exodus of young families from these neighborhoods. Skyrocketing suburban housing values have placed home ownership in the suburbs out of the reach of many young ethnic families. As a result, ethnic neighborhoods in the central city may no longer be staging areas for families preparing for an eventual move to the suburbs. More adequate data regarding the viability of ethnic neighborhoods need to be compiled. We also need to know more about ethnic residential patterns of third and fourth generation families who have moved to the suburbs. "Invisible ghettos" may exist in many suburban areas.

Table 1: Percent of Residents in Four Age Groups for 1970

	0-14 years	15-24 years	25-29 years	60 and over
Metropolitan Area	29	17	41	14
Ethnic Neighborhood	26	17	40	18

SOURCE: G. Baroni and B. Green, 1976:30.

ETHNIC CULTURE IN THE NEIGHBORHOOD

Our understanding of central city ethnic neighborhoods will remain partial and incomplete as long as the role of European ethnic culture in these areas is poorly understood. As a tool for studying diversity among groups in our society, European ethnicity has received too little attention. This is especially true in the human services. Clear thinking about the functions of ethnicity on our society has been hampered by conceptual confusion and the widespread acceptance of assimilationist assumptions in our society. It is too frequently assumed that all descendants of European immigrants totally adopt American working-class or middle-class culture in the United States. When the persistence of ethnic cultural differences is accepted, these differences are viewed as trivial and unimportant, such as differences between ethnic groups in food habits. There is increasing evidence that such assumptions require closer examination and reevaluation. In the human services, neglect of the evidence regarding the persistence of ethnic culture can lead to oversimplified understanding of family and community systems in the ethnic neighborhood.

Conceptual confusion in this area can be illustrated by the difficulties in defining ethnicity. Ethnic groups, for example, have been defined many ways by different authors. Different core elements are included in the various definitions of an ethnic group. Some, for example, include only the idea of common origin in their definitions. Accordingly, some define an ethnic group as a group of people who share a common national origin or presumed common origin. Broader definitions of an ethnic group include differentiation of the group on the basis of several elements such as race, religion, geography, or language (Greeley, 1974:291). The idea of a group sharing a common culture is frequently found in definitions of an ethnic group. Isajiw and Schermerhorn stress this element in their definitions. According to Isajiw (1974:122).

> an ethnic group can be considered to be an involuntary group of people who share the same culture or . . . descendants of such people who identify themselves and/or are identified by others as belonging to the same involuntary group.

Schermerhorn's (Greeley, 1974:291) definition is more elaborate but does not include the dimension of involuntary group membership,

> a collectivity within a larger society having real or putative common ancestry, memories of a shared historical past, and a cultural focus on one or more symbolic elements defined as the epitome of the peoplehood. Examples of such symbolic elements are: kinship patterns, physical contiguity (as in localism or sectionalism), religious affiliation, nationality, phenotypical features, or any combination of these. A necessary accompaniment is some consciousness of kind among members of the group.

Ethnicity may serve a number of social-psychological functions. For some, ethnicity is important as an element in their social identity and self-definition. Not much is known about the role of this aspect of ethnicity in the human services. In a recent study Erickson (1975) presents evidence that ethnic identity has something to do with outcomes in encounters between students and counselors. This study shows that when students and counselors share the same European ethnic background, counselors tend to make special efforts to help. Co-membership in the same ethnic group also appears to have positive effects on the communication between student and counselor.

Greeley points out that European ethnic groups continue to serve the function of providing a pool of preferred associates so that it is possible, if one chooses,

> to live almost entirely within the bounds of the community. One can work, play with, marry, attend church with, vote with and join fraternal organizations with people who are of exactly the same ethnic background. One can choose fellow ethnics to perform all the professional functions one requires, from interior decorator to psychiatrist to undertaker. One can belong to ethnic organizations, read ethnic newspapers, seek counsel from ethnic clergymen, play on ethnic baseball teams and vote for ethnic candidates in elections. [Greeley, 1971:47]

This function may suggest that access to certain services in the ethnic neighborhood might be facilitated if services are structured and organized as integral aspects of the ethnic subcommunity.

Although the evidence is fragmentary and incomplete, European ethnic groups may continue to function as bearers of distinctive cultural traits in a number of important areas. This issue has obvious relevance to our understanding of differences in individual and family systems. Giordano (1973), for example, has identified several studies which present considerable evidence of ethnic differences in areas such as value orientations, definitions of family roles, responses to physical and mental illness, utilization rates of mental health facilities, reactions of physical pain, and variations in the incidence of mental disorders.

Greeley (1974) has recently attempted to demonstrate that European ethnic groups in the United States continue to function as cultural systems with distinctive attitudes and behaviors. Through an extensive secondary analysis of existing data sources, Greeley has compiled fascinating evidence that many traits among descendants of immigrants in the United States appear to be consistent with ethnic cultural traits found in countries of origin prior to immigration to the United States. Greeley's data suggest that descendants of Italian-Americans, for example, are more fatalistic and less inclined than other groups to stress independence in children. Italian-Americans also seem less inclined toward democratic process and more restrictive in their attitudes toward male and female sexuality. These patterns are shown to be consistent with those found in southern Italy at the time of the groups immigration to the United States.

Greeley rejects assimilation as a model for studying European ethnic groups. The author points out that assimilation models are based on the assumption that ethnic culture begins to disappear when members of an ethnic group arrive in the United States. "Ethnogenesis," the alternative model presented by the author, suggests that ethnic groups as cultural systems do not disappear in American environment. Ethnic groups only adapt and change in the United States. Over time they take on new forms but do not disappear as cultural systems. Greeley concludes that ethnic groups continue to possess distinctive cultural traits which are different from other ethnic groups and different from those possessed by the group during the time of immigration to the United States. Ethnogenesis suggests that gross similarities between ethnic groups emerge as responses to a common culture in the United States, but important subtle cultural differences continue to distinguish one ethnic group from the other in contemporary American society.

Vecoli's (1974) position on Italian-Americans is consistent with the point of view that ethnic groups continue to function as bearers of distinctive attitudes and behaviors. According to this author, the way of life in the Italian-American white ethnic neighborhood is a compound of southern Italian and urban American folkways.

> It is in this anthropological sense that one can speak of an Italian-American culture today. Its core values are the primacy of personal relationships and of right behavior within these relationships. An unwritten code specifies the reciprocal obligations among members of the immediate family, relatives, and friends. Within the primary group, emotional intensity characterizes these relationships, and because emotions are not really repressed, feelings of love, hate, anger erupt freely. The purely contractual, legalistic, or economic relationships which is so typical of American society is foreign to such a value system. [Vecoli, 1974:31-43]

Vecoli goes on to identify the salient qualities of Italian-American ethnic culture. These include: the obligation of loyalty to family and friends; domesticity (enjoyment of home and family); the dominant role of the male; the importance of cutting a fine figure; overflowing hospitality; the passion for food and drink; and the respect for authority figures.

SOCIAL CLASS PERSPECTIVES ON THE ETHNIC NEIGHBORHOOD

Many believe that attitudes and behavior patterns in the working-class ethnic neighborhood should be attributed to social class rather than ethnicity. This issue is confusing. In the literature, the same group characteristics are often attributed to both ethnic culture and social class. Complex problems are involved in separating the influence of ethnic culture from social class. In spite of these difficulties, studies based on the social class hypothesis have contributed a great deal to our understanding of the working-class ethnic neighborhoods.

Social class can be defined in more than one way. The life-style definition of social class is particularly useful to human service issues in the ethnic neighborhood. In this approach to social class, society is viewed as consisting of four major life-styles associated with the lower class, working class, middle class, and professional upper-middle class. Class life-styles are seen, by some, as responses to available educational and occupational opportunities in the United States. The lower class consists of marginal and unskilled laborers. Stable semi-skilled and skilled workers are considered to be members of the working class.

One of the best illustrations of the class approach is Gans's (1968) study of the Italian neighborhood in the former West End of Boston. This study offers a richly detailed and insightful picture of life-styles found among lower- and working-class Italian-Americans. Gans's conclusions regarding attitudes, values, and behavior patterns are of considerable importance for human service intervention in working-class ethnic neighborhoods. Before reviewing some of the principle ideas of the study, it should be noted that a number of factors tend to limit the generalizability of the findings. Gans's conclusions are derived from participant observation rather than a representative sample in the ethnic neighborhood. Moreover, the study is now over two decades old, and it was undertaken during a period when the community was being threatened with demolition and redevelopment by urban renewal authorities. This external threat to the ethnic neighborhood may have influenced attitudes among members of the community.

Gans's study attempts to demonstrate that life among the working class of any ethnic background revolves around two primary groups, the family circle and the adult peer group. The family circle consists of collateral relatives, such as married siblings and in-laws, of the same sex, age, and stage in the family life cycle. A limited number of very close friends may also be members of the family circle. Adult peer groups consist of adults, relatives, and friends who may have been members of street corner youth groups. The compositions of these peer groups, therefore, remains relatively unchanged over time. Members of these unchanging peer groups tend to be of the same ethnic group and social class background. Peer group life, according to the study, is based on "sociability," which is defined as the routinized gathering of the group on a frequent basis. The social structure of the ethnic neighborhood is, in fact, considered to be a network of connected groups. Outside of employment, the majority of the residents spend a great deal of their time interacting with members of the peer group. This is not the case with all residents, however. Those who are more socially mobile do not spend as much time with peer groups in the ethnic neighborhood.

The density of this group life has important social-psychological consequences for the individual. The extensive involvement with kin and friends in the peer group society fosters a sense of belonging and social acceptance for the individual. Peer groups are also important for the individual since they frequently function as a vehicle for the exchange of needed goods, services, and emotional support. Within these groups, the individual is subject to considerable social pressures. Strong controls are exerted on the individual to conform to working-class values and behaviors. The family circle and adult peer group are the main avenues through which the working-class individual expresses his uniqueness and individuality.

The most important function of these groups, however, is the "person orientation" that they encourage. Person-oriented behavior is distinguished by the crucial importance placed on informal personal relationships. In the person orientation a great deal of value is placed on being a member of a group in which one aspires to be liked by others whom one likes in return. Social relationships are the principal aim of the person orientation. Gans concludes that the person orientation is one of the principle distinguishing characteristics of the working class. Social relationships in the middle, professional, and upper-middle classes are viewed as more likely to be colored by stress on goal or object-oriented individualism. This portrayal of the importance of informal group life among the working class significantly contributes to the understanding of life-styles in working-class ethnic neighborhoods.

ORIENTATIONS TO LOCAL NEIGHBORHOOD

Localism is the third concept essential to an understanding of working-class ethnic neighborhoods. Localism refers to the significance and attachment to people, places, and institutions of an immediate residential area. While important to most people, the significance and attachment to local areas is likely to vary depending on factors such as social class, sex, position of families in the life cycle, and physical properties of the area (Mann, 1970:537). Among the working-class ethnics, local people, places, and institutions have especially strong emotional significance.

Fried (1963, 1970), and Ryan (1963) offer an interesting picture of the importance of people, places, and institutions among residents of working-class ethnic neighborhoods. An underlying theme in their work is that middle-class professionals and planners seldom appreciate working-class commitments to neighborhood places and social arrangements. Fried points out that home is not merely a dwelling for many working-class ethnics. Streets and facilities, for example, may actually be viewed as extensions of home. The significance of local places beyond the dwelling is also likely to be reinforced when fellow ethnics and kin are concentrated in the neighborhood (Krickus, 1970). According to Fried, familiar local places are sources of considerable residential satisfaction even when the physical characteristics of a local area are not attractive by middle-class standards. In fact, Fried seems to suggest that it may be possible to distinguish between working-class and middle-class attitudes toward local space. Working-class structuring of space is viewed as territorial, that is, the structuring of local space in terms of a bounded area in which one belongs. The middle class, on the other hand, are viewed as more likely to draw sharp boundaries between their dwelling units and the immediate environs. The immediate area beyond the dwelling is not considered "ours." Attachments to places, among the middle class, is apt to be more selective and less focused on adjacent areas and places. Both Ryan and Fried stress the great importance of the local area. Its places and social arrangements are internalized aspects of a working-class group and spatial identity. In their view, a sense of spatial identity and belonging, most notably in the working class, is tied to externally stable places, facilities, and group networks in the local residential area. In assessing the impact of urban renewal on ethnic neighborhood dwellers, Fried suggests that relocation from the local neighborhood can produce a situational crisis associated with very strong grief reactions:

> Since most notability in the working class, effective relationships with others are dependent on a continuing sense of common group identity, the experience of loss and disruption of these affiliations is intense and frequently irrevocable. On the grounds, therefore, of both spatial and interpersonal orientations and commitments, dislocation from the residential area represents a particularly marked disruption in the sense of continuity for the majority of their group.

Ryan concludes that an expressive interpersonal orientation, centering on "friendliness," contributes to the significance of the neighborhood to working-class ethnics. Friendliness is defined as the feeling of commonness and mutual acceptance. Even if only an idea not always achieved, residents tend to view friendliness as the central attribute of local interaction. Friendliness according to most ethnics is what makes an area a neighborhood. In addition to providing an opportunity for cartharsis, commonness, and mutual acceptance, ethnic neighborhood relationships are a source of self-esteem and self-worth among residents.

The orientation to informal and friendly group life helps to explain patterns of local community participation among working-class ethnics. For the most part, members of the ethnic neighborhood participate in community associations mainly because they serve the purpose of providing additional opportunities for informal social activities, rather than cooperative work aimed at the accomplishment of abstract goals. The person orientation of group life in the ethnic neighborhood, however, leaves many individuals somewhat ill prepared for roles in task-oriented community activities. Participation in organizations that meet the needs of the peer group reinforces emotional ties to people and places in the local community. One study of the ethnic neighborhood (Fandetti, 1974) reveals participation in the following types of community associations:

Ethnic fraternal organization

Parent Teacher Association

Political club

Church societies

Social club

Veterans of Foreign Wars

Moose

Bingo club

American Legion

Knights of Columbus

The same study shows that a much smaller number, perhaps those more socially mobile, participate in newly formed social action and community development associations.

The Catholic church, perhaps more than any other institution, organizes the white ethnic neighborhood into a meaningful community system. As the center of a number of activities and associations, the church has an effect in keeping personal associations within the boundaries of the local community. Priests in the Catholic church have many important functions including the administration of the sacraments and rituals; confessional and periodic visits to homes in the parish; supervision of the moral training of children in parochial schools; and supervision of parishioners in church associations. Both priests and nuns are in touch with parish members at all stages of the life cycle from baptism to death (Warner and Srole, 1945:218). Even the Italian-Americans, who earlier demonstrated a traditional pattern of independence and ambivalence toward the church, are now more strongly affiliated with the Catholic church as an institution. With increasing acculturation and improved socioeconomic status, use of parochial schools has become more widespread. In some ethnic neighborhoods as many as 95% of Italian-American families have enrolled their children in parochial elementary schools (Fandetti, 1974).

Historically, groups such as the Polish have identified very strongly with the Catholic church. Thomas and Znaniecki (1958) describe the Catholic parish as one of the primary groups toward which the Polish developed intense feelings. Traditionally, the parish has been the locus of social solidarity. Socially oriented in nature, the church has traditionally offered a sense of participation through regular meetings, societies, and fraternaties. The intense feeling among the Polish for the Catholic church is also rooted historically in their association of the Catholic church with Polish nationalism (Thomas and Znaniecki, 1958).

In the ethnic neighborhood, the Catholic church has an important relationship to traditional family structure. In some respects it is a "cult of the family" with symbols and rituals filled with family elements. (Warner and Srole, 1945:123-124) The parochial school is an instrument of the family centered Catholic church which shares in the socialization and control of children. Among the institutions of the local ethnic community, the parochial school provides a secondary structure to supplement the control functions of the family (Warner and Srole, 1945:237-238)

IMPLICATIONS FOR SERVICE DELIVERY

An attempt has been made to introduce themes pertinent to the organization and delivery of services in Catholic working-class neighborhoods of southern and eastern European heritage. The discussion focused on several dimensions related to ethnicity, social class, and localism in the context of the ethnic neighborhood. Each of these concepts provided a useful focus in examining information and issues related to white ethnic neighborhoods. The issues reviewed appear to offer several useful concepts for service delivery in the ethnic neighborhood. The conclusions arrived at in the following discussion are primarily points of departure for those who wish to better conceptualize service delivery in the ethnic neighborhood. The problems and issues involved should become increasingly relevant as efforts are made to expand coverage in public services to the working class as well as the poor in our society.

Available evidence suggests that the role of European ethnic culture in shaping attitudes and behavior should be the subject of more intensive study in the human services. For many clients, the quality of diagnostically rendered case services could be improved if patterns in ethnic families were better understood. It would be extremely useful to know whether socialization is different among white ethnic groups such as the Polish, the Italians, and the Irish. There is a need to know whether ethnic groups have different styles of intimate behavior. In Greeley's (1974:321) terms, we need to know how the various ethnic groups "do" family, marriage, friendship, birth, and death. Efforts to adapt services to ethnic neighborhoods might also begin by establishing more in-service training programs on ethnicity for staff in social service and mental health facilities serving ethnic neighborhoods (Giordano, 1973:41). Evidence regarding the persistence of ethnic cultural traits suggests that staff involved in case services should be better acquainted with ethnographic and even literary sources on ethnic cultural heritage. Practitioners can have an important role in identifying issues and questions for further research. Practitioners also need to become more acquainted with theory on cultural value orientations. Social psychiatrist, John

Spiegel, for example, has recently developed a very useful framework for evaluating the interplay between psychological variables and value orientations in mental health and illness. Spiegel's material is particularly useful for case services because of its emphasis on sharpening skills in assessing values among clients of different social class and ethnic backgrounds. Advancing a social systems perspective, Spiegel points out that,

> psychotherapists, especially those who are psychoanalytically oriented, are especially sensitive to the psychological dimension that characterizes their transactions with a patient . . . they are rarely sensitized, however, to the variations in cultural and social role dimensions that are also important features in the field of transacting processes that characterize the patient-therapist interaction. [Papajohn and Spiegel, 1975:293]

At another level, there will need to be a stronger emphasis on neighborhood in the delivery of services aimed at reaching white ethnics. Some form of multi-ethnic service system located in the ethnic neighborhood seems to be required. Jenkins and Morrison (1974) sheds some light on the issues involved by identifying three basic approaches to making multi-ethnic systems a reality. These approaches include: increased representation and input from ethnic groups at all levels of service planning and delivery; changes in the law and administrative regulations of existing programs to make them more responsive to the needs of ethnic groups; and the creation of separate service systems conceived and administered by an ethnic group. Some discussion of each of these approaches will help to elucidate some of the pertinent issues.

Regarding the first approach, few would quarrel over the value of providing representation and input from residents of working-class ethnic neighborhoods, should additional efforts be made to introduce social services into these communities. Jenkins's second approach, changes in the law and administration, requires closer examination. The accent on localism in the ethnic neighborhood suggests that social service enabling legislation and administrative practices should facilitate a strong local neighborhood orientation, with local people, places, and institutions playing an important role in service delivery. Local resources have an advantage in service delivery because of their relationship to local life-styles. Administratively, social services can be viewed in terms of a hierarchy with less specialized counseling services and certain types of concrete resources located at the neighborhood level (Kahn, 1969:289). Many specialized services need to be located at the next level, outside of the neighborhood, to serve a larger geographic area. In the ethnic neighborhood, less specialized counseling services and some concrete resources, such as day care and programs for the aged, should be affiliated with local places and institutions. Some feel that counseling services could be organized to stress function rather than official buildings. That is, staff could be out-posted in familiar places and traditional institutions such as the parochial school, the church, or perhaps, union halls.

Case services might also be designed to utilize local people, such as housewives to perform some tasks (Giordano, 1973:41). The emphasis in such an approach is on informality and flexibility in the deployment of services rather than professional and structural rigidity. The neighborhood approach attempts to strengthen traditional structures of assistance, such as the church, which are effective institutions in the working-class ethnic neighborhood. There is evidence, for example, that ethnic families view the Catholic church as a preferred auspice for social utilities serving children and the aged (Fandetti and Gelfand, 1976; Fandetti, 1976). A neighborhood approach in ethnic communities attempts to create pluralism in the public-sectarian sense. Sectarian service auspices may facilitate initial acceptance of services in the ethnic neighborhood. Catholic residents of ethnic neighborhoods are not likely to favor monopoly in service delivery by government agencies. Such a system would, however, require public grants or purchase of service arrangements.

The emphasis, however, on neighborhood and affiliation of services with local places and institutions should not obscure limitations and problems in this approach. Some experienced organizers have reported considerable difficulty in their attempts to introduce services in the ethnic neighborhood. In some areas, ethnic community leaders have rejected social services, fearing that neighborhood residents might become less dependent on politicians and other leaders as they learn to rely on social service workers. Social services may be viewed as competitors by local politicians (IAM, 1977:62). Decentralization of services to the neighborhood level has its limits. No single neighborhood can contain the entire range of specialized services needed by residents. As indicated earlier, services deployment is hierarchical. Administrative issues, high cost, and low user density for some services require that certain services be located outside of the neighborhood to serve a wider geographic area. This suggests that parallel efforts in service planning need to assure pathways and linkage to needed services beyond the boundaries of the ethnic neighborhood. It can also be argued that a neighborhood emphasis in service delivery can reinforce parochialism and isolation of the ethnic neighborhood from the citywide social welfare network. The neighborhood focus should not be romanticized. Gans, for example, has shown how local cultural and emotional orientations among white ethnics can create negative results in service delivery. Strong ties to local life-styles can result in uneasiness, ambivalence, and even suspicion toward institutions of the wider society, resulting in delays in the use of needed services which are available outside of the ethnic community (Gans, 1968). Delays in the use of social services means lost opportunities for early intervention in potentially serious individual and family problems. The need for linkage and access to the wider network of service suggests that the neighborhood system also requires centers for the provision of information, outreach, referral, and general practice social work. General practice roles stress basic rapport with ethnic families and coordination of service aimed at overcoming discontinuity and obstacles to reaching required services.

This discussion of the value of strengthening rather than weakening traditional local structures in service delivery for the ethnic neighborhood would be incomplete without some reference to the family as an institution in these communities. Ethnic neighborhoods are traditionally family-oriented communities where extended family members often function as internal caretakers (Gans, 1968:159). Aunts and uncles, for example, aid in the rearing of children and care of aged family members. Too little attention has been given to examining ways in which extended family members might be assisted and encouraged to provide valuable services to family members. We may have too readily accepted and perhaps encouraged the transfer of many family functions to institutions external to the extended family unit. Our practice, for example, in services such as day care and some programs for the aged is to favor paying strangers rather than family members to provide needed services and care (Kahn, 1976). Insufficient attention is being addressed to the feasibility of providing increased financial incentives to relatives, who may continue to express a willingness to provide services for children and the aged. Expensive services are purchased from institutions but not from members of the family circle. Contradictions in this area suggest a need for closer attention to family oriented objectives in social service delivery. Family oriented, ethnic neighborhoods are likely to benefit from any increased efforts in social policy to strengthen the extended family as a source of assistance in our society.

The final approach to creating multi-ethnic service systems is that of ethnic separatism. The issue requires some clarification in the context of the white ethnic neighborhood. The need for such an approach in service delivery was first raised in relation to the needs of blacks in service delivery. Some see the creation of separate service systems, conceived and administered by blacks, as the only truly effective means of reaching blacks and counteracting institutionalized racism in the general social service system (Jenkins and Morrison, 1974:98). In this view, institutional racism and exlcusion provide the major rationales for the development of separate agencies and systems. While no attempt is being made to evaluate this approach for blacks, there appears little justification for extending the concept to southern and eastern European ethnic groups. Some discrimination against these white ethnic groups continues to exist in some institutions, but few would view this as a basis for separatism in service delivery for white ethnic groups. The neighborhood approach in single ethnic group areas might in effect create service populations consisting primarily of one ethnic group. Some ethnic interest groups might also attempt to bargain for resources to "take care of our own" or to fill gaps in services to a particular ethnic group. Multi-ethnic service systems for white ethnic groups, however, should not be confused with ethnic separatism.

REFERENCES

BARONI, G., and GREEN, G. (1976). Who's left in the neighborhood. Washington, D.C.: National Center for Urban Ethnic Affairs.

ERICKSON, F. (1975). "Gatekeeping and the melting pot: Interactions in counseling encounters." Harvard Educational Review, 45(February):44-70.

FANDETTI, D. (1974). Sources of assistance in a white, working class ethnic neighborhood. Unpublished dissertation, Columbia University.

——— (1976). "Day care in working class ethnic neighborhoods: Implications for social policy." Child Welfare, 55(November):618-626.

FANDETTI, D., and GELFAND, D. (1976). "Care of the aged attitudes of white ethnic families." Gerontologist, 16(6):544-549.

FRIED, M. (1963). "Grieving for a lost home." Pp. 151-171 in L. Duhl (ed.), The urban condition. New York: Basic Books.

FRIED, M., and GLEICHER, P. (1970). "Some sources of residential satisfaction in an urban slum." Pp. 730-745 in R. Gutman and D. Popenoe, Neighborhood, city and metropolis. New York: Random House.

GANS, H. (1968). The urban villagers. New York: Free Press.

GIORDANO, M. (1973). Ethnicity and mental health. New York: National Project on Ethnic America of the American Jewish Committee.

GREELEY, A. (1971). Why can't they be like us. New York: E.P. Dutton.

——— (1974). Ethnicity in the Unitid States. New York: John Wiley.

IAM (1977). 1:62-63.

ISAJIW, W. (1974). "Definitions of ethnicity." Ethnicity, 1(July):111-124.

JENKINS, S., and MORRISON, B. (1974). Identification of ethnic issues in child welfare: A review of the literature. Mimeo. New York: Columbia University School of Social Work.

KAHN, A. (1969). Studies in social policy and planning. New York: Russell Sage Foundation.

——— (1976). "Explorations in family policy." Social Work, 21:181-187.

KANTROWITZ, N. (1969). "Ethnic and residential segregation in the New York Metropolis, 1960." American Journal of Sociology, 74(6):685-695.

KRICKUS, R. (1970). White ethnic neighborhoods ride for the bulldozer. New York: National Project on Ethnic America of the American Jewish Committee.

MANN, P. (1970). "The neighborhood." Pp. 568-582 in R. Gutman, and D. Popenoe, Neighborhood, city and metropolis. New York: Random House.

PAPAJOHN, J., and SPIEGAL, J. (1975). Transactions in families. San Francisco: Jossey-Bass.

RYAN, E. (1963). "Personal identity in an urban slum." Pp. 135-149 in L. Duhl, (ed.), The urban condition. New York: Basic Books.

THOMAS, W., and ZNANIECKI, F. (1958). The Polish peasant in Europe and America (2 vols.). New York: Dover.

VECOLI, R. (1974). "The Italian Americans." Center Magazine, 7(July-August):31-43.

WARNER, W., and SROLE, L. (1945). The social systems of American ethnic groups. New Haven, Conn.: Yale University Press.

5

AGENCY AND FAMILY LINKAGES
IN PROVIDING NEIGHBORHOOD SERVICES

EUGENE LITWAK

In this paper some general principles of neighborhood programming will be developed. We will consider when large-scale formal organizations are most effective for handling tasks; when the small primary groups, like families and friends, are most effective; ane when organizations in between, like voluntary associations or small human relations structures, might be most effective. This first issue is central for dealing with the second and major aspect of this paper—establishing the principles by which social agencies might relate to community neighborhood groups. Should agencies seeking to reach the neighborhoods concentrate on mass media, decentralized storefront services, aggressive outreach programs, the use of indigenous people, or some combination of all of these? In addition, should the agency adopt an advocate's orientation or an enabler-facilitator approach? Finally, the larger question to which this paper will address itself concerns the circumstances under which each of these approaches might be justified.

AGENCY AND NEIGHBORHOOD PRIMARY GROUPS:
WHO DOES WHAT?

To understand the principles of neighborhood programming, we must first have a grasp of the more fundamental matter—which problems can be handled best by large-scale organizations and which by primary groups like families and neighborhoods? To start with there are some basic orientations in the field of social work that allude to this issue somewhat directly and which should be reviewed briefly. One approach, the large-scale bureaucratic organization (characterized by a stress on universalistic merit criteria, detailed specialization, long ladders of hierarchy, impersonality, stress on rules) is viewed, by some, as the most effective (Henderson and Parsons, 1974:354). The history of the Social Security Administration might provide a good illustration of this point of view. Effectiveness in administration of this agency has coincided with the use of large-scale machinery, like computers, and the increasing routinization of work. The suggestion of some that we move in a direction of negative income tax or some fixed family allotment plan in the field of income maintenance require such a rationalistic bureaucracy. The development of such rationalistic structures and their effectiveness in the field of social work has been documented by Wilensky and Lebeaux (1958:233-265). Carried to an extreme, such a position advocates that the sooner the formal organizations take over the handling of most social work problems the better off society will be. Thus children without an adequate parent should be put in boarding schools or the equivalent of a modern humane orphanage run by professionals; mentally ill people are best treated in closed institutions; delinquency is best handled in training schools; older people are best cared for in homes for the aged, and so forth.

In great contrast to such a position, there are at least two movements that suggest that the family, the neighbors, or the lay individual, not the expert, is the key to the solution of social work problems. One traditional social work position assumes that participation is the be all and end all of social work practice. The nonexpert must play a key role in all aspects of social work practice and the units of decision making must be small. Insofar as experts are used, they clearly cannot be part of a large scale organization. It would be very difficult, if not impossible to mobilize the staff of very large organizations to meet continually with their lay clients.

These traditional orientations were joined somewhat later by a movement in the middle and late 1960s (Reiff and Riessman, 1964) which stated that a significant number of activities now covered by the social work mantle were, in fact, activities which could be handled better by local indigenous people. The stress on indigenous people was often an indirect attack on the need for specialized training and large-scale formal organizations.

Between these extremes are those who view service delivery along a continuum of more or less formalized bureaucracies. Thus, those arguing that social work should move from a custodial orientation to a treatment orientation in mental hospitals and prisons were often also arguing that social work should move from a more rationalistic bureaucracy to a more collegial or human relations one. In addition, those arguing that we should move from closed institutions to halfway houses or to group homes were, in effect, arguing that we should move from highly organized structures to those which come very close to traditional primary structures like the family and neighborhood.

To more fully understand this first basic issue we need to recall why many people think large-scale rationalistic organizations are effective. Without trying to develop all of the details of the rationalistic structure, it should be quite clear that in contrast to primary groups, like the family and neighborhood, the rationalistic group can concentrate technical knowledge and organize large-scale manpower resources to achieve most goals far more efficiently. However, when confronted with this type of argument, some are overwhelmed by its logic and resist the image of a life dominated by large impersonal structures and the lack of participation by the ordinary citizen. They feel compelled to make a choice between efficiency and a democratic, humane way of life. The position taken in this paper is that there is no need to make a choice between being effective and being humane. Those arguing that the rationalistic bureaucracies are most effective have at best only a partial truth. There are indeed many tasks, equally important to those handled by the bureaucracy, which can best be handled by primary groups. Thus, the humaneness and warmth provided by primary groups are as essential to the effective achievement of most goals as is the rationalistic approach of bureaucratic organizations.

To fully understand this point we first of all need to understand that there are tasks for which technical knowledge provides no advantage. What might such tasks be? They are tasks which involve very unpredictable events; or situations where experts cannot be brought to the scene in time to make a difference; or tasks which require no more resources than the ordinary individual has in his own primary group. As a simple example, pulling a two-year-old child out of the path of an oncoming automobile is a highly unpredictable event which requires no more resources than the ordinary individual has in his everyday life. Using only specialists like policemen is not necessary or practical. Similar problems would arise for those with technical knowledge in more complex situations that had an enormous number of contingencies. In terms of the expertise itself, it is impossible to develop exact technical training and formal organizations for all tasks and all contingencies. Also, technical knowledge is not applicable (by definition) in frontier areas of any profession. For instance, psychotherapists do not have techniques and knowledge which enable them to handle problems like alcoholism, compulsive eating, or dope addiction. As a consequence, many therapists refer such clients to primary-like groups, such as Alcoholics Anonymous, who do as well if not better when all the costs are assessed.

In other words, the argument is made that where tasks involve great idiosyncratic influences, many contingencies, or frontier areas they require resources and knowledge that the ordinary individual receives from his everyday socialization. Therefore, in consideration of the nature of the tasks and the limitations in large-scale organizations, one begins to question the justification for rational bureaucracy. For purposes of clarification in the rest of this paper, we shall refer to tasks involving contingencies, frontier areas, and so on as *nonuniform tasks* and tasks which bureaucracies can best handle as *uniform ones.*

Keeping in mind the differences between primary groups and bureaucracies with regard to elements of organizational theory such as decision making, communication networks, division of labor, procurement of resources, and so on, we can begin to understand that primary groups are indeed more effective for handling nonuniform tasks and that bureaucracies are more effective for handling uniform ones. However, questions arise as to how extensive and important are the nonuniform tasks and how likely are they to survive in a world dominated by science and technology. Most experts agree that in current society such nonuniform tasks as the following are extensive and important: early care and socialization of the infant, the teaching of basic language, the preparation of food, the selection and purchase of clothes, the management of transportation by automobiles, the selection of one's spouse, etc. But debate still ranges as to whether or not formal bureaucratic organizations are indeed the most effective in a society dominated by science and technology. Those asserting the superiority of bureaucracies point out that more and more functions have been stripped away from the family and turned over to large formal organizations. The place of work has been moved out of the family into large-scale corporations and bureaucracies. This is true of medicine, of law enforcement (police bureaucracy), the manufacturing of clothing (clothing plants), the care of aged (social security bureaucracy), the protection against death (insurance companies), etc.

This analysis, while accurate, is only half of the tale. Although it is indeed true that for many preindustrial societies, dominated by kinship units the emergence of industrialization was accompanied by formal organizations taking over traditional family roles, that was only the first phase of industrialization. If the more recent phases are examined, one will discover that, in fact, there is clearly a distinguishable partnership arrangement between formal organizations and primary groups which often handle different parts of the same task. For example, if the family handles the cooking, the formal organization might handle the growing and merchandising of food. If the family handles the driving of the car, the automobile manufacturer and the garage handle the manufacturing and repair of the car, and so forth. Furthermore, if we examine the exchange between bureaucracy and primary groups which results from technological and scientific advances, we find a constant shifting back and forth between the two rather than the primary group losing and the bureaucracy gaining (Foote and Cottrell, 1955; Litwak and Figueira, 1968). Thus in the early stages of industrialization, transportation was handled through streetcars and large-scale organization. The development of the car gave the family control over transportation. Washing, initially done by the family, was eventually taken over by the laundries but currently is back in the family control as a consequence of the development of the home washing machine. Once this line of thought is highlighted, it becomes clear that there is an entire "do it yourself" industry that has been flourishing, which will flourish in the conceivable future, and which invariable indicates that some functions now being handled by formal organizations will be turned back to the community primary groups.

The reason we speak with such great assurance that science and technology will not lead to an elimination of nonuniform tasks (and therefore the effectiveness of the primary groups) is because there is no way to argue logically that science and technology invariably lead to economics of large scale. Instead they have an equal probability of leading to economics of small scale. We mean by the latter that science and technology are as likely to simplify and reduce the cost of a given procedure, so that the ordinary individual can use it, as they are to develop large-scale machinery requiring training so that only experts and large-scale organizations can house them. Thus, one may possibly argue that, in the logic of science and technology, airplane flying will be simplified so that ordinary persons will be flying their own airplanes just as they now drive their own cars, and that computers will be miniaturized and made so inexpensive and simple to run that ordinary individuals may have their own computers. It is hard to conceive of anything now being run by experts and large organizations which might not, through science and technology, be made simpler and inexpensive so the ordinary citizen with his everyday resources will be able to handle it. Of course, one may as easily make the reverse argument since science and technology do not, per se, move toward either economies of large scale or small scale. Rather they move toward economies; and as we have indicated, both economies of large scale and small scale have different virtues, but both are important. As such, we expect science and technology to continually produce both economies of small and large scale. Since these views have been developed more fully elsewhere, they will not be elaborated herein (Litwak and Figueira, 1968).

Recapitulating, we have said that *formal organizations should handle uniform events and primary groups should handle nonuniform ones if effectiveness is the desired goal.* As such, the practitioner is provided with crude criteria as to who should do what. However, these two groups are only extremes of an *organizational continuum,* and the two types of tasks are extremes of a *task continuum.* If the entire continuum is taken into account, then the number of alternatives open to a practitioner is considerably enlarged. Furthermore, we can view this continuum as a hierarchy of categories, with the absolutes and standardizations becoming fewer and fewer as the contingencies and variables ever become more and more. For instance, on one extreme we find the task of providing old age pensions as part of the social security system. This is a task which is relatively standardized and can benefit from large-scale resources such as computers, buildings for storing records, large staffs to process claims, and business administrators. Somewhat farther down the line of uniformity is the attempt to establish eligibility for income maintenance programs, although the rules for establishing such eligibility are not as clear cut as those of the previous category and have many more contingencies. Further on down the continuum is the social worker doing therapy, which deals with many more contingencies and involves many more areas of frontier knowledge and unpredictability. Still farther down the line are those people running halfway houses or group homes who must deal with the myriad problems of everyday living. Next are the volunteers who help out—making sandwiches for older people, helping with fund raising—and who require virtually no training or resources beyond that of the primary group. Finally, of course, we have the regular daily activities of preparing food, cleaning the shelter, succoring ordinary emotional problems, and so forth.

Parallel to these tasks is an organizational continuum. At the one extreme are the rationalistic bureaucracies, with object criteria of merit for appointment, detailed specialization, long ladders of hierarchy, detailed rules, and stress on impersonal relations. On the other extreme are the primary groups which stress just the opposite dimensions. However, in between we have organizational structures which can be described as exhibiting different amounts of each of the dimensions. This has been illustrated in Table 1. To show how to use the table, we will take one dimension, i.e., merit.

Rationalistic organizations utilize objective criteria of merit to cover almost all of their activities. Thus it could be argued that the Social Security Administration can give a test to most of its employees which can objectively grade their performance on all significant activities. In contrast, if we move down the organizational continuum to an organization which is slightly less rationalistic, we might find that their objective criteria of evaluation can only cover 85% of their activities. Such may be the case for welfare workers in major income maintenance programs, e.g., indigent women with young children. If organizations which have even less rationalistic structures are examined, like a small family therapy agency or a small closed institution which uses milieu therapy, then objective tests of merit can only cover from 60% to 70% of the significant activities. To evaluate performance in such situations requires much in the ways of subjective judgments and observing people in nonstandardized situations. Further down the organizational scale are the halfway houses or the group homes. Objective tests for evaluation performance may cover 20% to 40% of the activities.   .

When one considers both a task continuum and an organizational continuum, and the specific organizational structure which is best for fulfilling each task, many different alternatives require consideration. Implementation of a logical scheme based on this "continuum model" is not an easy matter. There are several major problems which must be dealt with.

First, there is a problem of measurement. At this point there are no quick and easy ways to measure organizations and tasks in the same way one can measure the length of an object by a tape measure. Generally, practitioners have to choose between one or two alternatives and the only measurement necessary is to say whether one structure is more or less rationalistic than another or one task is more or less uniform than another. For such crude choices, a scheme such as that suggested here might be useful.

Implied in the above illustration is a second limitation: often practitioners are not in a position to use maximum effectiveness as a criteria, when selecting a structure. Social norms or limited resources might prevent one from moving in the direction of what is the most effective, in which case the theory presented herein also suggests many alternative options which should be used. For instance, if the theory tells one that an entire class of people now in mental hospitals can be released to the community because their problems revolve around nonuniform tasks, but the law and social norms forbid this action, then the wise administrator might turn his attention toward making one part of his closed institution into a structure which closely resembles a primary-like environment. He may do this by moving toward a therapeutic milieu approach where the patients play a larger role in their own treatment; he may have volunteers come in who will provide primary group experiences; and he might seek to isolate this group of clients from those who have uniform problems. In effect this is what prison officials do when they feel that, with certain prisoners, custody (generally a uniform task) is not the key issue but rehabilitation (generally a nonuniform task) is the key. They seek to segregate those who need treatment from those who need custody and run two different types of prison administrations.

A third major problem area is based on the fact that at any given moment in time, empirical evidence might not permit one to determine whether the task is uniform or nonuniform. For instance, Freudian and neo-Freudian therapy, on the surface, seem to involve a more nonuniform definition of therapy processes than behavioral modification. Yet at this point in time the empirical evidence is not sufficient to say which, if either, is most effective. However, practitioners may have to make a decision in spite of the lack of information. The theory developed herein will not solve the immediate problem of which therapeutic modality is correct. Only more evidence will do that. However, it will indicate what kind of organizational structure is necessary once the practitioner made his choice.

A fourth limitation which is even more disturbing to some, is the understanding that the definition of uniform and nonuniform is often a value decision. For instance, in the field of social work, there are those who argue on the basis of morality that all people who are indigent should be provided food and shelter at a decent level—it is a human right. By contrast, there are those who argue on a different value premise: only those who display a willingness to

Table 1: Task and Organizational Continuum

Task Continuum	Extreme Uniformity[a]	Predominate Uniformity	Moderate Uniformity	Moderate Non-Uniformity	Predominate Non-Uniformity	Extreme Non-Uniformity	Multiple Tasks Uniform and Non-Uniform
	e.g., social security in U.S. or Automated Utilities	e.g. Establishing eligibility for welfare payments or unemployment insurance, custodial care of aged and mentally ill.	Psychotherapy of Freudian or neo-Freudian, or provision of direct family services like employment training.	Running of half-way home or group home, use of volunteers in fund raising.	Running of alcoholics annonymous, running small block clubs or intimate social clubs	Every-day activities such as driving, cooking, dressing, housekeeping, disciplining small children, etc.	Organization which has income maintenance and family counseling or housekeeping and billing departments as well as large treatment clinics. Mental hospital with strong custodial and treatment goals. Prisons with strong custodial and treatment goals.

Organizational Dimensions	Extreme Rationalistic[b]	Predominate Rationalistic	Moderate Human Relations	Strong Human Relations	Proto Primary Grp. Vol. Associations	Family, Neigh. & friends-Primary Grp.	Compartmentalized Organizations
% of tasks eval. by objective merit	90-100%	80-90	70-80	60-70	30-50	0-10	Sub unit 90-100 / Sub unit 60-70
degree to which job broken into small component for indiv. or machine specialization	90-100%	80-90	70-80	60-70	20-50	0-10	Sub-unit 90-100 / Sub-unit 60-70
Length of Authority ladder	Very long	Long	Shorter	Some Collegial	Collegial	Very Collegial	Sub-unit Long / Sub-unit Collegial
% of activities governed by rules	90-100%	80-90	70-80	60-70	20-50	20-50	Sub unit 90-100 / Sub unit 60-70
% of activities governed by impersonal norms	90-100%	80-90	70-80	60-70	20-50	20-50	Sub unit 90-100 / Sub unit 60-70
% of activities having a priori rights and duties	90-100%	80-90	70-80	60-70	20-50	20-50	Sub unit 90-100 / Sub unit 60-70
% of activities where administration and policy separated	90-100%	80-90	70-80	60-70	20-50	20-50	Sub-unit 90-100 / Sub-unit 60-70
Need for Balance linkages	Minor	Minor	Minor	Minor	Minor	Minor	Major

a. These are only points on the task continuum. There are presumably many more if we wanted to make even finer distinctions.
b. These are only points on the organizational continuum. At the very end we have included the compartmentalized which in turn can combine any two points on the task continuum. In addition, it is possible that the dimensions of organization will not vary together in which case we get even more organizational types. (See Litwak and Meyer, 1974).

work should be helped. Furthermore, since most people are inclined to cheat, to establish their true motives may require investigations. From the first value premise, the program of income maintenance would be defined as a uniform one with not too many contingencies. Only two things would be needed: first, that individuals say they are indigent; and second, a sampling check to see if their standard of living is below the minimum or not. However, by the second value premise, income maintenance programs would involve much more nonuniformity. Establishing desire to work involves many more contingencies and a continuous checking to see if behavior remains constant (is the person continually looking for work or only when the application is made, etc.). Unfortunately, there is nothing in the continuum model presented herein which enables individuals to say which value premise is right. Nevertheless, once the value premise is clearly stated, then the model could be used to indicate which form of organization might be most effective; and since many practitioners either have a value premise or one is foisted upon them by their employer, there is great virtue in having some scheme, such as ours, which indicates the next step.

Finally, we must consider a most important fifth area of difficulty. Any given organization may have to deal simultaneously with uniform and nonuniform problems. Thus if our theory and logic are correct, two kinds of structures will be needed. This issue is of central importance to the problem of agency-neighborhood programming. Following our hypothesis, an agency would handle uniform tasks while the neighborhood primary groups would handle the nonuniform tasks. Since our continuum model has indicated the need for different types of administrative structure to most effectively deal with these different types of tasks, the implication is that *an overall organizational structure with different subunits* is needed. Since these subunits stress somewhat contradictory elements of organization, it is generally felt that they should be isolated. Significantly, the need to coordinate these two subunits leads to the issue of agency-community linkage. The solution of this problem is what the rest of the paper will concentrate on.

AGENCY AND FAMILY LINKAGES IN
PROVIDING NEIGHBORHOOD SERVICES

In situations where agencies are developing services for neighborhoods and families, it is generally true that both uniform and nonuniform tasks are linked together. One typical way an agency will help a family is to provide extra resources where the family has broken down because of inadequate knowledge or resources. For instance, the family might break down because one member may have suffered severe physical or mental disability. The family as a primary group has the knowledge and resources to handle everyday forms of anxieties and minor illnesses of short duration, but it has neither the knowledge nor the resources to handle serious illnesses. At this point there is a need for a formal organization to take care of the uniform aspects so that the family can continue to handle the nonuniform ones.

A second typical way in which agencies provide service for families and neighborhoods is to provide them with information and organizing help in dealing with other large scale organizations in our society. Thus the man who is unemployed may not be familiar with the services he can get from the state unemployment agency; or a woman cheated by a store, tenants abused by landlords, or parents who seek to protest a school principal's arbitrariness, all may not know where to go or how to proceed. Such information tends to involve uniform tasks because these tasks generally require individuals who are very familiar with the organizational structure of the larger city or who have access to reference material which will enable them to find out about the various bureaucracies in question. Once this uniform aspect of the task is handled by the agency, the family can continue its nonuniform modes of action, e.g., boycott, refusal to pay rent, etc., in conjunction with the more uniform services supplied by the agency at issue.

The point which is central to the discussion is that neighborhood program-ming generally involves agencies in providing services around the uniform aspects of a given task, while, simultaneously, the family or some primary groups are assumed to handle the nonuniform aspects of the job.

The Balance Theory of Coordination

Our prior analysis suggests that such a division of labor is the most effective one. Thus, if an agency is seeking to provide services for the aged, it should never seek to supplant the primary group of a given option. A single aged person who finds it difficult to live by himself might best be helped by providing homemaker services, or by arranging for compatible neighbors in similar circumstances to live together, or by arranging for compatible kin groups to take the elderly person into the family. All of these solutions are characterized by retaining a primary group for the elderly persons and, as such, insuring that the nonuniform tasks in their life will be handled most effectively. However, the making of these arrangements might involve resources beyond the capacity of the elderly person, and this is where the resources of the agency come into the picture.

If this is all there were to the situation, the first part of the paper would be adequate to give direction for neighborhood service programming. However, it is now very important to point out that formal organizations, even those which are of the human relations-collegial type, have structures which stress behavior opposite to that which is stressed by primary groups: that is, the formal organizations stress the evaluation of individuals in terms of their merit (ability to achieve organizational goals); specialization not generalized diffused relations;

the need to follow rules and ladders of authority; and impersonal relations rather than continuous face-to-face contact.

This contradiction in structure raises a dilemma. The two types of groups must work closely together because uniform and nonuniform tasks are highly interdependent. At the same time, their structures are contradictory, and if the professionals and the members of the primary group work too closely together, this contradictory structure is likely to lead to the destruction either of the bureaucratic structure or of the primary group.

The conflict in structure manifests itself in the introduction of favoritism or nepotism in the formal organization with the workers giving better services to some of their clients than to others; or with the worker becoming overidentified with his clients and losing sight of organizational goals; or with staff losing sight of merit criteria altogether and accepting bribes for services. The contradiction in structure can also manifest itself in the introduction of bureaucratic norms into the family. Sometimes parents who are highly concerned that their child do well begin to treat their child like a teacher might treat a student. They make their parental approval contingent on the child's doing well in school, and they threaten to abandon the child if he does not do well. This same kind of instrumental contractual relationship sometimes develops when indigenous leaders of a local neighborhood suddenly begin to treat their friends and neighbors very instrumentally, once a target bureaucracy offers them a job and an opportunity for personal mobility.

It should be stressed that the dilemma of trying to coordinate tasks which have a contradictory structure is central to most social work agencies seeking to reach into the neighborhood. Thus, problems encountered are not a consequence of mismanagement or an overly rationalistic agency structure. The theoretical resolution of this dilemma, encompassed in the balance theory of "coordination," provides guidelines for almost all situations (Litwak and Meyer, 1974).

This theory states that the bureaucracies (i.e., agencies) and primary groups that are seeking to coordinate their activities must operate at some middle point of social distance. They must not be so close that their structures lead to conflict, and they must not be so far that they cannot coordinate their areas of specialty (that is, the handling of uniform and nonuniform aspects of the given task). They must continuously balance the costs of getting too close against those of getting too far and continuously seek the middle point where they can both minimize costs and optimize gains. This means that each practitioner or community person seeking to relate to the other has three possible distance diagnoses he can make: too distant, too close, or at the correct balance point. If the first is the correct diagnosis, he must seek linkages which close social distance, while if the second is the correct diagnosis he must seek linkages which will open social distance. If it is the last which is correct, he must seek linkages which maintain social distance.

There are many obvious illustrations of each of these conditions on the American scene. Thus Cloward and Epstein (1967) accused private social work agencies in the late 1950s and early 1960s of being too distant from the working class and very poor groups. They pointed out that these agencies did not stress services which would be useful to working class and very poor people and stressed the fact that their clientele was made up of middle-class people. The Community Service Society recently noted that there was one group of aged that was too distant from existing social agencies. They labeled these the "frail elderly"; they were those with physical and mental infirmities which prevented them from taking an active role in reaching agencies. Since most agencies had no outreach programs to get to these passive, low-resource people, they were never reached.

Another illustration of the problem of great distance occurs where agencies seek to locate a service in a hostile neighborhood. Thus, agencies seeking to locate group homes for children have found that middle-class neighborhoods are strongly resistant. The agency in this case is at some distance from the middle-class community. Agencies seeking to establish drug treatment centers meet with similar resistance. In general, agencies trying to deal with mental illness in lower-class neighborhoods may meet with great resistance because most families attach a stigma to mental illness.

The problem of closeness also may be manifested by certain client groups. Cloward and Epstein (1967), by suggesting that private agencies cater too much to the needs of the middle class, also illuminated the fact that because of the legitimization of psychotherapy among the more educated groups, the middle class is very likely to overuse such facilities if they are available; and, in this sense, this group may often be too close to the agency. When the Community Service Society launched a program (Friendship Center) to reach frail elderly people, they were swamped by older persons who were intact and aggressively looking for new facilities. From the point of view of the Community Service Society, this group was too close. In fact CSS referred these people to other programs and, in so doing, opened distance between these people and Friendship Center.

Finally, the problems of too great closeness also manifest themselves in the staff becoming overidentified with the client, as well as in the agency's providing services in a discriminatory fashion to given groups in the society.

LINKAGE MECHANISMS:
THE AGENCY REACHING INTO THE COMMUNITY

The balance theory suggests, in the case of too much distance, that the agency must use linkages to close distance; in the case of too much closeness, agencies must use linkages to open up distance. The theory of linkages will first be developed with regard to agencies seeking to intervene into the community and then with regard to community people seeking to intervene with agencies.

Agency Interventions

To begin this analysis, a list of typical ways in which agencies have reached into communities can be specified. This list is not intended to be exhaustive but only illustrative.

A Detached Worker Approach. The agency sends a paid professional into the home of the primary group, and the worker becomes a semi-member of the group in order to move it toward mutual goals. The youth worker who goes into the field to work with delinquent gangs is one illustration; the aggressive caseworker who seeks out a client who is too sick or passive to come into the agency might be another illustration; the community organizer who moves into the neighborhood he is seeking to organize is yet another illustration. This type of linkage can be used by any organization seeking to reach the community, not just social work agencies. Thus the church missionary often acts like a detached worker. The agricultural extension agent of the United States government will also often act in this capacity.

Indigenous Opinion Leaders of the Community. These leaders are not working for the agency. They either volunteer on their own to help the agency, or the agency might (through some other linkages like the detached worker) seek to recruit their help. Community organizers might typically work through such indigenous leaders as heads of block clubs, local clergymen, informal block leaders, etc. Such indigenous leaders were often the backbone of the old line political machines. Modern fund raising groups, such as those used in community chests, often use such people for raising money.

Decentralized Services. The agency brings physical facilities and professional services into close geographical proximity to the potential client. The settlement houses originally had this in mind when they were first established. In the 1960s the advent of storefront services suggested even greater decentralization of services. This kind of decentralization has also caught on in other areas of life and one of the more evident is the attempt to decentralize city halls in very large cities like New York.

Common Messengers. This is one of the more dramatic modes of interaction which uses indigenous people to link agency and community. This method differs from the use of local opinion leaders cited above in that the indigenous people are legally part of both the formal organizations and the community. There are basically three types of indigenous leaders. (1) There is the high powered lay person, such as a nonprofessional who is part of a governing agency board. Such people must be distinguished from (2) low-powered indigenous people, such as members of the community who are brought in as social work aids, custodians, or, in the school situation, as street crossing guards. These two groups must be distinguished from (3) the high-powered indigenous expert. This is the paid professional social worker who lives in the neighborhood. The reasons for these distinctions will become clear when we develop the theory of linkages.

Mass Media. Newspapers, television, leaflets, sound trucks, and so forth are another way agencies can reach the community. Often agencies seeking to raise money or to educate large numbers of people on problems of mental health or alcoholism have used the mass media approach.

Combination of Methods Plus Legal Authority. The use of legal authority is so distinctive that it has been highlighted as a separate form of linkage even though it overlaps with all of the above in terms of specific delivery mechanisms. The rationale for separating out linkages which can make use of legal force is the overwhelming character of legal force when used by a given agency against a given primary group. Thus the schools threaten to take parents to court and eventually to put the parents in jail if they refuse to give information to the truant officers. This possibility is so overwhelming that it gives the linkage distinctive character. The welfare department's capacity to punish clients for fradulent claims has this character as well. In Detroit, one well-known youth agency would pick up the delinquent gangs in the police station. The police who had caught the gang in criminal behavior had given the gang members the option of getting treatment from the youth worker or of going to training schools.

Delegated Authority. The example above is an illustration of a situation when a social work agency might find it advantageous to work through another formal organization. In the case just cited, the youth agency reached its delinquent gangs through the police. They might also work through the schools, the churches, and business organizations.

Voluntary Associations. This linkage is a favorite way by which agencies reach into the communities. Thus, mental hospitals can establish a group of community volunteers to come in and provide recreational activities for the clients. Voluntary associations are the backbone of major fund-raising activities. Many programs on the aging depend heavily on volunteers to help chauffeur aged people to hospitals and recreational centers. Organizations like the schools have parent-teacher associations which explicitly link the school to their community, while churches have lay church groups which do the same.

As mentioned above, the list of linkages is not meant to be exhaustive but does present typical ways in which agencies reach into the community. Those methods will be used to illustrate the major principles of linkage. If the linkage theory is correct, then it should give the practitioner general guidelines for assessing when a given linkage will close or open distance. Also it should help to indicate when one might ideally use each of the above linkage procedures, what sequencing might be appropriate, and how to assess new linkages which are not mentioned herein. It might even suggest guidelines to new linkages which must be built in the future.

Selective Listening and Sender Initiative

When one examines the literature on efforts by formal organizations to close social distance (such as persuading people to buy government bonds or convincing enemy soldiers to surrender), there has been an important common finding: the people who are most deviant from the agency are the ones who are least likely to listen to the message. For example, when a Democratic party politician gives a television speech or comes to a town to address a political rally, the people least likely to come to the speech or tune in the program are the rabid Republicans, and the people most likely to do both are the enthusiastic Democrats. The process by which the people most distant from the message sender avoid listening to the message has been labeled "selective listening" (Hyman and Sheatsley, 1947).

In the past many investigators have concentrated on the psychological mechanisms by which people avoided messages. Investigators have sought various ways to alter mass media messages. They have not given equal priority to major variations in the structure of alternative forms of linkage which would permit the message sender to overcome the problem of selective listening. Therefore, what is obviously needed to overcome selective listening is a linkage procedure which gives the sender initiative (rather than the target group) as to whether or not the message will be heard. If we examine the various linkages (Table 2), we see that there are some which leave initiative in the hands of the target population while others give more initiative to the sender. For instance, most forms of mass media leave the initiative in the hands of the target group because it takes very little effort on the part of the target population to turn off the mass media. To turn off the television channel takes only a flick of the wrist; to turn off a newspaper article takes only a minor adjustment of the eye muscles; and so forth.

To understand how little effort it takes to turn off the mass media, one must contrast it with such mechanisms as the detached worker. In this case, the agency is paying the professional at least eight hours a day to go to the home of the target group and stay with them until contact is established. In this case the members of the target population have to continuously speak to the detached worker if only to say they don't want to have anything to do with him. This requires far greater effort on their part than flicking a channel or moving an eyeball.

On the other side linkages such as voluntary associations give even greater discretion to the target population than mass media because mass media can generally force people to at least acknowledge the presence of an opposing view. That is, the newspapers (by virtue of a headline) or the mass media (by virtue of spot announcements) can generally make the most hostile person aware of the message even though the target population can avoid the details of the message by very simple efforts. But the use of linkages such as the voluntary association, opinion leader, and the settlement house without other backups depends almost exclusively on the target group taking the initiative even to hear the message. It should be clearly understood that all linkages (e.g., those listed in Table 2, those which people have used in the past but not listed, and those which people will invent in the future) can be assessed by the amount of initiative they give to the sender. The same point holds for the other dimensions discussed below.

Thus, our first point with regard to linkage theory is that practitioners must assess any given linkage in terms of sender initiative if they are interested in moving toward a balance point. The practitioner must make a diagnosis as to whether the community is too distant or too close. Then he must look at the linkages available to him and assess them in terms of the sender initiative they permit. Where the community is too distant, the practitioner must have linkages which give the sender or the agency great initiative. Where the community is too close, there must be linkages which are passive, that leave the initiative to the community. Where the administrator is faced with a mixed population, he must have linkages which have high sender initiative for the distant population and low sender initiative for the population which is not distant.

Selective Interpretation and Primary Group Intensity

Several earlier investigations studied linkages under conditions in which the sender had great initiative. These researchers discovered that getting people to listen to a hostile message does not necessarily mean that the message will get through. They found that people forced to listen to a message which was antithetical to them, engaged in a process of selection interpretation, which occurred in one of two ways.

First, people often take a complex message and select out the parts that were congenial to their views and ignore the rest. For instance, Paul F. Lazarsfeld points out that the simple question, "Why did you buy this book?" can be interpretated as Why did you buy rather than steal? Why did you rather than someone else buy? or Why did you buy a book rather than some other object? Where the message is much more complex, the opportunities for reinterpretation are much greater. A classic illustration of this process was described by investigators in the area of prejudice who told jokes that belittled prejudice to prejudiced people and were astounded to find out that the prejudiced people would often reinterpret the story so it turned out to be supportive of their views.

Another type of reinterpretation was found to take place over a period of time. A different group of researchers found that people might absorb a hostile message, but as time passed they would gradually forget that part of the message which was hostile and remember only those parts which were congenial.

In order to overcome these elements of selective interpretation, the various investigators suggested: (1) the need for continuous face-to-face interaction with the target group to allow for immediate correction of misinterpretations; (2) this face-to-face contact must be in many different areas of life to prevent the respondent from confining the message to one limited area; and (3) for this process to be fully effective it must eventually involve personal trust. In other words, although they are often unaware of it, these investigators have suggested, in actuality, that the linkage procedure must have something resembling a primary group character if selective interpretation is to be overcome. Prior investigators have produced empirical evidence which has led to a similar conclusion. Presently, however, we feel that an underlying theoretical explanation can better be supplied by using the balance theory. Basically, all that is necessary to make earlier writers consistent with the balance theory is to assert that they were dealing with primary groups and generally, had nonuniform tasks in mind when speaking about primary group intensity.

The high effectiveness of primary groups is due to their short lines of communication, ready availability of members to one another, and willingness of members to take risks for each other in times of uncertainty. In relation to balance theory, primary group-like linkages would result in faster communication, more flexibility in looking at alternatives, and lower cost for society. However, this type of linkage would not avoid problems of selective interpretation when uniform tasks were involved. Past investigators did, indeed, recognize this separation where uniform tasks were concerned.

If we now reexamine the linkages in Table 2, we see that they vary in their ability to provide primary group intensity. Nevertheless, this is not necessarily related to their capacity to provide sender initiative. For instance, the use of legal force, which might have high sender initiative, generally has low primary group intensity. Linkages such as opinion leader and settlement house, which may have low sender initiative, can have very high primary group intensity.

The central element in rating the linkages on primary group intensity is the extent to which they permit the agency (through its linkages) to have much face-to-face contact, as well as the extent to which they permit the generation of positive feelings of trust (rather than impersonal relations). The detached worker does permit all of these aspects. Thus, the youth worker with delinquent gangs is empowered to spend as much time as necessary (eight or more hours a day) to engage in a variety of activities with the gang and to develop positive trust relationships. Settlement house programs which run group therapy sessions may also have this characteristic. The opinion leader approach can have primary group intensity much more than any other linkage because it consists of real life primary groups. The same is true of linkages which we have called common messenger linkages (such as the indigenous worker). By contrast, mass media and large voluntary associations may be very low on this dimension.

Table 2: Theoretical Criteria for Evaluating Linkages Typically used by Agencies Reaching into the Community

Empirical Listing of Typical Linkages	Sender Initiative	Primary Group Intensity	Bureaucratic Intensity	Scope
1. Detached worker—professional sent into client's home	High	High	High	Lowest
2. Opinion leader—indigenous leader works on the agencies' behalf on a voluntary basis	Low (with regard to Agency)	Highest (with regard to Primary group)	Lowest	Moderate
3. Decentralized service—agencies locate physical facilities with paid professionals in close geographical proximity to client population, e.g., storefront services, settlement houses, etc.	Lowest	Moderate	Low	Moderate-High
4. Voluntary associations—agency uses volunteers to connect with community, volunteers to connect with community, e.g., fund raising for community chest, volunteers used to drive aged to doctors' appointments, visit sick patients, provide recreation for those in 24 treatment facilities.	Lowest	Moderate	Low	Moderate-High

Description				
5. High powered lay common messenger, e.g., lay person who is part of agency and group agency seeks to reach, e.g., member of the board of directors where agency seeks to get aid in fund raising, or where agency seeks to communicate with client groups such as community health planning boards.	High	High	Moderate Low	Moderate
6. High powered expert common messenger, e.g., paid professional who also lives in the area where he works such as settlement house worker who lives in the area.	High	Moderate-High	High	Moderate
7. Low powered indigenous common messenger—indigenous people who are hired for low powered jobs such as social work aids, street crossing guards, lunch room attendants, etc.	Moderate-Low	High	Moderate-Low	Moderate
8. Mass media—television, radio, newspapers, posters, etc.	Moderate-Low	Lowest	Moderate	Highest
9. Delegated authority, e.g., use other agencies	High to Low	High to Low	High to Low	High to Low

Complexity and the Use of Bureaucratic Intensity

Former investigators have pointed out also that sometimes a message was not communicated because it was so complicated that the audience could not understand it, even though sympathetic to it. The assistance of an expert was required for the target group to truly follow the message. Such a formulation could be reinterpreted under balance theory to state that the agency's efforts to communicate uniform tasks required people with technical knowledge and resources that permit economies of large scale. In balance theory, linkage which indicates some element of bureaucracy is called "bureaucratic intensity." This term means that the practitioner must rate linkages in terms of their ability to put experts in contact with clientele.

Again, however, we make the point that there is not necessarily a relationship between the amount of sender initiative, the amount of primary group intensity, and the amount of bureaucratic intensity a linkage permits. For instance, in Table 2 the detached worker approach permits all three types of qualities—high initiative, high primary group intensity, and high bureaucratic intensity. By contrast the mass media has moderate to low initiative, low primary group intensity, and low bureaucratic intensity. The settlement house generally permits high primary group and bureaucratic intensity but little else, and legal authority permits high initiative but generally allows little else.

Not only do linkages vary in their ability to handle the various dimensions crucial to closing social distance, but also families and neighborhood groups must be assessed along these attributes (i.e., the extent to which they are distant and the extent to which they must be approached on uniform or nonuniform tasks). As a consequence, the practitioner ultimately must have independent evaluations of each dimension of linkage.

Community Size and the Question of Scope

There is yet one other element which past investigators have stressed when dealing with problems of reaching distant groups.They were concerned with the numbers of people to be reached by the message. In some instances, social work agencies seek to reach many people, such as in fund-raising drives. Such programs require widespread coverage to be effective. However, at other times, agencies deliberately set up programs which are designed to reach relatively few, highly circumscribed groups of people. For instance, the Community Service Society recently mounted a program to reach the "frail elderly." As already mentioned, these people are the aged who are sick, frightened, or for whatever reason unable to leave their apartments. To reach such people, CSS set up a small drop-in center in an area which had a high density of single older people. They also used leaflets and spoke to local opinion leaders. These are all linkage procedures which have high to moderate scope. In fact, they attracted the normal and aggressive aged in numbers which were equal if not larger than the fragile aged. This meant that the linkages they used had too large a scope. The possible danger of such an overflow was that the robust aged would seek to get the agency to change its program to serve them rather than the frail aged. The agency resisted these efforts and used distance opening linkages to push the more robust group into other services. In their next phase, the Community Service Agency intends to use a detached worker approach, which has a narrower scope to it, and to concentrate on the harder to reach population.

If the linkages in Table 2 are examined with the dimension of scope in mind, one can see that some of them are geared to handle very large numbers of people while others are geared to handle very few. For instance, a very strict detached worker approach is supposed to have one paid professional to one group. Clearly an agency with 20 members on their staff cannot deal with more than 20 groups at any one time. By contrast, people using the mass media in the United States might be able to reach 60 million families. In between these extremes one can argue that voluntary associations can reach many more people than the detached worker, but not as many as the mass media. The settlement house can reach more than the detached worker, but generally not as many as the voluntary association, while the common messenger can reach more than the detached worker, but generally not as many as the settlement house. In summary, there does seem to be some relationship between the demands for small scope and the demands for primary group intensity; and the more intense the primary group stress of the linkage, the less the scope.

Nature of Linkages and Nature of the Community

The above analysis suggests that practitioners planning neighborhood programs must be able to make an assessment regarding the distance of their clients. In addition, they must decide whether the agency's efforts to help the community involve shoring up of nonuniform tasks or uniform ones or both, and how many people the agency seeks to reach in the community. With this information in hand, the practitioner can then look to the various strategies of linkages, such as those outlined in Table 2, and decide which ones or which combination of ones they will use. Where the community is distant, the practitioner must use a linkage with high sender initiative; where the agency must intervene on nonuniform tasks, the practitioner must use linkages with primary group intensity; where the agency must intervene on uniform tasks, the practitioner must use linkages with bureaucratic intensity; and where it must reach many people, the practitioner must use linkages with high scope.

The top row of Table 2 provides the practitioner with the basic dimensions of linkage. With these dimensions the practitioner can assess any new linkage and decide what it will do. Alternatively, the practitioner might decide to develop new linkages using the theoretical dimensions as a guideline. If the agency is faced with a changing population, the practitioner might have to alter the linkages with changes in the population.

If no single linkage meets the needs of the practitioner, he might have to program a combination of linkages. For instance, a community agency dealing with a community which is very distant might use detached workers to recruit community people and quickly move them to a local settlement house. Although the local settlement house lacks initiative and therefore cannot be used to recruit people, once recruited it can develop the same intensity as detached workers and has the advantage of providing more scope. By combining the detached worker and the settlement house, one can maximize initiative, intensity, and scope.

Given the limits on space, we cannot point out the major defects and advantages of various linkage procedures (Litwak and Meyer, 1974); rather, these linkages have been used as illustrations to show how the balance theory principles can be used for developing, in a systematic way, agency neighborhood programs. In Table 3 are suggestions how the practitioner might put together assessments of community needs and the linkage capabilities to form an agency program for the community. A more detailed classification of family, neighborhood, and linkages has been developed elsewhere (Litwak and Meyer, 1974).

LINKAGE MECHANISMS:
THE COMMUNITY REACHING INTO THE AGENCY

It turns out that much of an agency's work involves helping community members reach into other agencies. Although the balance theory can be used as a guide and the various dimensions of linkages still hold, there are considerable differences in emphasis from the situation where the agency is reaching into the community. The differences revolve around the fact that a primary group as a source of linkage is a far different structure from an agency. For instance, most primary groups cannot afford the use of linkages which require trained experts. To use such linkages they must either first develop a voluntary association or seek aid from a friendly bureaucracy. A second significant difference is that the bureaucracy as a target group is far different in structure and type of activity than a primary group as a target of action. The chief difference is that the bureaucracies tend to stress very uniform tasks. Also even the nonuniform tasks are part of a structure which has large scale resources. In other words, primary group members might not be able to intervene in bureaucratic organizations on uniform matters simply because they do not have the technical knowledge to evaluate the staff's response.

If we consider nonsocial work examples, the case is obvious. Passengers cannot vote on how the pilot should land an airplane; patients cannot vote on how the surgeon should cut out the heart valve; clients cannot determine if the automobile mechanic is lying or not when he says a new clutch is needed; and so on. Clients seeking to deal with the social service administration on their income maintenance decisions have found it is difficult, if not impossible, to know whether the staff is telling the truth or not regarding the law and regulations. They have found it very helpful at times to have a former staff member who "knows the ropes" to act on their behalf (Cloward and Elman, 1967). In some cases, they even need a lawyer because they do not know the law well enough to know if their rights are being violated.

Even where the community is seeking to change a nonuniform element in the bureaucracy, the very size of the staff often makes the problem different from that of the typical family. Thus the community might not be able to present its case by changing one person or even five persons on the staff. They might have to change a very substantial part of the staff and this can range in the thousands in very large governmental agencies.

The differences between the two processes can be seen also by studying how the very same linkage has many different implications, depending on whether the primary group is using it to influence bureaucracies as opposed to bureaucracies influencing primary groups. For instance, what constitutes opinion leaders in a bureaucracy? In most open bureaucracies opinion leaders overlap with formal authority so that opinion leaders are the top leaders in the bureaucracy. Who is most likely to know and influence such opinion leaders? Generally people of equal or greater status. Since heads of organizations generally come from the middle and upper class, the opinion leader mechanism is likely to work in the direction of the upper classes unless the organization takes special precautions. This has even greater validity for when applied to indigenous linkages. The heads of the organization are indigenous members of upper-class neighborhoods. With regard to the mass media, bureaucracies often have the ability to maintain a full-time advertising program in newspapers and on television. Family primary groups, at best, can hope for dramatic events to get news coverage. This in turn is likely to lead to an ad hoc form of mass media coverage.

The same point can be made more clearly if one examines the types of linkages which are typically used by communities to reach bureaucracies. Communities might turn to advocate organizations (e.g., law firms) or develop their own advocate operation (Jewish Defense League, NAACP, Welfare Mother Organizations, etc.). The community might seek out organizations for information or advice (that is, enable type organizations like the information centers set up in England described by Kahn et al., 1966). The community might use mass media, various forms of indigenous people, systematic boycotts or strikes, mass marches, ad hoc violence, petitions, or individuals in face to face contact with bureaucratic staffs. Bureaucracies seeking to influence primary groups are less likely to use linkages such as boycotts, strikes, mass marches, and petitions to get primary groups to change their posture on a given issue. The differential

Table 3: Illustration of General Programming Strategies for Agencies Given Some Generic Family and Neighborhood Characteristics

Nature of Task, which Agency seeks to reach Community	Majority of Families Support Agency		Majority of Families do not Support Agency	
	Minority of Families Also Support Agency	Minority of Families do not Support Agency	Majority of Families Also Support Agency	Minority of Families do not Support Agency
Non-Uniform Tasks, e.g. help with homemaking, changing attitudes and values about urban living, teaching everyday care for infants.	*Wide Scope, Primary Group Intensity, Low Initiative Linkages* Settlement house, voluntary association type programs with modest forms of mass media. The settlement house staffed by indigenous lay people. For instance, programs like alcoholics anonymous are examples.	Two Diff. linkages: (1) *Wide Scope, Primary Group, Low Initiative for Majority* e.g., settlement house and (2) *Small Scope, Primary Group. High Initiative for the minority*, e.g. detached worker indigenous lay worker combination or detached worker opinion leader combination	*Wide Scope, Primary Group, High Initiative Linkage* e.g., detached worker settlement type of links but modified to be staffed by indigenous lay people with very modest training such as in homemaking programs, and programs like alcoholics anonymous but dealing with other issues.	Two Different Linkages: (1) *Wide Scope, Primary Group with Low Initiative*, (2) *Narrow Scope Primary Group with Low Initiative* The first case would be illustrated by detached worker settlement house combinations staffed by indigenous lay people with modest training. The second would be small voluntaristic groups with no active recruitment.
Uniform tasks e.g. delivering information on job retraining or unemployment compensation, delivering therapy to mentally ill, giving information on filling out government forms for needed services, etc.	*Wide Scope, Bureaucratic Intensity, Low Initiative Linkages* Mass Media and Settlement house but different from above in that staff is highly trained. May have regular classes teaching skills in various occupations, etc.	Two Different Linkages: (1) *Wide Scope, Bureaucratic Intensity, Low Initiative, Adult Education* classes, etc. and (2) *Small Scope, Bureaucratic, high initiative linkages,* e.g., job counseling for hard to employee who go to the clients homes.	*Wide Scope, Bureaucratic Intensity, High Initiative linkages,* e.g., Need a massive door to door recruiting procedure couples with decentralized adult classes in churches, businesses, store fronts as well as schools.	Two Different Linkages: (1) *Wide Scope, Bureaucratic Intensity, High Initiative,* e.g. detached workers with decentralized services in schools, businesses, churches, etc. (2) *Narrow Scope, Bureaucratic intensity with low initiative* e.g., centralized adult classes without mass media or detached workers.

a. In this table no attempt is made to capture the full complexity of the situation and therefore the full complexity of the programming. Rather it is an attempt to illustrate how the principles of balance theory provides a general guideline for programming decisions. The more details of the given situation can be provided the more accurately the principles of balance theory can be used. For instance, where an agency faces a majority group who approves and a minority which objects to the agency policy the programming decision depends on the extent to which the minority is tied to the majority on other issues. If they are indeed tied to the majority on many issues then the agency might use the opinion leaders of the majority to deal with the minority. However, if the two groups are polarized then the use of opinion leaders is not a good procedure and the two procedures suggested in the table above would be better. In table no attempt has been made to deal with the situation where both uniform and non-uniform tasks must be simultaneously dealt with. There are a variety of ways these can be handled, that is some mechanisms permit both such as the detached worker and the indigenous expert. Brevity in space prevents the full presentation here.

frequency of use of linkages originated by primary groups—as opposed to those originated by bureaucracies—is a rough indicator of the symmetry of linkages when agencies are seeking to influence primary groups, as compared to when primary groups are trying to influence agencies. Despite these differences, the reader must keep in mind that certain central features remain in both situations. In each case, it is necessary to keep in mind the concept of social distance, the need to maintain some midpoint of balance, the need to differentiate uniform from nonuniform tasks, and the need to keep in mind the central components of linkages (that is, primary group intensity, bureaucratic intensity, scope and distance).

Selective Listening in Bureaucratic Organizations

Like individuals, bureaucratic organizations can engage in selective listening. However, the processes of selective listening in a bureaucracy are much different. For instance, the bureaucracy might not receive the community's message because the community might not lodge its message in the right bureaucracy. As Kahn et al. (1966) pointed out, there are so many different bureaucracies which touch upon people's lives that the ordinary citizen cannot possibly keep them all in mind. To do so requires a person with a full-time job and sufficient reference material. Furthermore, even if an individual does manage to locate the right bureaucracy, he often does not know where to enter the bureaucracy. To enter a very large bureaucracy at the wrong place may mean that the message gets lost or takes so long to be transmitted to the right person that it is too late to do any good. Finally, in those cases where the individual manages to find the right bureaucracy and the right entry place, his message might still be sidetracked by a hostile staff person who offers some technical objection to the message which the community member is in no technical position to challenge. To overcome selective listening, such as those examples cited above, clients require the assistance of people with technical knowledge to represent their needs and interests.

Community members may be involved also with bureaucracies on matters which are nonuniform. These are tasks which the community member can assess without the help of technical knowledge such as the following two examples: the welfare agencies make an administrative ruling that henceforth people cannot use taxicabs to come to the agency; and an agency makes an administrative ruling that all welfare allotments will be cut 10% across the board. In such cases, community people can close distance with the bureaucratic organization using linkages which have low bureaucratic intensity even though they have high sender initiative.

To sum up, community members seeking to reach into the agency must assess each linkage in terms of the sender initiative. With regard to each they must further determine which gives them primary group intensity, bureaucratic intensity or both toward closing social distance. Looking at the linkages in Table 4, we find that both a tentative rating of sender initiative and an indication of whether or not this initiative is good for uniform and nonuniform tasks. Linkages such as advocate bureaucracies, strikes, boycotts, and, in some cases, indigenous workers have high community sender initiative. By contrast, individual contacts and enabling bureaucracies generally have very low sender initiative. Linkages such as mass media, public marches, and ad hoc violence have moderate sender initiative. Furthermore, an advocate bureaucracy would have especially high sender initiative if uniform tasks were at issue, while strikes and boycotts would have high sender initiative if nonuniform events were at issue.

Such an analysis suggests that when communities are being abused by organizations on uniform tasks and they cannot protest directly or hope to win, they must work through an advocate expert who knows the organization thoroughly. On the other hand, when communities are being abused by organizations on nonuniform matters, they can indeed move on the organization

Table 4: The Theoretical Dimensions of Linkages Typically Used by the Community to Reach the Bureaucracy

	Sender Initiative	Primary Group Intensity	Bureaucratic Intensity	Scope
1. Advocate Bureaucracy, e.g., law firms, unions, NAACP, welfare mothers organizations, etc.	High	Low	High	Moderate
2. Enabling Bureaucracy, e.g., the English civilian advice bureaus, university research centers, etc.	Low	Low	High	Moderate
3. High powered centralized pay boards	Moderate	Moderate	Low Moderate	Low
4. High powered decentralized boards	High Moderate	High	Low	Moderate
5. Indigenous experts	Moderate	Moderate	High	Moderate Low
6. Low powered indigenous messengers	Low	High	Low	Moderate
7. Mass media, mass marches, petitions	Moderate	Moderate High	Low Moderate	High
8. Systematic picketing, boycotting, or violence	High	High Moderate	Moderate	Moderate
9. Ad hoc picketing, boycotting, riots, etc.	Moderate	High	Low	Moderate Low
10. Personal face-to-face contact	Low	High	Low	Low

through the use of voluntary associations and threats of strikes and boycotts which have very strong primary group dominance. In the past, some community people have argued that all organizational tasks are within the knowledge boundaries of laymen, and they have justified direct community involvement on these grounds. Staffs, however, have suggested that all activities in the bureaucracy require technical expertise and justified the exclusion of lay persons on that ground. We suggest that both are wrong. The staff is wrong in asserting that all matters are technical ones and wrong in assuming that the community cannot intervene where the tasks are technical; they can intervene, but through advocate experts. The community is wrong in assuming that all tasks are nonuniform and that community members cannot intervene through advocate experts when the task requires technical knowledge.

With these thoughts in mind, we can suggest that community linkages, which are cohesive in character, should be used where the bureaucracy is distant. Such cohesion can be based on primary group control when the issue to be dealt with is nonuniform and can be based on the use of advocate experts when the matter is uniform in character. On the other hand, where bureaucracies are friendly and the task requires technical knowledge, the community member should operate through enabling bureaucracies or through the staff of the target bureaucracy. If the task is nonuniform, the person should operate through direct individual contact (e.g., visit, telephone, or use of some printed form).

Selective Interpretation in Bureaucratic Organizations

Granted that the bureaucracy has heard the message, it does not mean that it will necessarily do anything about it. Recalcitrant staff members can sabotage any agreement. To handle technical sabotage, the community must have some organizational expert who can monitor the situation. This, of course, deals with the uniform tasks. It means one must have a procedure with focused expertise; the outside expert must stay close to the scene of action.

When seeking to change nonuniform tasks (like prejudiced behavior among the staff), the community members can directly participate. For example, one can sit in on staff-client contacts to monitor them for racial remarks. This of course would be tolerable only in cases where the community and bureaucracy were very hostile to each other. Otherwise such close contact between staff and community member would run the risk of favoritism and nepotism.

When community members and staff are close, the recommendation for monitoring uniform events might be much simpler. The agency could have a subgroup of its own experts to act as monitors. In the army there is the well-known Inspector General's Office which can be activated by complaints of individuals. Such internal monitoring of units is appropriate when the community and the bureaucracy are close together. Such a self-monitoring technique is inappropriate when the bureaucracy and community are distant.

When nonuniform events are at issue and the community and bureaucracy are close then the monitoring is generally done through some central policy board made up of lay people (such as the Board of Education) or through a single person who is an acknowledged political appointee meant to represent the basic values of the community (like appointed police commissioners). Such lay governing boards are kept isolated from the staff, or the agency, having contact only with the professional head of the organization. However, policy boards do have power over general policy issues which are often the basic nonuniform tasks of organizations.

If we look at Table 3, we can see that there are certain procedures which are good for supervising nonuniform tasks because they permit very close contact in a primary group way (such as the local board of education). Perhaps the indigenous expert might also provide some close monitoring resources as well. By contrast, neither advocate or enabler experts provide much in the way of monitoring skills nor do systematic strikes or boycotts for nonuniform tasks. Again looking at the table, we now examine those mechanisms which are good for close monitoring when uniform tasks are involved. We suggest that the enabler bureaucracy, the advocate bureaucracy, and the indigenous expert all have high monitoring capacity.

Scope: Reaching Many and Few People

Whether the community will seek to reach large numbers of people or only a few, in part, depends on whether or not the larger community (of which the protest group is part) is supportive or nonsupportive of the target bureaucracy. For instance, where the community seeking change finds the bureaucracy is cooperative but the larger community is hostile, they might want linkage procedures which have low scope. If they find a staff with cooperative individuals but with the majority hostile and the larger community hostile, then they might want linkages with even smaller scope. On the other hand, if the bureaucracy is unfriendly and the larger community is very friendly, then the subcommunity seeking change might want a linkage with very large scope so that it might enlist the larger community on its side.

A classic case in point concerned the flouridation controversies during the middle 1960s. If those people who were advocating for the use of flouridation were to rely on public referendum, they would be defeated. However, if they bypassed consulting the larger community and went to the mayor and the city council and had them pass a resolution, they would win. This was clearly a case where having linkages with the wide scope led to the defeat of a program. In another case in the late 1960s, when the farm workers' union was locked in conflict with the grape growers, they successfully used linkages with wide scope (e.g., mass media, picketing) to enlist the aid of middle-class consumers who eventually provided further support through their boycotts. Using this same type of reasoning we would argue that the conflict strategies advocated by Alinsky in the early and middle 1960s would work only where the larger community was indifferent or friendly to the cause of the minority. Where the larger community was actively hostile, the type of controversy which was advocated would serve to organize the larger community as well as the group he was interested in.

If we examine the various mechanisms, it is clear that the mass media, systematic strikes, boycotts, and public marches are all useful mechanisims for developing wide scope. The advocate bureaucracy can work in either direction. The indigenous expert often has very limited scope, since the probability of having an indigenous expert in any given community one is seeking to organize is very limited, unless one is speaking of high status neighborhoods.

What we have suggested is that various linkages are good for closing social distance in a bureaucracy, and these may or may not be the same as those which are useful for monitoring the changes of the bureaucracy or those which have wide or small scope. We have especially stressed the need to differentiate between uniform and nonuniform tasks where seeking to influence bureaucracies because this factor determines if the primary groups can intervene directly or must do so through advocate organizations.

The same problems or sequencing and grouping can be developed here as in the prior discussion on bureaucracies seeking to reach community primary groups. In addition, social workers involved in such programs must have some ability to diagnose organizations as distant or close on uniform and nonuniform tasks. Such diagnoses require knowledge that is far different from those used in diagnosing such qualities in families and neighborhoods. It requires sophistication in theories of organizational structure as opposed to theories of family and neighborhood structure (Litwak and Meyer, 1974).

Furthermore, we point out that problems involved in getting the bureaucracies' attention might be far different from those involved in getting them to change. Thus a strike or boycott which may be excellent for getting attention might not be suitable for instituting change.

Finally, in order that the reader might have an idea of how distances of larger community, target bureaucracy, and the character of the task intertwine, Table 5 has been prepared. This table, like the others, can be used as a rough diagnostic tool indicating to the community member or the practitioner what must be evaluated in an effort to design linkages that will permit the community member to intervene successfully in organizations.

ORGANIZATIONAL STRUCTURE AND LINKAGE MECHANISM

Thus far in our analysis we have not directed our attention to the relationship between the organizational structure and that of the linkage it uses to reach the community. We have drawn a distinction between rationalistic organizational

Table 5: Ideal forms of Linkages by Community, Reaches Agencies Given Varying Distance of Larger Community and Nature of the Tasks

Type of Task	Larger Community Supports Subcommunity		Larger Community Does Not Support Subcommunity	
	Target Agency is Distant	Target is Close	Target is Distant	Target Agency is Close
Task is uniform, e.g., getting school to develop a text book on black history, writing a new law on income maintenance which incorporates the features of negative income tax, legal representing a community member against a landlord in violations of rent control laws, etc.	1. *Wide scope, high bureaucratic intensity, moderately high initiative*, e.g., use of friendly advocate bureaucracy such as political party, ethnic defense agency, etc.	2. *Wide scope, high bureaucratic intensity and passive initiative*, e.g., through personal but formal contact ask the agency's own staff to handle the matter. For instance, parents ask friendly school staff to develop history text, community ask friendly police department to develop technical criteria for evaluating good police work.	3. *Low scope, high bureaucratic intensity, and high initiative*, e.g., use of indigenous experts. Community members can go to one of their members who is also an expert in the target bureaucracy and through him get the agency turned around without necessarily alerting the larger community.	4. *Low scope, high bureaucratic intensity, and moderate initiative*, e.g., community member informally contacts friendly staff member and asks the staff member to institute new course and new textbook.
Task is nonuniform, e.g., community getting school to adopt a policy of income maintenance based on need, getting community to boycott stores that discriminates in hiring personnel, getting people not to pay rent in a rent strike.	5. *Wide scope, high primary group intensity and moderately high initiative*, e.g., use of ad hoc boycotts, picketing, mass marches, and petitions which will also tend to mobilize the larger community	6. *Wide scope, high primary group intensity, and low initiative*, e.g., use of personal contact and centralized nonexpert people such as boards of education, boards of trustees, etc.	7. *Low scope, high primary group intensity, and high initiative*, e.g., personal contact with indigenous nonexperts such as decentralized boards of education, indigenous people in high power position.	8. *Low scope, high primary group intensity, low initiative*, e.g., personal contact with indigenous people in high or low powered position, e.g., social work assistants, secretaries, janitors, etc.

structure and primary group character, and we have suggested that where organizations must deal with the two tasks—one highly uniform and one highly nonuniform—they should be governed by the balance theory. But we have been dealing with situations where the two tasks could in fact be handled by different organizations, one a bureaucracy and one a primary group. However, for many situations both types of tasks have to be carried on within the same organization. This concept is especially true of closed institutions; and the evolvement of informal groups within such closed institutions has been noted by many social scientists. Theories developed in this paper help to explain why these informal groups are likely to arise, and once they do arise which kind of problems they are likely to handle more effectively than the more bureaucratic aspect of the organization.

We have suggested also that to fully understand the interaction of primary groups and monocratic bureaucracies within the same structure, one needs something like a linkage mechanism to keep the proper point of balance for two separate groups. Although we think the situation is somewhat different from two semi-autonomous organizations (family and bureaucracy) relating to each other, we believe the basic idea of linkage mechanisms for isolating and coordination is correct. For more open agencies, which have to handle uniform and nonuniform tasks, the same problem appears in a far milder form but calls forth the same logic. A good illustration of the latter is a local social service center of welfare departments in Michigan. It combined an income maintenance program with a direct delivery service program. The income maintenance program was defined as being involved in relatively uniform tasks as compared to the program for direct delivery of services. Putting these two programs together in the same organization often led to friction because they required somewhat opposing structures. As a consequence the two subunits within the organization required linkages which follow the logic of the balance theory.

In the remainder of this paper no further attempts will be made to elaborate on the above point (Litwak and Rothman, 1970). Rather we will concentrate on organizations which have conflicting substructures (because they must deal with some tasks which are highly uniform and others with moderate uniformity) as compartmentalized structures. We can delineate four types of organizational structures which clearly differentiate significant parts of the organizational continuum. This delineation will permit the analysis of the relationship of organizational structure to the types of linkage an organization can use to reach community primary groups.

One of the four organizational structures has already been mentioned, and it is the rationalistic bureaucracy on one end of the organizational continuum. Somewhere in the middle would be the compartmentalized organization and further along would be another type we had previously delineated, the human relations structure. Still further toward the primary group side of the continuum would be the large organizations which are characterized by nonmerit. They differ from family and friendship groups in that they are much larger and ostensibly are oriented to handle uniform tasks.

Structural Consistency

Although the above typology is not exhaustive (Litwak and Meyer, 1974), it does permit a good illustration of how organizational structures put limits on the type of linkage one can use. The general principle which guides this relationship is one of structural consistency. Agencies seeking a link to the community must use linkages which are consistent with their internal structure. Thus organizations seeking to develop a linkage which has high initiatives, and moderately high primary group and bureaucratic intensity, such as the detached worker, must have an internal structure that approaches that of the human relations organization. That is, to operate effectively this linkage must have decentralized authority, must permit the development of positive trust, and cannot be circumscribed by a priori rules. If one tries to run such a linkage out of a highly rationalistic organization, it will fail. There will be enormous conflict between the people seeking to fulfill the mandate of their linkage and those involved with the internal operations of the organization.

A typical case in point was the attempt to operate a detached worker program out of a highly rationalistic school structure. The principal of the school would not permit the detached worker to leave the school building until he indicated what his schedule would be for the day, who he was meeting, and where he could be reached. This was impossible to do since the detached worker must be free to alter his plans at a moment's notice depending on who he meets in the field. He is often in no position to know who he will meet, once he has made his first contact. Conversely, where the agency is using a highly centralized linkage procedure like mass media, it may be much better to have a single person in charge and detailed rules and regulations regarding when the news release will go out, the format, and so on.

Thus, practitioners must be very sensitive to the relationship between the linkage and the type of organizational structure they must operate out of. If they are in no position to change the structure, they might reject certain types of linkage procedures. Alternatively, they might seriously consider changing the structure of the agency before launching into any community programs. If they do not keep their linkages consistent with their organizational structures, they will find that the linkages only become a paper structure which is not implemented, or that the staff implements the linkage but does so by keeping its behavior covert so that supervisors, in fact, do not know what they are doing. Sometimes there is enormous conflict between those seeking to implement the linkage and those administering the internal structure of the agency. Table 6 summarizes these issues.

Although we will not develop the point here, a similar consideration faces the community trying to intervene in organizations. There are, in fact, a variety of types of family and neighborhood structures. Some of them are much more congenial than others to the use of various forms of linkages (Litwak and Meyer, 1974).

SUMMARY AND CONCLUSION

In this paper we have sought to address ourselves to several fundamental issues which relate to agency programming in the community. We have tried to suggest some criteria for determining what it is that an agency should do, what voluntary associations should do, and what primary groups should do with regard to such problems as whether older people, children, delinquents, or drug addicts should be put in closed institutions, halfway houses, foster homes or group homes, or left with their kin. Central to our analysis was the need to distinguish the task continuum, which ranges from activities which require technical training and resources to activities which can be performed by individuals on the basis of their everyday socialization and resources. The former tasks we called uniform tasks, while the latter tasks we called nonuniform ones. We pointed out that the rational bureaucratic structure (long ladders of authority, specialization, merit appointments, impersonal relations, and a priori rules) were best able to handle the extreme uniform tasks. The opposite type of structure—the primary group—with short ladders of authority, generalist, nepotistic appointments, positive affect, and stress on total group face-to-face meetings was better able to handle the nonuniform tasks. We suggested that the human relations organizations were best able to handle those uniform tasks which were closer to the uniform part of the continuum, while voluntary associations were better able to handle those nonuniform tasks which were closer to the nonuniform part of the continuum. We pointed out that where a given task had both extremes, that is, nonuniform subpart and uniform subparts, they could be located in separate organizations, such as a bureaucratic organization and a primary group. Their relationships would then be governed by the balance theory of coordination. This states that the organizations must operate at some midpoint which balances the danger of their contradictory structures, causing them to destroy each other, with the danger that their complimentary tasks are not properly coordinated.

It was suggested that this balance theory provides a guiding orientation in setting up neighborhood programming for agencies. That is, agencies must be able to assess whether a given linkage closes distance or opens distance. More specifically, the people involved in programming must be able to assess the following qualities of the linkage: degree of sender initiative, degree of primary group intensity, degree of bureaucratic intensity, and scope. These factors could

Table 6: Agencies Seeking to Reach the Community, Taking into Account Distance from the Community and Agency Structure

Organizational Structure	Nature of Linkages	Neighborhood in Support of the Agency		Neighborhood Not in Support of Agency	
		Minority of Families in Support	Minority Not in Support	Minority of Families in Support	Minority of Families Not in Support
Human Relations structure	Linkages which permit decentralization, positive affect, e.g., detached worker	Bad—Too close to all groups	Good for minority and bad for majority	Good for majority but bad for minority	Good for all groups
Rationalistic structure	Linkages which encourage long ladders of Hierarchy, impersonality, and rules, e.g., mass media	Good for all groups	Good for majority and bad for minority	Good for minority Bad for majority	Bad for all groups—too distant
Either structure	Linkages which stress the opposite dimension, e.g., detached worker with rational or mass media with human relations	Bad for all groups—internal friction	Bad for groups—internal friction	Bad for all groups—internal friction	Bad for all groups—internal friction
Compartmentalized structure	Linkages with decentralization attached to human relations part and linkage with long ladders of hierarchy attached to rationalistic part.	One part good while other part bad—too close	Good for all groups—majority and minority.	Good for all groups—majority and minority	One part good and one part leads to error of too much distance.

exist very independently of each other and all linkages can be assessed in terms of them. This requires an assessment as to whether the problems lie in uniform or nonuniform tasks areas or both, whether many or few people must be reached, and where the target group welcomes or does not welcome intervention. We pointed out that the problem of agencies reaching into community primary groups had differences from community groups reaching into agencies, though both operate within the context of the balance theory.

We also stressed that to really understand the problems of balance we must have some understanding of the organizational structures of agencies and that of primary groups. We pointed out, in this connection, that unless the linkages were consistent with the organizational structure, they could not operate effectively. Therefore, before launching any community linkage program, the practitioners must be sure that it is consistent with their organizational structure. Though the point was not developed specifically, an extension of this idea is the notion that only certain kinds of primary group structures are consistent with certain kinds of linkages.

Finally, we discussed that certain kinds of indeterminacy exist in the defining of uniform and nonuniform tasks. These indeterminacies are a function of imprecise knowledge and differential value emphasis. With regard to both problems, neither the theory developed here nor any other theory is likely to settle such problems. Practitioners must often act even where they do not have precise knowledge or consistent value mandates. The balance theory does not tell one how to make such value decisions, but, once they are made, it tells one what type of organizational structure and what kind of community linkages must be used to optimize the value position.

To point out the limits of the balance theory is not to deny the hope that an exciting basis now exists for collaboration between practitioner and social scientist. Together we may be able to develop a more systematic program for agency services.

REFERENCES

CLOWARD, R.A., and ELMAN, R. M. (1967). "The storefront on Stanton Street: Advocacy in the ghetto." In G.A. Brager and F.P. Purchell (eds.), Community action against poverty. New Haven, Conn.: College and University Press.

CLOWARD, R.A., and EPSTEIN, I. (1967). "Private social welfare's disengagement from the poor: The case of family adjustment agencies." In G.A. Brager and F.P. Purcell (eds.), Community action against poverty. New Haven, Conn.: College and University Press.

HENDERSON, A.M., and PARSONS, T. (trans. and ed., 1947). Max Weber; The theory of social and economic organization. New York: Oxford University Press.

HYMAN, H.H., and SHEATSLEY, P. (1947). "Some reasons why information campaigns fail." Public Opinion Quarterly, 11(fall).

KAHN, A.J., GROSSMAN, L., BANDLER, J., CLARK, F., GALKIN, F., and GREEWALT, K. (1966). Neighborhood information centers: A study and some proposals. New York: Columbia University School of Social Work.

LITWAK, E. (1961). "Models of bureaucracy which permit conflict." American Journal of Sociology, 67(September).

LITWAK, E., and MEYER, H.J. (1974). School, family and neighborhood: The theory and practice of school-community relations. New York: Columbia University Press.

LITWAK, E., and ROTHMAN, J. (1970). "Towards the theory and practice of coordination between formal organizations." In W.R. Rosengren and M. Lefon (eds.), Organizations and clients. Columbus, Ohio: Charles E. Merrill.

PURCELL, F., and SPECHT, H. (1967). "Selecting methods and points of intervention in dealing with social problems: The house on Sixth Street." In G.A. Brager and F.P. Purcell (eds.), Community action against poverty. New Haven, Conn.: College and University Press.

REIFF, R., and RIESSMAN, F. (1964). The indigenous nonprofessional, a strategy of change in community action and community mental health. New York: National Institute of Labor Education.

WILENSKY, H.L., and LEBEAUX, C.N. (1958). Industrial society and social welfare. New York: Russell Sage Foundation.

6

OPTIONS FOR DELIVERY OF SOCIAL SERVICES AT THE LOCAL LEVEL: A CROSS-NATIONAL REPORT

ALFRED J. KAHN
SHEILA B. KAMERMAN

Little progress will be made in improving social service delivery systems systematically and on a broad front unless there is prior clarity as to objectives. Little progress will be made in defining and testing alternative approaches without prior attention to basic concepts and to the specific content of options.

BACKGROUND

First it is necessary to distinguish "social service" or "human service" programs, the larger overall category, from the "personal social services." In general international discussion, "social services" means: health, education, income transfer programs, housing, and—perhaps—employment, *as well as* what Americans call "social services" and the British call "personal social services." We adopt the British usage to avoid confusion. Personal social services include family and child welfare, certain services to the aged, community center programs, and so forth (see below). In the U.S. there is a trend to use the comprehensive term "human services" where others prefer "social services."

Efforts have been made over the past decade in the U.S. to organize service delivery on "human services" principles. In effect, this means multiservice or integrated approaches to service delivery covering a number of the major systems. One of us reviewed a decade of experience with multiservice neighborhood service centers and found that they seldom cover all—human, social—service systems despite announced goals and claims, that components are seldom coequal and that colocated services are seldom effectively integrated.

The achievements usually relate to visibility and convenience of place, not to basically changed delivery (Kahn, 1976).

Nor is this development surprising given the differences among the several systems (health, education, housing, income transfers, employment) with regard to mission, professional culture, need for special equipment and space, intervention orientations, types of relationships with clients, and social control sanctions and mandates. To this, one must add the normal tendency of bureaucratic systems to wish for identity and visibility, both of which are essential to building constituencies and to obtaining political and fiscal support for program maintenance and expansion. These imperatives and realities are reinforced and protected by a pattern of regulations, directives, and reporting requirements and by the unique character of federal-state-local or public-voluntary relationships within each system. One need only compare education and health, or employment and housing, to illustrate these points.

Thus, while the professional rhetoric simulates unanimity on the issue of multiservice delivery outlets and integration of all social services/human services as a goal ("to end fragmentation"), multiservice delivery, where successful, means two or three subsystems integrated on a well-focused task, where roles can be clearly defined (child abuse, community care for a specific group of the handicapped, an employment program). Or it means colocation, but no greater service integration than where there is no colocation. Or it means posting "intake" and "access" staff from a variety of services (nursing, housing, employment, public assistance) in one place to facilitate client access to the specific service system by referral back to the "main" or "central" facility of the system. Or one system gives its core service in the office, while others refer back to their own main centers. And we do not know of any evidence that indicates this is necessarily a bad thing.

Modern society invents and reinvents the division of labor for good reason. Medical care is not the same thing as education. Employment counseling is not identical with health service. And family and child welfare or personal social services to adolescents are not to be confused with any of these or with education, income maintenance, or housing administration. Close integration of two or three systems around specified tasks, which require integration, may work very well where roles are clearly defined (pediatrics and child welfare in re child abuse, social work, nursing and geriatric medicine in social care of the aged, etc.). However, one need not conclude that we do not need system boundaries, role differentiations, or operational separation at all among the human services!

Considerable efforts have been made over the past five years in the U.S. Department of Health, Education, and Welfare under a rubric known as "service integration" and "capacity building" to encourage local and state governments and service systems to achieve better case integration, improved accessibility, and less program fragmentation by means of improved information and referral services, more comprehensive management information systems, and revised delivery structures (Kamerman and Kahn, 1976). Our assessment of the effort is that certain efficiencies and improved access can be achieved by means of information and referral services as well as management system reform, but that the evidence for significant case integration progress has not been offered. By this we mean that the effective meshing of the simultaneous and sequential service and treatment activities with complex cases, interventions which clients cannot coordinate for themselves and in which meshing is the precondition of effectiveness, has not been achieved. Such service integration efforts often seem to become preoccupied with management solutions at the higher level and do not ordinarily reorganize service delivery on the front line. Or, if they do consider service delivery, it often is a matter of placing a case manager at the doorway who, in effect, refers to service specialists or draws upon resources (like homemakers), but neither delivers service himself nor is accountable for service integration. This is not to deny continued efforts in this direction (Lynn, 1976).

Thus, to summarize, our close monitoring and research review of service integration developments and of the emphasis on efforts to organize for comprehensive human service delivery in the U.S. leads to three conclusions:

(1) Program coordination and shared service doorways are sometimes possible and useful. They may add to accessibility and convenience; they may provide the base for specific joint or cooperative activity among two or three of the human services around a class or category of services or need.

(2) Comprehensive integration of all human services in one delivery system is neither sought nor achieved, despite the rhetoric of the promotional activity. The five basic systems apparently need, and protect, their core identities and autonomies.

(3) The personal social services take service integration efforts most literally among all the systems, and then quickly submerge themselves in efforts to erase system boundaries and to experiment with new delivery modalities, service roles, levels of staff qualification—all designed to achieve human service integration. Since the other systems "give" very little, the personal social services suffer from loss of identity, disorganization, and decreased effectiveness. This is a serious consequence since personal social services are in any case poorly conceptualized and organized.

Obviously, related service systems need to be coordinated. Certainly core policies should and must be harmonized. However, we now believe that only as each of the six systems develops and matures, becoming clear about its own character, contribution, and identity, will essential and realistic coordination work on a system-wide and a local basis begin.

Indeed, such clarity exists to a large extent already within the traditional systems of health, education, housing, income maintenance. We would argue that without comparable clarity regarding boundaries and functions, the personal social services can only be viewed as minor adjuncts to the other systems. As a result, little interest or support will be available for development and improvement of services for those who need, want, and use them.

A first prerequisite, therefore, is a careful analysis of the personal social services aimed at conceptualizing and organizing the components into a coherent service system. The remainder of this paper, then, poses the question: What are the organizational options available to us as we search for ways to improve service delivery at the local level? We begin with some essential clarifications.

WHAT ARE THE PERSONAL SOCIAL SERVICES?

An eight-country study of personal social services was carried out by teams in the United States, Canada, the United Kingdom, France, Federal Republic of Germany, Poland, Yugoslavia, and Israel between 1973 and 1975, and an integrated overall analysis and perspective was completed in 1976. All country reports and an overall volume have now been published (Kahn and Kamerman, 1977).

On a descriptive level, personal social services cover such familiar program activities as:

- Child welfare (including adoption, foster home care, children's institutions for the dependent and neglected, and protective programs for children)
- Family services and counseling
- Community services for the aged
- Protective services for the aged
- Homemakers and home helpers
- Community centers
- Day Care
- Vacation camps for children, the handicapped, the elderly and average families
- Information and referral programs
- Congregate meals and meals-on-wheels
- Self-help and mutual aid activities among handicapped and disadvantaged groups
- Counseling programs for adolescents
- Protected residential arrangements for youth
- Specialized institutions for several categories of children and adults.

However, we note that probably more important than the program specifics are the functions which these programs assume in the several societies and their roles in the total picture of family and community activity. These programs strive to contribute to daily living, to enable individuals, families, and other primary groups to develop, to cope, to function. While the names of the programs and weighting of their functions differ across national boundaries, there is no difficulty in communicating concepts about them.

The personal social services, as we have observed them, are addressed to one or more of the following tasks:

— Contributing to socialization and development, that is, offering daily living and growth supports for ordinary average people (not just problem groups), a role shared with other nonmarket services but involving unique programs.

— Disseminating information about and facilitating access to the services and entitlements in all six social services areas.

— Assuring for the aged, the handicapped, the retarded and the incapacitated a basic level of social care and aid necessary for them to function in the community or in substitute living arrangements.

— Arranging substitute institutional or residential care or creating new permanent family relationships for children whose parents are not able to fulfill their roles.

— Providing help, counseling, and guidance which will assist individuals and families facing problems, crises, or pathology to reestablish functional capacity and overcome their difficulties.

— Supporting mutual aid, self-help, and activities aimed at prevention, overcoming problems in community living, advocating changes in policies and programs, and service planning.

— Integrating the variety of programs or services in response to consumer needs to assure maximum benefit.

— Controlling or supervising deviant persons, who may harm themselves or others, or those who may be harmed, while offering care, assistance, and guidance.

In general, the personal social services seem to have focused increasingly on developmental and socialization tasks and on what is often called "prevention." The remedial functions and treatment services remain urgent, however, and command the majority of resources.

Everywhere these services are expanding and appreciated. They are clearly important. They are not for the poor alone, anymore than community care of the aged, services for alcoholics or drug addicts, family life education, protective services, marital counseling, child guidance, or adoption are for the poor alone. Services improve and expand as countries can afford them. They are not "cashed out" in favor of marketplace organization and not made redundant by development of socialist economies. The trend to universalism is accompanied by a strong interest in localization—decentralization. Services, to be responsive, often can and should be adapted to local circumstances and priorities.

But everywhere, personal social services are inadequate in size and scale and have not coped with the internal subcategorization and fragmentation that comes from their histories. They were not developed as one system after all. Rather, in the U.S. and many other places, they are the product of decades of incremental responses to problems, crises, and needs of population subgroups, variously conceptualized, perceived, explained—and responded to.

Nonetheless, modern societies have sought from time to time to increase responsiveness and access, to add to efficiency, and to consider principles of organization and administration. Trial, error, and administrative logic have combined to create organization and reorganization. Professional developments have added to the initiatives. As a result, those who would strengthen and organize the personal social services may not begin to discern alternative organizational approaches.

Here we summarize and characterize the major patterns as seen in our cross-national studies. No country is a pure case, and all have continued to evolve. No one-time snapshot looks like any live and growing system. Nonetheless, efforts to describe "ideal" types and to identify their potential advantages and "costs" (however artificial and outdated by events) may contribute to programming initiatives and research and to the selection from among options.

DIMENSIONS

So little has been done by way of systematic service delivery research that there are as yet no widely recognized categories for analysis. The following questions, which are based on our experience in characterizing systems, yield much of the essential data about what exists in a neighborhood, city, or country and makes basic comparison possible.

(1) Does the country have one personal social service system or are there two or more categorical systems (child welfare, aged, etc.)? If one system, what is its scope; if categorical systems, are they in any sense interconnected?

(2) Are the personal social services free-standing, a recognized separate entity, or are they adjuncts to other services or service systems? If free-standing, what linkages are provided? If adjuncts, what are the host services and what provision exists to achieve coherence and identity?

(3) What is the local service outlet: an office, a center, a detached practitioner? Is it an outlet for the personal social services alone or for other systems, too, such as health or employment services?

(4) Are the practitioners generalists or specialists? If the latter, how are roles conceptualized and interrelated? What level of training or education is expected? Is the delivery unit a "team" or a "practitioner"?

(5) What is the major service content: developmental, therapeutic-helping, access, social care, or what? How are services conceptualized?

(6) To the extent that there is a personal social service system, several interrelated categorical systems, or relatively separate categorical systems, what is the provision for assuring or facilitating

   − quality service, which is quantitatively sufficient
   − access to service by potential users
   − meshing of concurrent and sequential services to an individual or to different family members (case integration)
   − interrelating program operation and planning (service integration and coordination)
   − evaluation, feedback, accountability?

(7) What of all this is part of a public system; what are the roles of the several tiers of government? What is the province of industry or labor unions; what is located in the voluntary, nonprofit sector? Are any of the services carried out by profit-seeking (proprietary) groups? If several sectors are involved, what is the thinking about their roles and the provision for their interrelationships? Where is the lead; what is the provision for accountability?

(8) To what extent is (are) the delivery system(s) conceived and organized to serve (a) all citizens, under "normal life" circumstances; (b) all citizens, but only if there are special problems or crises; (c) subcategories of citizens only and, if so, which (the poor, disorganized, minorities, etc.)?

Because countries do differ on these dimensions, comparative analysis heightens awareness of what is involved in some of the implied choices.

In what follows we deal only with major dimensions, not pursuing many of the subissues. We remind the reader that we have moved from empirical reality to the construction of ideal types. Our objective is to make a contribution to analysis and discussion while facing the reality that systems grow, change, respond to societal developments (the recent inflation-unemployment cutbacks) even as reports are written and publications are processed. In brief, we discuss:

   − a comprehensive, integrated, personal social service system (the U.K. is the closest model);
   − personal social services based in many institutions and, then, coordinated-integrated locally as needed (France approximates this);
   − the parallel public-voluntary system, which may be subdivided into child welfare and "other" services (Germany provides one of many illustrations);

— a system under which given institutions carry major personal social service responsibilities at different points in the life cycle (Poland represents this pattern).

A COMPREHENSIVE SYSTEM

The United Kingdom has made the largest commitment to a free-standing, comprehensive, personal social service system with a delivery outlet in each locality. It serves, thus, as an excellent point of departure for highlighting the diverse approaches of alternative models described subsequently. Furthermore, our assessment of the U.S. and the international scene has led us to conclude that the British experience has particular significance for Americans.

In brief, the U.K. moved away from stigmatized "poor law" social services early in the 20th century, gradually establishing financial aid by right and on demographic principles, but retaining a residual assistance category. Services could then be developed separately, and the distinctions between services for the poor and those for other citizens could gradually be wiped out by a functional rather than an income-basis system of public administration. In a search for more effective child welfare services, with a mission in prevention as well as protection and substitute care, the British, in 1948, set up local authority children's departments to be responsible for the child care services previously provided by public assistance and education departments, and, in the 1960s, encouraged them to develop preventive family welfare services. They discovered, at that point, that family and child welfare have uncertain boundaries. Once this is faced, one must ask whether certain services to the aged, handicapped, and ill are not most effectively delivered through the same structure. The Seebohm Committee studied these matters (Committee on Local Authority, 1968); its recommendations should be seen in the context of a series of major governmental reorganizations affecting local government generally as well as the various components of the health services.

Since 1971, each British local authority has had a fully autonomous department for personal social services, a major unit of local government organized on social work and social care principles. Like other departments of local government ("local authority" is the U.K. term), the social service activity is guided, inspected, and supervised by a major committee of the local legislature, a council committee for social services, which has an influential chairman who is usually closely related to the work of the local authority social services director. Called a "social services" department in Scotland, this local governmental unit is charged with providing a comprehensive range of domiciliary daytime care and other residential services for people in the area, as well as carrying out long-term planning.

With some exceptions, the service is very broad, covering all the population groups, circumstances, problems, and needs traditionally assigned social work or personal social services. There is major stress on social care (assistance to the frail and handicapped to permit them to remain in their own homes), emergency aid, assisting in access to concrete benefits-services, and obtaining financial and other entitlements, as well as on a program of "social treatment," counseling, and casework. In the U.S. vocabulary, each local social service department covers much (but not quite all) of what would be described as family and child welfare; services to the aged; services to youth; psychiatric after-care; community social services to the handicapped; shelter; detention; residential treatment for dependent, neglected, delinquent, disturbed children; and related services. Because social care and concrete services are very important, as is day care and residential care, the social workers actually constitute only 10% to 15% of the work force. The program is intended to be universal and nonstigmatic, not limited to the poor alone or to those considered disorganized and unable to carry responsibility for themselves. Because demand is heavy, resources are in short supply and need is not equally distributed. The poor and low-income groups are, of course, served more than the affluent middle class.

The pattern of organization and professional operation is still emerging. While certain services (care for dependent, neglected, delinquent children; community services to the disabled and the aged, etc.) are mandated by national legislation, other services are permissive or only encouraged, varying by local preference and resources. The locality has options and range, and local programs are not all alike. However, the forward thrust is general and there is actually much sharing of patterns of administration and practice. This commonality, despite what is technically much decentralization, may be explained by a strong Local Authority Social Services division in the Department of Health and Social Security; technical assistance; a requirement that formal plans be submitted (a ten-year "rolling plan"), and centrally approved capital funding plans; the importance of central government's annual financial subvention to local government (a "block grant" or general revenue sharing in the U.S. vocabulary); and the influence of shared professional participation through research, social work education, task forces, and ongoing national discussion.

When the consolidated social service departments were created by local government in 1971, they brought together staffs from units which had earlier carried out child welfare programs; services to the aged; services for the mentally ill, the retarded, and handicapped; as well as others who had specialized in medical and school social work, work with unwed mothers, and so forth. The expansion and immediate heavy service demands on the new programs required creation of a new structure of management and professional leadership. As a result, the line staff was new and inexperienced, and operational patterns are still being shaped.

The departments are broad but do not include some services which are covered elsewhere. The original proposals called for adding what is commonly known as school social work and social work in housing to the assigned tasks, but the legislation did not mandate this. (Some local authorities, nonetheless, do cover social work in schools in these departments.) Hospital-based social work was initially left out, too, but was taken over in April 1974. Nationally, probation and parole remain as part of the "correctional" system under "justice," but a somewhat different act in Scotland created children's panels to replace the juvenile court and assigned the social service, probation, and after-care functions to local authority social services. As most of the responsible local authorities cover rather extensive areas and/or large populations, most social services departments set up headquarters and area (not called district) offices. As many of the area offices covered population units of 50,000-100,000, they in turn developed "field work" teams for smaller geographic units, sometimes working from a local suboffice. However, no particular form of localization of delivery is mandated, and many authorities are still working out the most suitable form of decentralization and localization for their particular area.

Each local authority has a central administration under a director which encompasses all of the functions of a sizeable public department. In addition, it usually has one second-level administrator (deputy) in charge of area teams, one in charge of residential services, one responsible for domiciliary social care services, and, increasingly, one for research and development services and/or financial administration. These three arms of the program are interdependent, coordinated, and in a position to function in a far more integrated fashion under the new organization. Positive results (good continuity from residential treatment to community care, good after-care, service integration where there are several "needs" or "problems" in a family) are visible in some places, but are yet to emerge in others.

The area social work teams offer access, case assessment, case integration, follow-up, and a modest amount of social treatment (casework and group work). They facilitate self-help, mutual aid, and some community organization. The central tasks are case assessment, access to resources and referrals, and such concrete aid as home helps, foster home placement, adoption, arranging residential care, and helping with emergencies. Time for other activity is limited.

The tendency early in the development has been to organize the work by geographic teams, with persons of several backgrounds and levels of training/experience, and for each to "rotate" in "intake" and to function with a general load, exercising all functions. However, some special expertise was brought to the program and some has evolved because of different proclivities. Thus, even though the organization requires a caseload that goes across the board from child welfare, to the aged and handicapped, from concrete benefits and social care to social treatment, there is no legislative or administrative requirement that all social workers do exactly the same job. Recent reports from the U.K. suggest that within generic teams individuals may begin to specialize in knowing about certain population groups or resource clusters, in carrying out certain liaison functions with other human service systems (health, education, employment, housing, etc.) or in functioning with special skill in specific circumstances (group therapy, individual intensive casework, organizing client mutual aid, etc.).

Unlike the U.S. counterpart, the U.K. personal social service department has a large and respected domiciliary care service which carries major responsibility for facilitating community living for the elderly, handicapped, mentally ill, mentally retarded, and terminally ill. The services—offered on a scale unknown in the U.S.—include home helps, many types of day care centers and sheltered employment, meals-on-wheels and congregate eating arrangements, a large transportation service, personnel and supplies to adapt people's apartments to their handicaps, so that they may remain at home (Morris, 1974).

The local authority department's residential unit covers what are variously thought of as institutions and community group care for dependent, neglected, and delinquent children; foster home care; short-term shelters and more-secure detention; special residential arrangements for the elderly and the handicapped, if not otherwise available. There are often emergency arrangements for homeless families and sometimes "training" houses-rooms-apartments for families unable to function on their own in normal community living and who have been evicted.

The U.K. has a long tradition of voluntary (nonprofit) social services, and there are still many voluntary agencies nationally and locally. However, as public responsibility for a coverage service has increased over the past several decades, the position taken has been that it could be assured only through a public service. Voluntary programs continue, but in an increasingly secondary and supplementary role. Where public departments call upon voluntary children's homes, programs for the elderly, or voluntary community service, they may or may not pay for the care, depending upon local circumstances. Payment is quite common, however, and carries with it relatively strong requirements and inspection.

The U.K. system is not without operational problems and current (1977) resource cutbacks are leading to a variety of solutions in different local authorities, including new interest in the voluntary sector. As yet, this system has not invented dramatic new devices for case integration, beyond case conferencing, liaison work, and practitioner accountability, but the area team mission does encourage accountability and continuity of care and may facilitate the process of keeping vulnerable clients and complex cases visible.

The British have a comprehensive, universal, and personal social services system which is developing in form and function. The vast majority of clients are low income but policy and practice open the system to anyone and it is used by all social classes. Its generic area-team practice may yet evolve some specialities within it. There is much emphasis on social care and other concrete services. The program has achieved initial acceptability and status in local government. Despite movement toward a pattern of locality-based outlets for the field teams, there are issues of function, boundaries, staffing, and administration now being recognized and discussed.

Critics complain that some categories of clients are favored over others, that intensive long-term social treatment gives way in form to social care and emergency services and that practitioners do not develop the expertise that more extensive specialization could achieve. Proponents see these and other problems as transitory, and they note that major growth and positive public response followed the implementation of the plan and that only the U.K. financial crisis has inhibited further development.

PERSONAL SOCIAL SERVICES IN MANY INSTITUTIONS

Under the major alternative pattern of the French—which we here sche-matize—each major societal institution develops those personal social services essential to its function or to deal with the problems which develop for those who deal with the institution. The stigma is decreased or disappears as personal social services appear in many places: schools, social security programs, family allowances, offices, trade unions, factories, social (cash) assistance offices, maternal and child health centers.

The foundation of the French system (one-quarter of staff) is a program of polyvalent social workers, sometimes called family social workers, who cover all geographic areas. These social workers, mostly female, are trained in a system which combines basic social work with some elements of public health nursing. The relevant law requires coverage by one polyvalent worker for each "sector," a geographic area with a population group of some 5,000. Coordination legislation includes a procedure under which agencies meet to allocate coverage responsi-bility, so the local polyvalent worker may actually be employed by the public health program, a sectarian private family agency, an agricultural program or a family allowance office. Whoever the employer, there is a mandatory system of office hours in portions of the sector on set days (a "permanence," involving specific times and places where the social worker may be consulted), required visiting after child-birth, and—beyond this—openness to referral or self-referral.

While it is reported that they do not work in great depth or with expertise of specialists, these polyvalent workers constitute a detached coverage system; they work as individuals, in the field, where people are. They do not close off self-referrals or referrals to categorical programs or more specialized services, but they do help directly, give information, and refer to specialists as needed. They take on supervision and planning for neglected and dependent children, for example. Many people rely on them as "last resort" helpers.

The other social workers are either specialists (child care, psychiatric work, etc.), or they are polyvalent workers serving categorical programs (railroad workers, trade unions, etc.). A principle of universalism leads to other forms of proliferation. There are social workers in prisons, refugee programs, and so on. Recognizing the problems of overlapping, competition, and discontinuity, the French began to enact coordination legislation in 1959. The solutions sought are not here relevant, but we must note that the search for principles and patterns for case integration and accountability is constant. New initiatives, which resemble U.S. human service integration, began several years ago.

On the positive side, this multiple access system is pluralistic, precludes monopoly, and has many manifestations and locations to encourage universalism. But, as institutions uncover new needs, this is to be balanced against the monetary and social costs of fragmentation and constant proliferation of social services as well as against the inadequacy of solutions to the problem of case integration and accountability where there are multiple administrative bases.

Practitioners tend to be generic (polyvalent) or specialized. They concentrate on casework, but do not function in a standardized organizational matrix most likely to maximize the advantage of the division of labor. On the other hand, social work is valued, services are not clouded in stigma, and some are used extensively by the middle class.

PUBLIC-VOLUNTARY; CHILDREN-OTHER

Many countries initially developed personal social services as part of the investigative task of the public assistance ("poor law") eligibility worker. Then, because of broader need and to decrease stigma, they tended to spin off (or develop separately) what became known as child welfare services. Later, when public assistance or supplementary benefits were assigned to other, independent income maintenance systems (separated from service delivery), these countries were left with two subsystems in the personal social services: child welfare and "other." While the "other" category should cover the family, the "young and single," and the aged categories, only the services to the aged have seen significant expansion in recent years.

Because the West German situation suggests certain similarities with the U.S., it may be worth noting some of the factors which have contributed to the development of this "dual system."

Historically, F.R. Germany has placed particular stress on income maintenance, health, and employment. Social insurance benefits are uniformly high, with pension levels and unemployment benefits among the highest in Europe. Health insurance coverage is extensive, too. Furthermore, for some time—and until very recently—F.R. Germany has had close to full employment. Moreover, a central social policy instrument has been the use of cash benefits, in other words, the "cashing out" of those services which indeed might still be needed by families.

Those personal social services, going beyond remnants of old poor law and private charity, therefore, emerged for those categories of people whose needs could not be met by an income (and employment) strategy, especially when the need for service created a demand which could not be met by the market at a reasonable price and within a realistic time frame. Thus services were provided first for children and second for the aged. Certainly not an unfamiliar development, although one which was maintained far longer in Germany because most basic needs for productive adults could be satisfied.

In time, in Germany as in other industrialized countries, other needs emerged—or were acknowledged—and other services developed. Inevitably, among these were services for the inadequate or deviant. Increasingly, however, services are created in response to normal needs such as counseling around marital problems or decisions regarding having a child. These services are now emerging on a haphazard basis, usually outside the two major service delivery systems, thus adding to the fragmentation.

Furthermore, this type of fragmentation is often cross-cut by another, the public-voluntary split. At the very least, the result is a "four-field" system: child welfare and other ("social" office); public and voluntary. There are also local health offices. All apart from the local offices, which deliver means-tested, safety-net cash assistance. (Or the "social" office also houses the social assistance unit—the old pattern.)

While the several states have considerable prerogatives and therefore show variations, the F.R. Germany may be cited as representative of a common pattern. A constitutional preference for voluntary agencies, even if publicly-funded, is a relevant part of the picture, balanced by increasing conviction that services are a "right." As a result, personal social services may be estimated as half delivered under public and half under voluntary auspices. In general, child and youth services have developed more extensively and to a higher level of professional practice than the others. The new thrusts are toward the needs of the aged. Welfare offices deal with homeless, dependent, and problem-inflicted adults, but family services per se are limited.

The evidence suggests that the complexity of the system is of concern; overlap, duplication, fragmentation, and discontinuity are major problems. The public offices grow and are used despite the legal preeminence of the voluntary services; they are more visible, standardized, a right. Moreover city after city is experimenting with one form or another of multiservice center or combined service system in which there is: (a) colocation of health, youth, and social offices, to increase visibility, case integration, and accessibility; or (b) assignment of roles out of two or three systems to a single social worker, so that an integrated, coherent service may be delivered, whatever the statutory separatisms; or (c) colocation of offices for the three systems in one center and creation of cooperating teams from each office, to meet the specific needs of complex cases (case integration, in short).

Among the experimental variations included in current initiatives are approaches which build medical, nursing, psychological, and psychiatric services into the teams; approaches which break down a long-standing and dysfunctional German distinction between internal work (eligibility, internal administration, paying benefits) and the external "field" work; approaches which include what the U.S. would describe as probation and protective work.

Our own impression is that as efforts are made to assure service rights and coverage, there is a logic that calls for geographic assignment of responsibility, generalist practice and a front-line role which includes case integration and basic counseling and service brokerage here and everywhere. We interpret this as the force behind the various experiments.

The current F.R. Germany pattern illustrates what is probably the prevalent arrangement in the more industrialized countries. It also serves to recall the argument for organization on age principles which cuts across systems: health-housing-income-personal social services to the aged; maternal and child health-income-personal social services in the early years of life, and so forth. A full version of such principles will be seen in the final "model" pattern, below. Clearly, such an approach runs contrary to the functional organization of modern government: housing, income security, medical care, and so on. To split administration by demographic or problem category is to create havoc for planning and operations.

Income maintenance is best administered as a unity (or in tandem with the tax system), not by age group, or territory, or the absence or presence of means tests. Education cannot be divided by family role or sex. Employment systems should be coherent, and so on. Thus, we ask whether, given a pro-family orientation and a concern with primary group relations and neighborhood coherence, personal social services are viable if the public-private and the child-adult splits are operationally continued and reinforced.

The alternative principle is to organize personal social services for the aged under medicine; they need medical care, social care, and related personal social services. But this approach emphasizes a pathology and treatment orientation where the philosophy is normalization and community service. Why not health care in a health system and personal social services in a system of its own, which is family and community oriented? Similarly, while one could argue for attaching child abuse services to a hospital medical program, this would detach it from a needed family social work base organized on broader principles.

The strongest argument for subcategorical delivery systems based on age or problems are their political appeal (they attract constituencies) and their ability to create their own imagery, which can, as appropriate, be stigma free. This type of attractiveness may well defeat approaches like the comprehensive, integrated U.K. system, which clearly, in the short run, did trade-off the interests of some categories in favor of broader priorities.

LIFE-CYCLE APPROACH

What we think of as the Polish pattern may evolve only early in a country's social service history (and only then under centralization), but it is nonetheless interesting. Under this approach (not fully conceptualized as such), the social institution which is most critical to a life-phase is the base for service from all social service systems: health through age 3; education after age 3, until a youth enters employment; the enterprise and unions for most of one's own life (labor ministry); and, then, from the age of retirement, once again, health. There are obvious exceptions, such as a correctional system which deals with some youth and adults.

The approach allows for excellent integration, such as day nurseries (day care centers) with child health, or—at the other end of the span—geriatric medicine and social service. However, there are major problems of continuity-discontinuity (the transition from a health-related infant nursery to preschool at age 3) and, in effect, limited development of the diversity of services possible, where cohort need and not institutional imperatives dominate programming.

One notes pressures, under this system, to create a more comprehensive personal social service program. Such a system would be less tied to health, since there are other needs to be met which involve people of different ages at the same time (the family as a unit, for example). Moreover, the service delivery base could then be in the community not in the enterprise or unions, since there is a case for separation of some problems from the work place and the school and for dealing with the family or household as a whole in its daily-life environment. The system could evolve in the French direction; or the current health base of social welfare services could create new office specialization and growth on the British pattern.

What is unique about Poland is the large dependence on volunteers. Some 65,000 retired civil servants and professionals (many are themselves old age pensioners) devote considerable time each week (2-3 days) to serve as what social welfare professionals might call case finders, referral agents, "brokers" between services and those in need, or informal counselors, Only their out-of-pocket expenses are reimbursed and there are some modest amenities by way of recognition. Each volunteer covers a small, intimately known local population group: a village in a rural area, a block in a large city. In short the practitioner—not a *team*—is the service person.

The pattern, established in 1959, is familiar in Eastern Europe. It is these volunteers who offer the core services in the social welfare system. They operate in their local residential areas, and are thus quite decentralized, but they have ties to district social welfare offices based in health offices. Their linkage is to some 15,000 professionally trained social workers who supervise their work, though loosely, take on complex tasks and referrals or resource authorization, and will increasingly take on "in-serve" training.

This back-up system was launched in 1969 and is only partially implemented. The corps of professionally trained social workers is inevitably thin, but plans have been made to expand from the present 13 social work schools to 49, one for each region, both to allow a professional/volunteer ratio of from 1 : 6 to 1 : 10 and to provide qualified staff for complex ongoing situations. It is recognized that expertise and professionalism do meet certain needs best. The model toward which the system is pointed involves eventual population coverage of one volunteer worker per 2,500 persons in urban areas and one per 5,000 or 6,000 in rural areas. There are some signs that, as professionalization develops, roles change and this, in turn, poses alternative organizational options.

MULTIPLE SYSTEMS

Each of the above generalized models has its several variations and diverse manifestations. The operational reality also contains another pattern, visible in the U.S. and Canada, for example. This is really a multiple system model. It may involve a British -type pattern as outgrowth of public welfare, in some parts of the U.S. South, Midwest, or Far West, under which a relatively comprehensive and integrated public-social service delivery system is in place in many countries or throughout states. Elsewhere in the U.S., the pattern is more like that in the F.R. Germany. The Northeast offers plenty of examples—parallel public and voluntary systems—perhaps for families, perhaps for the S.S.I. categories, perhaps for the adolescents, and so on.

On top of this, everywhere, seldom systematically related to these systems, are personal social services attached to hospitals, schools, courts, unions, settlement houses, churches, and courts. A French-type system, not in any way subject to coordination and service integration provision, is now assigned sanction to create a system for these services.

Next, and in addition, complicating it all and dramatizing the urgency for more systematic programming, are the unrelated and parallel systems or components of personal social service growing out of the remnants of the U.S. anti-poverty program ("community action") of the previous decade, or out of housing and community development, or out of community mental health, where many of the components are closer to personal social services in content than they are to psychiatry or to medicine.

Finally, there are states which have wiped out distinctions among systems by creating "single state agencies" for several social service systems (mental health, child welfare, aged, corrections, and rehabilitation, for example), and have organized for human service, not personal social service delivery. Another form of multiservice center is the local outlet. The state organizational pattern does not affect the original local categorical outlets at all. We have evaluated these efforts above: they never quite "come off"; they seldom lead to integrated case service delivery. Of special interest is a Canadian variation, in Quebec, under which health and personal social services are located in one basic system with good geographic representation. There is one office outlet at the first line of access. Each system is specialized at the next level.

Almost all reviews of social services in the U.S., which look at what exists from a consumer's perspective, note the lack of standardized locally based access services, the lack of standardized and reliable provision for service integration, even where the need for protection, outreach, and continuity are acknowledged, as well as a pattern of excessive fragmentation among and between competing or unrelated models, systems, and outlets. The social service budget is not inconsiderable, but the urgency of reform in delivery is acknowledged. With some exceptions, this is also the Canadian picture.

If a British system may make a planner worry about monopoly and its effect on freedom of choice, the U.S. system approximates anarchy in its waste of resources and lack of accountability. The former system is, in fact, flexible enough around the edges and leaves enough out so that the theoretically derived "monopoly" problem is not experienced. The U.S. pattern reminds one of the need to protect some elements of pluralism in any solution, but present experiences document the desperate lack of system and coverage as well as the larger price paid by those needing help!

Provision under U.S. Title XX (Social Security Act) legislation permits considerable progress (as does recent Canadian legislation). States are, in effect, given social service bloc grants, if they plan and meet a limited number of other requirements. Federal regulation now permits considerable waiving of administrative requirements under the categorical social service legislation for children, youth, the aged, or the handicapped, if states or local government wish to move toward increased service integration and more systematic planning and operation. A "single city" agency or "single county" agency could repackage categorical programs to create an integrated personal social service system, if there were a will to do so.

CONCLUSION

The personal social services are standardized societal responses to developmental and socialization needs, on the one hand, and problems which demand treatment and help, on the other. While some of the services-benefits are simple and meet needs of completely competent people in one-time contracts, others involve complex interventions requiring program coordination, case integration, and accountability. If such programs are to be effective per se and to cooperate as well with others among the human (social) services, the personal social services need to be organized as integrated, visible, localized delivery systems.

The experience in the U.S. has underscored the problems in service delivery which emerge: (a) if there is no clearly defined, coherent personal social service system; and (b) if efforts are made to integrate all so-called human services, when only some are distinctive and visible while others are diffuse, amorphous, unrecognized and, thus, invisible. Quantitative increases in specific categories of services cannot solve the problem of fragmented, haphazard, and disparate delivery efforts. On the other hand, improved delivery systems can maximize the use of scarce resources and may highlight those services in most demand, thereby documenting the need for additional provision.

Our ultimate concern here is with improving the delivery of services at the local level. We have described and analyzed several alternative models as illustrated by the experience of other countries. (As part of this, we are committed to the profession of social work and to the centrality of the profession to the personal social services and vice versa. The implications of this for social work training and education are of major significance. We leave this subject for subsequent discussion.) Recent British developments offer a particularly interesting model, although attractive elements exist in other models, too. Progress demands deliberate choice and the analysis of ongoing experience. Faddisms and rhetoric often guide what occurs today but the payoffs of the past 15 years have not been impressive. To improve *how* services are delivered may require a clearer sense of *what* is being delivered.

REFERENCES

Committee on Local Authority and Allied Social Services (1968). Report. Cmmd. 3703. London: Her Majesty's Stationery Office.

KAHN, A.J. (1976). "Service delivery at the neighborhood level: Experience, theory, and fads." Social Service Review, 50(1).

KAHN, A.J., and KAMERMAN, S.B. (1975). Not for the poor alone. Philadelphia: Temple University Press.

––– (1977). Social services in international perspective. Washington, D.C.: U.S. Government Printing Office.

KAMERMAN, S.B., and KAHN, A.J. (1976). Social services in the United States. Philadelphia: Temple University Press.

LYNN, L.E., Jr. (1976). "Organizing human services in Florida." Evaluation, 3(1-2):58-97.

MORRIS, R. (1974). Toward a caring society: The report of a U.S. study team. New York: Columbia University School of Social Work.

7

SERVICE DELIVERY AT THE NEIGHBORHOOD LEVEL IN ISRAEL

DAVID MACAROV

The importance of neighborhoods on the physiognomy of Israel arises from a number of factors. In the early days of the resettlement of the country, dating back to the beginnings of the 19th century, immigrants from various countries, regions, and even cities sought each other out for mutual support and settled in contiguous areas. This tendency toward ethnic identification was reinforced by the social welfare system of that time, such as it was. Collections taken up abroad for the support of "the poor Jews in Palestine" were distributed on the basis of the collection area—monies collected in Galicia went to Galician Jews in Palestine, monies from Bessarabia to Bessarabians, and so on. Thus, being part of the community, emotionally and geographically, was required for participation in the distribution. Hence, there still exist in Jerusalem, for example, neighborhoods known as the Greek Colony, the German Colony, the Russian Compound, the Bokharian Quarter, the American Colony, and others. In addition, the Old City of Jerusalem has been divided since time immemorial into Moslem, Christian, Jewish, and Armenian quarters. Even new towns and neighborhoods may be distinctly of one country, such as Iraq; or one region of the country, like Kurdistan; one city; or even one or two extended traditional families. Eighty percent of the population of the Arab village of Abu Ghosh, for example, are of the Abu Ghosh tribe.

In addition to such geographically based and ethnic enclaves, there are also areas where religious Jews of various subsects live together, regardless of national origin. There are followers of Chassidic Rabbis, like the Lubavitcher Rebbe or the Satmar Rebbe, in their own neighborhoods or even villages, just as the extremist Netura Karta ("Guardians of the City") live close to one another.

Christian and Moslem Arabs tend to live in their own areas, as do Circassians, Druse, Bahai, and adherents of other religious groups.

Then there are neighborhoods marked off by geographic features. Haifa, for instance, includes the port area, downtown, the slopes of the Carmel, and the top of the Carmel, each of which is so designated, as well as neighborhoods set off from the rest of the city by deep valleys, like Wadi Rushmieh, or by the Kishon River.

There are also large-scale housing projects, sometimes including thousands of apartments, in or near most cities. Some of these are only tenuously connected by transportation or by sentiment to the cities which they border—Upper Nazareth, for example, or Upper Affula, or Upper Tiberias, are geographically noncontiguous with the nearby city. On the other hand, there are equally large housing developments within cities—French Hill, in Jerusalem, for example. Such housing projects may be virtually self-contained, in terms of schools, stores, community centers, health clinics, and so on.

Finally, there are deliberately designed development towns—usually rather small—set in previously unoccupied areas, and often quite isolated from any other community. These were established in pursuit of dispersion of the population from the areas of the large cities, and were intended to be self-contained. Between 1948 and 1972, over four hundred new villages were established. The lure of the city is such, however, that in 1973 only 16% of Israelis lived in rural areas, with the remaining 84% in urban settings. Of the 16% in rural areas, 3% of all Israelis lived in voluntary agricultural collectives (*kibbutzim,* s. *kibbutz*).

Many of the neighborhoods depicted above have acquired distinctive characteristics in addition to those mentioned—they are populated by certain ethnic groups, by new immigrants, or by old-timers; they are industrial, one-industry, service-employment oriented, or have a negligible employment base; they are deteriorating, well-kept, newly built, or being rehabilitated. Some are known as pockets of poverty or other kinds of problems, while others are seen as economically flourishing, or even luxurious. Moreover, neighborhoods in Israel tend to keep their characteristics over long periods of time. Since most housing in Israel, including apartments, is purchased rather than rented, geographic mobility is very limited. People tend to stay in the place they have purchased, and neighborhoods therefore change as people's circumstances change, rather than by a change in population.

The concept of Israel as a mosaic of neighborhoods is reinforced by the fact that there are no administrative or legal units between the national government and localities—no states, counties, provinces, parishes, or other intervening political subdivisions. Although some governmental departments divide the country into regions for their own administrative convenience, these are not units of self-government. The only units which subsume neighborhoods under other political entities are cities.

Cities, in turn, can be subdivided between those large enough to be termed "municipalities," of which there are 31, including two Arab municipalities; 115 local councils, including 46 Arab and one Druze; and for units too small for self-government, 49 regional councils, including one Arab. Local authorities sometimes combine for purposes of sanitation, hospitals, secondary education, and so forth, but without abandoning local prerogatives. When a local or regional authority is unable to function properly, it is governed by appointed officials of the Ministry of the Interior, which restores self-government when capacity has been demonstrated.

These two factors—the multiplicity of neighborhoods and direct links between the local and national authorities—result in counteracting tendencies. On the one hand, there is a need for, and a desire to furnish, differential services based upon the varying needs of neighborhoods. On the other hand, centralization almost always moves toward standardization of services. Services in Israel reveal the effects of this dilemma, but in order to examine these effects it is necessary to distinguish between the delivery of services on the local level and the participation in or control of service delivery by local people.

Within the confines of the culturally pluralistic society which Israel is, the education system, for example, is highly centralized insofar as planning, policy, and administration are concerned. However, services are differentiated for large sectors of the population and delivered on a local level. Schools in the Arab sectors are taught in Arabic, with the Koran as the basic text; American schools are taught in Armenian; while Jewish schools are taught in Hebrew, using the Old Testament as a base. The syllabi in each system, however, are mandated by the Ministry of Education, and within each section, there are no differences in the material offered in the schools in a depressed urban area and that in a prosperous farming community; or between that in a village of Moroccans, and in a neighborhood of South Africans. Local bodies do not determine school curricula, and although there is a parents' association, there is no parent-teachers' association, and certainly no parent-teacher-students' association, as there are in some countries. There is a national high school admissions examination (the *seker*) which was originally intended to determine stipend eligibility on the basis of attainments, but which has come to be used as a selective device. This is a standardized national examination, administered on the same day and at the same time throughout the country, as in the matriculation examination administered at the end of high school. There are no arrangements for regional, local, neighborhood, or cultural variations in the content of these centralized, standardized examinations.

On the other hand, although the examination questions are the same throughout the country, extra points are automatically added to the scores of new immigrant children, those living in "culturally disadvantaged" sections, and some other categories. In addition, there are sanctioned differences in the curricula of kibbutz schools, religious schools, and general schools. In addition to a required core curriculum, differences in other required and optional courses are allowed, although these differences, in turn, are standardized for the various types of schools. Again, although education is free, compulsory, and universal only through the eighth grade nationally, it extends to the 10th grade in certain disadvantaged areas. In social welfare terms, these are categorical or selective policies added to what are basically universal programs in an attempt to find a middle course.

Further evidence of the search for middle ground in the educational system is the current "reform" of Israel's schools. Instead of eight years of elementary school and four years of high school, the pattern is being changed to six years of elementary school, three years of junior high, and three years of high school. In addition to any formal educational reasons which might exist, this change is designed to move children out of neighborhood elementary schools, which tend to be de facto segregated along ethnic lines due to the housing pattern mentioned above, and into regional schools, which are more integrated by virtue of serving an entire region, two years sooner than would have been the case under the former pattern.

Turning to the health area, medical care in Israel is insurance-based, although the government is not the insurer. The largest portion of health care in Israel is administered through the Sick Fund of the general, well-nigh universal, labor union known as the Histadrut, and through several other smaller sick funds. Most of these are employer-employee contributory, and cover every health exigency, including examinations, laboratory tests, prescriptions, hospitalization, surgery, and recuperation, as well as mental health care. The major exception to this coverage is dentistry. Nonemployees, including the self-employed, housewives, the aged, and others can join some of these funds through monthly payments, while new immigrants are automatically covered for their first six months in the country. Since there are, nevertheless, some uncovered portions of the population, and some complaints about the quality or process of service, there have been increasing calls for nationalizing health care in Israel, either by requiring every one to take out insurance, or through government administration of the existing insurance plans, or through the establishment of a government health service.

There are obviously fewer regional, local, or ethnic varieties of medicine than is the case in education or social welfare, and it is no surprise that medical services tend to be standardized throughout the country. The delivery of health services, however, is almost entirely locality-based, with few exceptions.

One of the most ubiquitous institutions in Israel is the *Kupat Cholim,* the Sick Fund Clinic. There is hardly an isolated locality without its own clinic, and these are usually especially constructed buildings, rather than parts of homes, in office buildings, or in other community services. Such clinics deal primarily with diagnosis and treatment, with very little emphasis on preventive medicine. It is in the case of more sophisticated diagnostic techniques and tests that the client may have to go outside the neighborhood, and, in the case of small settlements, even to another city. Similarly, if the treatment calls for hospitalization, this, too, is in the neighborhood only by chance. The existence of an ambulance station is therefore an urgent need in some neighborhoods—a need which is met to an insufficient degree.

The neighborhood character of medical service is also lessened by the fact that hospitals in Israel do not, by and large, serve the neighborhood in which they are located. Admission to the emergency ward, for example, is rotated on a daily basis among the hospitals in a city, so that regardless of whether or not a patient lives close to a hospital, he or she must turn to the "duty hospital" for that day for service other than a severe emergency. The "duty hospital" is listed in every daily paper, as are the emergency pharmacies and hospitals open on the Sabbath. At such a time, one may have to travel a great distance to be served.

On the other hand, one of the most successful services in Israel is in the field of preventive medicine. These are the well-baby clinics operated by the Ministry of Health. In these neighborhood-located clinics, services begin with prospective parents, continue through pregnancy and delivery, and only conclude at the end of infancy. This is a universal service, originally free but now charging a symbolic fee, patronized by every strata of Israeli society. The clinics offer no curative medical services, instead referring parents to other medical units if necessary. Although there is little diversity in the service offered, the process of offering service often differs according to the presumed need of the parents. Thus, in one area the nurses may try to wean mothers away from dependence upon folk remedies or witch doctors; in another, to change traditional diets to those preferred or available in Israel today; in still another, to organize discussion groups of overanxious mothers.

In both education and medicine, as noted above, service delivery tends to be neighborhood based, but with little involvement of neighborhood people or groups as such. This is also true of some social welfare services, whereas others are heavily dependent upon neighborhood inputs.

Every local authority in Israel is required by law to establish a social welfare office, and in the large cities, of course, there are several. Such local offices are not, however, as numerous or as widespread as are schools and Sick Fund clinics. However, many social services are universal and do not require personal visiting at welfare offices. Not only are salaries in Israel geared to family size and the cost-of-living index, there is also a family allowance paid by checks mailed from the National Insurance Institute. Retirement pay, maternity benefits, survivors' insurance, and workmen's compensation are all handled in this manner. Unemployment insurance is one of the newer features in Israel, the country having a history of labor shortages and unemployment rates of less than 1% most of the time. Too little experience has been garnered by this program to date to allow for analysis.

The influence of neighborhoods on the delivery of services is more evident in social welfare than in education and health. In small villages, for example, it is the responsibility of a local welfare committee to report to the social welfare office regarding individuals or families in need of help. Since a large proportion of Israel's present population came from settings in which the government was viewed as an enemy, the thought of requesting help of a government agency was foreign to them. Indeed, it was unwise in their home countries to call any government official's attention to oneself. Hence, even in Israel, friends and neighbors are called upon to publicize to the client, and initiate for the agency, the help-giving process.

There is also a widespread network of voluntary agencies in the areas of child care, youth services, disability, dread diseases, and so on. These are mostly membership organizations with chapters in every settlement of any size, offering services to and through the membership. Such organizations also tend to offer standardized services, devised in the national office for all the chapters.

Education for social work, on the other hand, is far from standardized in Israel. The school of social work at the Hebrew University focuses mainly on casework; that at Bar-Ilan University on group work and community organization. The Tel Aviv University school is based on fields of service—child care, aging, etc.—while the Haifa University school emphasizes rural social work, including work in Arab villages.

Perhaps the largest step toward neighborhood participation in both devising and offering services is also the latest, and that is the newly established network of community centers now being established throughout the country. This network was initiated by the Ministry of Education as an aid in the process of immigrant absorption, as well as recreation, sport, and youth activities. In the last few years, however, these centers have taken on a congeries of activities, including those of a social welfare nature, such as services for new immigrants, the aged, returning soldiers, local planning bodies, preventive health, improved housing, and social action.

The original plan for these centers envisioned 30 centers, in the most disadvantaged neighborhoods in Israel, engaging in leisure-time activities. Present plans call for 200 such centers, in almost every neighborhood, including some regional centers for settlements too small to support their own. The major spurt in activities took place during the Yom Kippur War, when the centers took the place of other community services which were inoperative, reduced, or missing. As citizen groups and other agencies requested the centers to undertake additional activities, they began to move toward a multiservice operation.

In order to guard the autonomy of the center movement as a whole, and each center in particular, a government corporation for the operation of centers was established removing the centers from direct control by the ministry. The governing body of the corporation includes representatives of philanthropic organizations, technical experts, and public-spirited citizens. Whereas the corporation owns the physical buildings of the centers and employs the directors, the buildings are constructed only after a series of community surveys and self-surveys concerning citizens' preferences and needs, and the establishment of local committees concerning various phases of the center-to-be's operations. Similarly, the director of the center is chosen in consultation with local groups, who have veto power over the choice. Each center has its own autonomous board, and all center employees other than the director are employees of the board. Financing derives from the national corporation, the local authority, and membership dues and fees.

The involvement of local people is not limited to the preliminary survey and later board membership. Some centers conduct regular neighborhood surveys concerning newly proposed activities, as well as requests for new ideas. Almost every center employs a trained community organizer to identify community problems with which the center can become engaged. As a consequence, activities of centers vary with local needs.

One center has an all-day-care program since mothers are employed full time in a local factory; another has a half-day program for mothers who work part time, or do not work at all. Still another has a three-day-a-week program for two groups, since this is the work pattern of the mothers in that neighborhood. In many localities, the center provides a library in which children can do their homework, but in one city it became apparent that resources were available to add rooms to apartments, and the center took the lead in expediting this project. In one section of Jerusalem the center is involved with new immigrants from Russian Georgia, who arrive with their own needs, prejudices, and behaviors; in another the predominant population is from Yemen, with quite a different pattern.

Although the move from community centers to multiservice centers has been rapid in this new service, and the involvement of local populations—at least on the advise and consent level—important and successful, there are structural considerations which have so far prevented the full fruition of this move. In the first place, the centers were initiated by the Ministry of Education, which is controlled by the Labor Party; the Ministry of Social Welfare is usually controlled by the National Religious Party; and the Ministry of Health is under the aegis of another faction. Consequently, considerations of territory and prestige enter into moves to combine, for example, welfare offices, well-baby clinics, and vocational training into one center.

Second, social welfare offices are considered to convey an aura of need and problems (i.e., to be for "social cases") and whether locating them in centers would remove the stigma, or would stigmatize the center, is an open question.

Finally, there are questions of accountability to the board of the center as such, vis-à-vis accountability to the sponsoring ministries, with consequent possibilities of conflict.

As a consequence of these problems, there is little formal referral from the center to local welfare offices and vice-versa. There is, however, a network of citizens' information bureaus throughout Israel. These were originally volunteer services, manned by experts in various fields—law, taxes, health, and so on. With demonstrated effectiveness, they began to come under the aegis of municipalities, with employed (if relatively untrained) staff, and are now being developed into a national service. In many localities, they are physically located in the local center, and play the role of information and referral in a wide sense.

The structural considerations mentioned above also have impact on the method of staffing the centers. In order to assure a high standard in the centers, directors and senior staff are required to be university graduates (the BSW is the terminal degree for most Israeli-trained social workers, and undergraduate training is the mode for most service occupations). Specializations may, however, include not only education and social work, but recreation, economics, political science, and others. To overcome the deficiencies and differences thus engendered, senior positions in centers are increasingly available only to graduates of a one-year post-Bachelor's program, jointly established by the schools of social work and education at the Hebrew University for this purpose. Recognizing that the bulk of applicants do not hold social work degrees, the program includes elements of group and community work, administration, and social planning. Graduates of this program who direct centers are paid at the same level as principals of high schools.

Although both community centers, representing the local scene, and university-based researchers, representing a broader perspective, have been useful in identifying unmet needs—for example, supportive services for unmarried girls whose boy friends or intended husbands were lost at war, as well as for widows and parents; or problems of young Arab workers in large cities—there is no formal, specific unit in any ministry or service charged with monitoring the quality of life, social indicators, or emerging social problems. Feedback concerning social services is most often in statistical form, derived from the local welfare agency through supervisory and administrative personnel to the Ministry of Social Welfare. There are, in addition, the inputs of concerned members of voluntary organizations which, on reaching "critical mass," make for new services on the part of such organizations. Finally, there are concerned citizens' committees, such as the Trust for Expanding and Improving Services for the Aged; ad hoc governmental bodies, like the Prime Minister's Committee on Disadvantaged Youth; and new services sponsored by overseas organizations, like the Joint Distribution Committee. Concern with local community matters is also exhibited in the plethora of community organization efforts. Almost every ministry, agency, or organization has such a department, including the Housing Authority, the labor union, municipalities, and community centers. Hence, there are depressed areas in Israel which have been overresearched to the point that inhabitants refuse to answer additional questions, and the expressed, if facetious, need is for someone to coordinate the efforts of coordinators.

There is a final factor to be taken into consideration when viewing neighborhood delivery of services in Israel. This is the fact that although a country of mass immigration, with the successful absorption of immigrants both a value and a goal throughout every service, there is no consensus on the ideological level as to whether the goal of absorption is or should be assimilation, a melting pot, or cultural pluralism. Hence, the effort to respond to neighborhood differences in the delivery of services can be approved as helping to maintain—or, at least, to recognize—cultural differences, but it can easily be attacked as deterring homogeneity, national loyalty, or even good intergroup relations. This question has not been resolved on a level that will inform programs and shape activities.

In summary, it can be said that Israel exhibits great effort and relative success in attempting to deliver those services on a neighborhood level which are not, by their nature, better centralized and standardized. There is less clarity, and therefore less success, in involving local people in policymaking and service delivery, with the exception of the newly created network of multiservice centers.

8

NEIGHBORHOOD SERVICE DELIVERY: FRANCE

JACQUELINE ANCELIN

A BRIEF OUTLINE OF THE POLICY

The Vth (1966-1970) and VIth (1971-1975) French plans of Economic and Social development have, among others, given priority to the development of social services.

Solidarity

The common denominator of all activities undertaken under the VIth Plan—with a view toward solidarity—is the attempt to ensure the autonomy of and groups; to preserve that autonomy when it is threatened; and to restore it when it has been lost. The aim is to enable each individual, whatever his handicap, to take his share of initiative, responsibility, and satisfaction. Each person should have at least a minimum of means that are his by right—and not received as charity. Measures regarding allowances to the aged and handicapped are directed along these lines.

This view also means that an individual must be able to acquire and complete, at any period of his life, the education and training which are today the essential conditions of his independence. Finally, it means that priority in every sphere of social action must be given to preventive measures, to reeducation, and to action affecting the regular daily life of the people involved—especially families, the aged, and the handicapped.

Action

According to these guidelines, overall action will be developed within limited community areas. It will be based on the social centers, service aids, and all the teams working in the area. It will serve as the unifying framework for all specialized action. Three categories of population will be given priority: families, the aged, and the handicapped.

Families

Services intended for families will be developed, particularly those to help the working mothers of young children. The capacity of day nurseries will be increased, both creches and home nurseries. There also should be an increase in the number of social workers who can prevent children from being placed in the public care in the event of a mother's illness or absence, or where a mother has to stop work to nurse a sick child. Policy to prevent abandonment of children will be enforced, and adoption will be facilitated. Better coordination among all children's services will be implemented. In rural areas and at the district level, families will benefit in general from the sociocultural and socioeducative facilities.

The Aged

Services for old people (apart from the guaranteeing of minimum income) will aim at keeping them in their own homes. First will be the development of low rental housing programs. In these homes, light and diversified social facilities will be installed and will also be open to other old people from the outside. These facilities will include restaurants, clubs, and information centers in old people's homes.

Action for the aged will mean also a better understanding of the medical needs of old people. Instead of allocating facilities arbitrarily, between those who are able and those who are disabled, the emphasis will be on specific possibilities of treatment and functional readaption. For example, for those whose isolation or health require home aid or home care, such services will be available. Thus, instead of the present system of undifferentiated accommodation by a variety of formulas, policy will be based on an assessment of long- and medium-range needs. Whenever possible, restored independence of the elderly will be the goal.

The Handicapped

Services for the handicapped and maladjusted will aim at ensuring, as far as possible, that individuals retain their independence through the prevention of handicaps and maladjustments as well as reintegration into working and social life. Policies will be given priority during the VIth plan and will be adapted according to the age of the handicapped or the maladjusted.

Coordination of services will be most important at all levels: national, regional, and at the level of direct action. *Sectorization* will be stimulated as functional links are established between the service authority and the operational teams.

Focus

Thus far we have briefly pointed out the three populations receiving priority under the VIth Plan. The remainder of this paper, however, will focus on the delivery systems. Two major aspects of the delivery system which have developed or changed in France during the last decade are: the sectorization of social services (mentioned above) and the social centers. A few remarks on social research and pilot experiments will also be included.

THE SECTORIZATION OF SOCIAL SERVICES

The Social Services Reform Act of 1972

Social Services, employing various types of skilled social workers, are organized by three categories of institutions: the public ones (ministries and the Directions Depatmentales de l'Action Sanitaire et Sociale [a "department" is a local unit of government, similar to the county. There are 95 departments in France.]); the semi-public ones (for instance, the Family Allowances agencies); and the private ones (diverse assocations, factories, etc.).

During the past few years, beside the social workers (the *assistantes sociales*), workers from other disciplines have taken an increasing role in the field of social action. Educators, who used to work mainly in children's institutions, have become sociocultural leaders (the *animateurs socio-culturels*) in the social centers. Nurses, after complementary training, have left the hospitals to work at home in the families for maternal and child health protection. Home economic teachers, with complementary training, also have left adolescents groups in school to do counseling (the "counseilleres en economic sociale et familiale") for adults. Consequently, we have now in the field of social action a diversity of social workers who have different training and who are employed by various services. Because of newly recognized social and individual needs, and in relation to the development of social sciences, these social workers are asking for more training and postgraduate training.

As of 1974, we have about 20,000 assistants sociaux, 17,000 nurses, 9,000 specialized educators, 6,000 monitors/educators, 5,300 helpers, and 2,100 economics counselors. Overall, the total is about 50,000 social workers for a population of about 52.5 million. In a recent book entitled *Les Exclus,* Rene

Lenoir, the Minister for Social Action and Social Rehabilitation, wrote that one out of 10 French people is an *exclus* (is on the fringe, a marginal one).

Types of Social Workers

Among the assistants sociaux there are different categories important to know if one wants to understand how the French system works. They all have the same training and the same state diploma, but they are differentiated according to the type of work they do with "users."

The *assistants polyvalents de secteur* are social workers (also called family social workers) who work in a specific geographical area (the *secteur*) with all the population and all the family members in that area. They must have a comprehensive approach to the sanitary, social, economic, and psychological problems of families; and they must help them to find solutions and remedies with the help of the specialized services for particular situations.

The *assistants polyvalents de categorie* have, in principle, the same attributes as the assistants de secteur, but they work with specific categories of people—for instance, families in which the father works on the French railways or in the army.

The *assistants specialses* take care of one particular person, or a particular problem, for a limited period of time, in collaboration with the assistants polyvalents de secteur—for instance, social workers working in mental health, in the prisons, or with judges.

In 1971, we had about 24.38% polyvalent social workers, 17.5% categorial polyvalent social workers, and 43.42% specialized social workers.

The Coordination of Social Service

The social services have not been rationally spread all over the country. Many were established by private initiative before the ministries and public services organized their own services. In addition many services were created according to resources, rather than needs. Consequently, there has been much development in the big cities with many rural areas remaining underserved; some areas have had several social workers serving the same family; other times there have been lapses of energy and means or anarchy in the interventions; and sometimes there has been no response at all.

For these reasons, the law of August 4, 1950, on the Coordination of Social Services tried to organize territorial planning of social work services. That law aimed at avoiding overlapping so that a family would not be cared for by several social services (and, in doing so, it aimed at protecting the intimacy of the family and reducing loss of energy in the services); avoiding the reverse situation—that one agency, considering that the other was responsible, would leave out a family in need; and avoiding that some families would be deprived of necessary help because they would not know which agency to call.

Organization of coordination committees was created in each department as a liaison between public and private social services. Each committee, which had jurisdictional capacity, was regrouped under the Presidency of the Prefect (the representative of the government in each department). The committee consisted of the director of health, the director of population, the *conseilleres generalles* (elected), representatives of family associations, and social workers elected by their colleagues.

After listing all the private and public social services in the department, these representatives to the committee had to declare in which category of social work they wanted to practice. Next, a coordination regulation was established which distributed various functions between the services, taking into consideration their vocation and real possibilities, the population density in the various geographical sectors, and the users' categories. The basis of social service had to be the polyvalent social worker in the sector; and the sectors had to be delineated—a "ward" in cities, a "canton" in rural areas. These coordination regulations had to be approved by the Ministry of Public Health and Population.

Organization resources of the committee involved a secretariat, files, and a system of documentation. Resources were provided by public and private employers according to the number of social workers they employed; by contributions from commercial and industrial enterprises and public utilities according to the number of insured people or beneficiaries of family allowances; and by grants from public, semi-public, and private institutions.

Evaluation of the system followed a long, slow, and difficult organization. On January 7, 1959, a *decret* redefined the role of the committees and gave them one year to work out the regulation. If it was not done by that time, the prefect was authorized to submit a regulation to the ministry.

In spite of the stricture, only 60 departments established regulations; and these were not always applied. The reasons for that half-failure might have been the lack of personnel to cover some sectors mainly in rural areas, the reluctance of some services to give priority to the polyvalent social workers when they employed mainly specialized or categorical workers for their own population, and, possibly, the reluctance of social workers themselves to accept polyvalent work. The latter was an extremely difficult job, for a polyvalent social worker, isolated in a geographical area with sometimes 15,000 inhabitants, had too many tasks and heavy responsibilities.

In 1966, when reform took place, coordination worked really only in Paris and in about thirty departments. (We will come back to the situation in Paris.)

Reform: The Sectorization of Social Services

As part of a broader reform of the external services of the Ministry of Public Health and Social Security, the law of July 30, 1964, reorganized the administrative services of the prefecture and the powers of the prefects. The different services of the prefecture—including population services, health services, social assistance, health, and social services of the schools—were unified into one service. The new service was the Direction Departementale de l'Action Sanitaire et Sociale. All the public social work services were united under this single direction as well. The guideline of such a policy was to organize one unique service, focused on polyvalence de secteur. It aimed at a better territorial implantation of social workers.

In 1965, the tasks of the new service were defined. Those tasks were maternal and child health and social protection, including medico-social protection of children and adolescents, who were "normal" and who were "in danger"; medico-social protection against social diseases; family social work; contribution to the training of social work students; and unexpected tasks, those not covered or not completely covered by other existing services (such as care of the aged, marginal families, etc.); and those cases which constituted an emergency (disaster). Focus had to be on prevention and early detection, with priority given to the most underprivileged people.

In addition to the polyvalent social work, the only specialized services (public ones) are: services "d-Aide Sociate a l'Enfance" (Aid to dependent children); services *de prevention* (aid to neglecting families and children in danger); services for prostitutes; and mental health services and services dealing with social diseases (tuberculosis, cancer, veneral diseases, etc.).

The organization of the sectorization is specified more precisely in a memorandum of December 12, 1966. For the first time, the sector is defined; we call it *circonscription.* It is a geographical area with 50,000 to 70,000 inhabitants, divided into sectors of polyvalence of 3,000 to 5,000 people, and each circonscription must have an administrative center.

The organization is at the level of the department. There is a chief social worker who under the authority of the "directeur department al de l'action sanitaire et sociale" functions as technical counselor, studying and organizing the circonscriptions to define the methods of work, to enable the liaisons with the other services, etc. She is assisted in these tasks by several specialized social workers. In each circonscription there is one *assistante de circonscription* who organizes the doctors and the various types of social workers (also the nurses, home helpers, educators, etc.). This assistant also coordinates the work of all social personnel employed by the direction departmentales; controls their work and facilitates and develops team work, an interdisciplinary method, and organizes field work for the students. The polyvalent social workers have to work in close contact with that assistante de circonscription and get technical help from her in case of need.

Relationships with the other social services (semi-public and private) grew in importance as a result of the reorganization of the public services. The 1966 memorandum says that all the polyvalent social services must have their place in the circonscription. Without prejudice of the rules and technical supervision specific to the services which are their employers, the polyvalent social workers will be integrated into that new organization, if the employers have signed an agreement with the Direction departementale. (The public services employ only 33% of the social workers.)

Evaluation of the reform is still difficult to make accurately until more time has passed. However, several problems have become evident in the application of the reform. First, many private and semi-public agencies were opposed to a reorganization of social services which appeared as stronger "state control." On the other hand, services had different policies, and taking part in the sectorization meant losing at least part of them. Also, the assistante de circonscription, to assume her organizational or consultantive role, needed specific training (which later was organized). Finally, in most of the circon-scriptions, the polyvalent social workers and the assistante de circonscription were employed by the same agency (the *homogeneous circonscription*). But, in others, the polyvalent social workers had various employers and, beside the assistante de circonscription, they kept their own hierarchy. One can easily imagine that in these heterogeneous circonscriptions the durability of hierarchies might be difficult to live with.

The National Funds for Family Allowance decided in 1967 to collaborate with the reform seeing advantages in a better distribution of social workers, a better knowledge of needs, and a more comprehensive approach to social problems. However, among the local family allowances agencies, not all followed that recommendation and signed a *convention* (an agreement) with the Direction Departementale de l'Action Sanitaire et Sociale.

The great majority of the big semi-public social services, those attached to Social Security or Rural Social Mutuality, kept their specialization. The same was true for most of the private social services. However, most of the social services attached to local authorities (mainly in the big cities) did enter into the system.

What happened to the previous coordination system established in 1950? It still exists in some departments and is often the support of postgraduate training "refresher" courses for social workers of all categories.

Other services beside the social services have been sectorized as well. The unified service for children, inside the Direction Departementale de l'Action Sanitaire et Sociale, was established in 1969. It unifies all the services concerned with the protection of children (maternal and child health protection, maladjusted children, and school health). The psychiatric sectorization was created in 1960, defining the role of the psychiatric team in each geographical sector, and assuring the continuity of action from prevention to after care rehabilitation. Additional services include the national education and its

Table 1: Circonscriptions (January 1974)

	1971	1974	
The plan	730	759	
The reality	299 +217 projects	466 +150 on preparation	
Geographical dimension		193 <50,000 inhabitants 220 : 50 to 75, 000 67 : 75 to 100,000 47 : >100,000	

circonscriptions with a medico-pedagogic committee, and social assistance with its administrative circonscriptions. A major problem has been the harmonization of all these sectorizations, as each system is sectorizing according to the norms specific to its own field of action.

Conventions signed between the Direction Departementale de l'Action Sanitaire et Sociale and other services are:

Local Authorities	12 + 7 projects
Rural Social Mutuality	24 + 9 projects
Family Allowances Agencies	35 + 20 projects
Illness Social Security Agencies	5 + 4 projects
Private Services	18 + 5 projects

Paris and the Coordination of Social Services

Because of the urban economic and social context of Paris and the region surrounding the city, the need for coordination was obvious. Even before the public authorities made the official decisions, a system of coordination was established in January 1948 and remained functional until the new law of July 30, 1964. The latter reorganized the external services of the ministry and divided the Paris region into six departments, each one having its own Direction Departementale de l'Action Sanitaire et Sociale. However, the department of Paris still keeps the system of coordination after several decrets and memoranda.

The prefect is the president of the liaison and coordination committee of the social services. Among the 58 members, there are representatives of the Council of Paris (eight), the Social Security (12), the Social Workers (eight), and the Bureau d'Aide Sociale of Paris. The committee has to elaborate the coordination regulation, apply it, and vote the annual budget.

The *Regulation of June 1973* says in its preamble that it is aimed at the coordination and harmonization of all the social services within the department of Paris. The goal is the efficient and rational use of existing social resources to avoid overlapping, while at the same time respecting the independence and proper vocation of each service and the free choice of families. The functioning of the coordination is assured by the Service departemental de coordination.

The *central service* includes among its personnel head social workers, inspectors of the coordination secretaries, documentalists, administrative assistants, and so on. Apart from the usual administrative tasks, the central service has the important function of documentation and information, mainly about the social and medico-social services in the region of Paris and sometimes in France. It also publishes several bulletins for social workers and organizes conferences every month.

The *arroundissements* are where the practical work gets done. There are 20 arroundissements in Paris, and each is under the responsibility of a social worker, the *deleguee a la coordination,* chosen among the polyvalent social workers and nominated by the prefect. She is assisted by secretaries with the correspondence, the files, and the documentation. She must assure the functioning of the secretariat, assure the liaison with city hall, the Bureau d'Aide Sociale, and all social services in the arroundissement, and organize study groups with the different kinds of social workers, and so on.

For reasons of efficiency, since 1962, the major services have decided to regroup their personnel in the same arroundissements. As a result, the Prefecture of Paris is covering six arroundissements, the Family Allowances Agency six, and the Social Security five. The other arroundissements will be regrouped later.

Resources come mainly from the budget of the City of Paris and the Family Allowances and Social Security (20%).

The *functioning* of the social services in the department of Paris in 1970 involved the following: six services with 301 social workers, *polyvalentes de secteur;* 29 services with 330 social workers, *polyvalentes de categorie;* and 457 specialized services, with 1,882 social workers (1,119 doing specialized social or medico-social work, and 763 working for the personnel in factories and public or semi-public administrations). In total there are 492 social services, employing 2,513 social workers.

There is a great diversity of services but unfortunately an insufficient number of polyvalent social workers. Forty-four percent are employed by public administrations, 16% in the semi-public sector and 40% in the private sector. These various services have their own techniques and are working with people of all ages and social classes. To avoid overlapping, the Service Departmental de Coordination tries, as much as possible, to organize the polyvalent services and to establish liaisons. Actually, a network of polyvalent social workers covers the department which is divided into 269 sectors. All referrals are registered by the secretariat and addressed to the service which asked to take care of the family. Two hundred thousand families, referred to the social services or using them, are registered in the 21 centers. However, despite these efforts at coordination, the improvement of the coordination between polyvalent services and specialized services remains one of the main preoccupations of the Service Departmental de Coordination.

SOCIAL CENTERS

Thus far we have described how social work services are actually organized in France. Another field of social action has developed during the last decade which is also very closely related to the delivery of social services—the social centers (*centres sociouse et socio-culturels*).

After World War II we had a very acute housing problem and had to develop social policy also in that field. Little by little we saw new wards with new houses, new buildings, and new towns. However, this urban development created new social problems—the adjustment of people to these completely new housing conditions, and the problem of isolation, the adjustment of people from rural areas to an urban way of living, and the adjustment of those who used to live in very poor houses. Also there were environmental problems. Because of these problems, the social center became an integral part of planning in the field of housing and urban development.

Functions

In 1970, a memorandum of the Secretariat d'Etat for Social Action and Social Rehabilitation defined the function of the social center: it will be more than a shelter for services and activities; it is a device for the animation of social life in the geographical areas for the organizers who are associated with it. The social center will have an educative, preventive, and promotional function in trying to have a comprehensive approach to the user's problems. It will be open to all age categories, infants and children, adolescents, adults, and old-aged. . . . Open not only to individuals but also to families and groups with an objective of community action. And—this is an important point—the users must effectively participate in the management, the activities, and in the global animation of the center. Initially, the social center offers an easy way of assembling and coordinating a number of public and private services, both social and medico-social, which are necessary for the population living in a limited geographical area. In that way the access to services will become easier and expenses for the collectivity will be less. The social center is polyvalent.

Presently, there are about 800 social centers in France, and the VIth Plan has provided for 180 more. An enquiry made by the National Federation of Special Centres a few years ago showed that about 200,000 families were using the centers (48% children, 26% adults, 12% adolescents, and 4% aged). In these 800 centers, there were 2,200 permanent employees, among them 1,650 social workers (various categories), 2,700 part-time employees, and 5,000 benevolents (volunteers).

Services

Usually the social center starts with a few services—maternal and child health clinics and *halte-garderie* for young children. Staff is composed of social workers and home economic counselors. New services are created after consulting the people about their needs and wishes. They also take some part in the creation of such services. In the third stage, the social center becomes a place where the "dynamic forces" of the sector can meet and organize their own activities, and take an active part in the management of the center (comanagement). At this point it is a real "neighborhood house," where social workers and benevolents work together and where the needs of the people and the needs of the community can be expressed.

We usually distinguish between small centers (less than a surface of 500 m), medium centers (between 500 and 1000 m2), and large centers (more than 100 m2). The respective percentages are 65%, 25%, and 10%. In a small center, one will find an infant clinic, a halte-garderie, a library, a room for pottering, the social worker's office, and the home economic counselor's room. In the larger centers, there will be also collective services, a dispensary, the home-helper's office, and sometimes a Social Security and Family Allowances paydesk.

Resources

For the construction of the centers, the state pays 40% and the Family Allowances Agencies pay 40%. The functioning expenses are covered by the local authorities, the Family Allowances Agency, and, since 1973, by the state. Users are also participating in a small way.

Evaluation

There are financial problems but mostly there are problems regarding the users. They are not always those for whom the services are intended; more often they are middle- and upper-class people. It happens also that some groups of people are "monopolizing" the centers, excluding, little by little, those who do not share the same aspirations or ideology. In some cases, centers become more "politic" than "social," and it is often difficult for the social worker or the sociocultural leader, who is responsible for the center, to distinguish between politically oriented objectives and socially oriented ones.

Finally, there is the question about the desirability of one big center which groups all of the services in the same building versus different services in several small buildings in varied locations. The second formula is recommended, as it seems to facilitate access for a larger number of people.

RESEARCH AND PILOT EXPERIMENTS

I have selected from research some of the results or hypotheses which appeared of particular interest with regard to the problem of social services delivery. Previously we have described some of the organizational means used to facilitate access to social services. Now we have to question, through research, the real results of policies and practices. Some questions we should seek answers to are: (1) Do the people use the social services? (2) Who are those who use them, and those who do not? (3) Who is using what and why? (4) What would people like as social services?

We obtained much information from a socioeconomic research project on "Needs and Aspirations of Families and Youth" sponsored in 1971 by the Caisse Nationale des Allocations Familiales (National Funds for Family Allowances). The objectives were to get a better knowledge of changes in the families, fecundity, women's work, family relationships, attitudes toward the various sorts of help to families, the presentation of social equipments and services, and attitudes toward "collectivity." The sample consisted of 2,000 families, having zero to five children, who were interviewed for long hours.

Before saying a few words about the social equipments and services, it is important to mention that the great majority of families are in favor of cash benefits, and that increases when going down the "social ladder"; and it is associated with a position of "turnback" toward the organized collectivity. When there is an option between social services or cash benefits, young couples more frequently favor social services. When the mother works, there is a demand for housing in the lower classes and for day care centers in the upper classes.

The usage of social equipment and services has been analyzed with reference to the resources (salaries and cash benefits) and the sociocultural status (social origin, education, and profession). It is the last variable—the sociocultural status—which appeared to be the most discriminating. Some services are effectively redistributive; the rate of usage increases when the sociocultural status decreases. A few examples are home-helpers services, holiday camps functioning during the day only, and some services in the social centers, such as dispensary and social workers' services. The nonredistributive services are holiday camps for children, "holiday houses" for families, and, in the centers themselves, leisure and cultural activities. But it is important to note that, when these last activities are offered in a social center, there is less equality than when it is offered outside. Services for children show more equality, but the rate of usage still increases with family resources. One could think that cultural brakes appear to be stronger than economic ones. One indisputable fact is that there is a big lack of information among these families. For instance, 50% did not know if there was a home-helpers service in their surroundings or not. And ignorance is more frequent among poor families. However, the issue is not a simple problem of noninformation. The director of the research indicates that a systematized policy of information would certainly have some positive if limited effect. The real problem seems to lie in the way services are produced. The models, norms, and values on which they are based are often those of certain categories of families which other families are "supposed" to follow. The risk is reproduction of the market mechanism.

THREE EXPERIMENTS

Social Action for Holidays

In 1973, after much social research conducted in the field of "social action for holidays," one of our Family Allowances Agencies in Angers, started an action-research—a pilot experiment on "Holiday Information."

The objective was to have a better understanding of that problem of information in a field which was not sufficiently redistributive, to understand the economic and cultural mechanisms, and to experiment with new methods of information. The research team was composed of a sociologist, one social worker, and one home economics counselor, with the collaboration of all the social workers of a specific urban area.

Initially, the team made a brief survey of the population and analyzed the existing information and the formal and informal channels of information. Next, they experimented with new methods. Beneficiaries living in the area agreed to have visits or phone calls from everybody. Little booklets (strip cartoon types) were distributed, mainly by the research workers standing in the street (like the Salvation Army!) or the market place.

Although the experiment is not finished nor completely evaluated, the researchers already write that "information is a false problem." It is not due to lack of information that some people do not use services they would be entitled to. Rather, their "reluctance" is of a more complex, global nature (although it was noticed that people appreciated and used information most when social workers were standing in the street!).

Day Care

Another study involved day care for young children. For many years, day care in France was an underdeveloped field. Now, however, it is receiving priority.

As a result of the new focus, an experimental center was organized in 1973 in Paris (14th arroundissement—180,000 inhabitants) supplying information and counseling for the care of children up to three or four years of age. Again, it was an action-research conducted by psychiatrists, a sociologist, psychologists, and social workers.

The reasons for this experiment were: (1) the desire to protect the mental hygiene of young children whose mothers had or wanted to work; (2) an attempt to coordinate the efforts of all those who are concerned with young children (social workers, teachers in the kindergartens, doctors, local authorities, family associations, representatives of public or private social agencies, etc.), so that day care services might really correspond to the global needs of children and their families; (3) the wish to help parents, through information and counseling, to find their best individual solution for the day care of their young child. An area of particular focus grew out of the observations of these psychiatrists in their practice. Frequently, they saw that mothers of young children had ambivalent or guilt feelings about working and were often confused about the solutions from which to choose—foster home, creche, or *ecole maternelle* (public school for children from two to six, before entering the compulsory school). Contributing to each woman's personal dilemma is the attitude toward working women in France. Even though changes are rapidly developing, attitudes vary greatly according to social status.

Socially Handicapped Families

Research on socially handicapped families and social action was sponsored by the Caisse Nationale des Allocationes Familiales a few years ago. One of the main reasons for such research was the feeling that social work services had failed with these poor families. This conclusion was based on passivity of these families and their very limited use of social equipment and services. When the research team, with the help of 15 social workers working in poor areas, analyzed the situation, it appeared that there was a big gap between what the families expressed as their needs and what the representatives of social action agencies thought their needs were. The main observations were also that social equipments and services were used by these poor families only when they were physically close to them, when equipment and services were specific to them, and that an individualized and continued relationship with them was indispensable to help them to go toward social equipment and services.

CONCLUSION

In France, the development of social services is certainly considered as an indispensable complement of a cash benefit policy. Services are mainly aimed at certain categories of underpriviledged people. Due to a long history of social action, the administration of social services has been a complex one in the public, the private, and the semi-public sectors. Public health and social action have not always known a happy marriage.

Certainly there have been important efforts made during the last decade to "rationalize" the system, to coordinate services, to sectorize and unify them (to associate public and private), to develop the *action concertee* (one more new concept!), and to decentralize. The aim of these efforts is to save energy and resources for the benefit of the users and to offer them a more coherent and a larger range of services.

Failures might be due to the fact that means have obscured ends. Also, because social policy is so linked to the political scene, "fights" for power have made successes more than desired. However, because we really are concerned with people—individuals, families, groups, and communities—the main problem remains the nonredistributive role of many social services in spite of many attempts to organize a better delivery system. The question is still open: Why do some people, especially those who we think are the most in need of services, not use the social services we have so well planned? Therefore, the answer might be, for the coming years in our situation, not only to improve access to social services, but to help people create the services they really want.

BIBLIOGRAPHY

(Addresses are included for those readers wishing more information)

Action Sociale et Familles socialement handicapees Etudes C.A.F. N 13, 63 boulevard Haussman, 75008 PARIS

La reforme de Service Sociale des Directions Departementales de l'Action Sanitaire et Sociale, Revue Francaise de Service Social; n2: 1972. A.N.A.S. − 3 rue de Stockholm, 75008 PARIS

Les besoins et aspirations des familles et des jeunes−Etudes C.A.F.−C.N.A.F. − 47 rue de la Chaussee d'Antin, 75009 PARIS

Les Centres Sociaux et socio-culturels. Fie Sociale − 12-1973. C.E.D.I.A.S. − 5 rue Las Cazes 75007 PARIS

Les exclus−Un francais sur dix. Rene Lenoir. Edition de seuil. 27 rue Jacob, 75006 PARIS

Les experiences pilotes et l'action sociale. Informations Sociales: 11-1973. 63, boulevard Haussman, 75008 PARIS

Reglement departmental de coordination des Services Sociaux de Paris: Service departmental. 21 place de Pantheon, 75005 PARIS
VIth Economic and Social development Plan (1971-1975) La Documentation Francaise:
  29-31 Quai Voltaire — 75007 PARIS

9

SOCIAL SERVICE DELIVERY IN ZAMBIA: THE PRIMARY GROUP

ELIZABETH BROOKS
VUKANI G. NYIRENDA

The idea of social services in Zambia is as old as the Zambian society itself. However, the meaning and approaches to service delivery have changed. Service-rendering in traditional Zambian society meant quite a different thing from what it means now in a modern state built around a money economy. The need for institutionalized services, located in formally organized agencies, has also changed. Our view is that there is a greater demand for such services now than previously. Thus, we feel much thought is necessary to determine how to best organize such services so that they really *reach* the people for whom they are meant.

In this paper, an attempt has been made to identify a service delivery structure which would or does permit accessibility of needed services to the Zambian community. This is not a new model; rather, what we have done is to identify some existing approaches which have in the past tended to be ignored, despite their potential effectiveness.

In arriving at this conclusion, we first take a look at the nature of the Zambian society. Like all other societies in the developing world, a large percentage of the population is found in the rural areas with communal living based on kinship ties. In these areas, there are built-in institutions from which the individual or group draws help. The urban areas, on the other hand, are populated by a society which predominantly is in transition. Here the traditional and the modern meet in what has been termed "cultural dualism." The majority of the urbanites depend on tribal customs and traditions in order to cope with uban living. This is an important factor to note in organizing services for the Zambian urban dwellers.

A casual look at the conventional patterns of social service delivery in Zambia reveals the serious problem of irrelevance which renders services either unacceptable or counterproductive. However, a closer observation reveals that, while there are some community-based patterns which produce relevant and effective services, they have not received sufficient emphasis. In our conclusion, therefore, we appeal for a rediscovery and emphasis of those patterns which are both flexible and relevant and which allow the service users to be coplanners as well as consumers.

THE ZAMBIAN SOCIETY

In Zambia, like in many other developing countries and former colonies, the characteristic approaches to social policy formulation have been to borrow, in carbon copy form, ideas, policies, and service models from developed countries and former colonial powers (Clifford, 1966; de Jongh, 1969; Forder, 1966; Mukundarao, 1969). However, when this approach is followed, the services are either rejected by the potential users or the services have an adverse effect on the very people who were supposed to benefit from them. For this reason, we would argue that a discussion of any service model must be preceded by an analysis of the community or society which is supposed to be a beneficiary of the intended service.

In this section, the writers will identify the basic elements in the social organization of the Zambian society. This will provide a base for a model of service provision. Our analysis will focus on three variables: patterns of residence, kinship networks, and social relations. These variables will be applied in looking at both the rural and urban communities in Zambia.

Rural and Traditional Social Systems

The Principle of Village Living

The most universal aspect of rural life in Zambia is the village. This pattern of social organization is found in all Zambia tribes, without exception. It is also common in many other African communities throughout this continent. Maquet (1972:76) has included "living in a village" among his 34 elements which contribute to the "contents of Africanity"; and Gluckman et al. (1949:7) have observed:

> One social group occurs in all the tribes, whatever their environment and whatever their social organisation. This is the village—a discrete group of people who usually reside in adjacent huts, who recognise allegiance to a headman, and who have a corporate identity against other similar groups.

Members of the village community are normally linked together by varying ties of kinship and affinity. It is these ties that define the community. In the olden days (and to a great extent in the majority of the more remote villages in Zambia today), all members of the village community had to prove a genealogical relationship with the headman in order for them to belong. Today, however, an individual can gain a "residence permit" in any village through any one of three types of relationships: kinship and affinal ties; clanship; and ties of friendship, acquaintance, and shared common experience.

An individual member retains his place in the group as long as he has good character and displays appropriate behavior. The significance of such requirements becomes crucial when one realizes that a village community in Zambia is considered to be more than a social grouping; it is an "ethical unit" whose goodness depends upon the character of its members. The implications of this concept of villages are far-reaching and of maximum importance. Since the most cherished element in village living is what Callen Young (1937) once called the "great-hearted comradeship," if the others fear that an individual's conduct might "spoil" the group, then the community will not hesitate to withhold or withdraw such rights of association.

Composition and Community Boundaries

Another important factor in the principle of village living concerns the composition of village communities and the determination of group boundaries. What is crucially important is the fact that a Zambian village is a corporate group of relatives whose members are related to one another and ultimately to the leader—the village headman. Tribes are grouped into three categories of patrilineal, matrilineal, and bilateral groups. These categories are reflected in the village communities through the composition of the entire community and especially of the nuclear group. Among the patrilineal tribes, this nuclear group consists of male siblings, their wives, and their children. Among matrilineal groups, the nucleus is composed of the village headman, his sisters, and his sisters' matrilineal descendants. These two patterns are combined into the bilateral group where the nucleus is composed of a headman, his wives and children, and his collateral kin from both his father's and mother's side, i.e., those who he may have won over through his conduct and generosity.

An important conclusion to be drawn from this discussion is that village membership in Zambia is synonymous with membership in a kinship group. The village must be considered as a community of kinsmen, cooperating in production and consumption activities. The rules that govern membership in a kinship group equally apply to members of a village community. Interpersonal relations among villagers can only be understood by referring to rules that govern kinship relations.

Spatial Organization

As Zambian villages are basically kinship units, their design is only governed by functional requirements. As George Kay (1967:30) once wrote:

> it is perhaps sufficient to note first, that no strict adherence to any geometrical pattern nor to any formal layout is customary (in Zambian villages). Secondly, that the general shape and the disposition of buildings within a settlement is largely a product of the social organisation of the inhabitants.

A study of the Mossi of Upper Volta by Peter Hammond (1959:241-242) reveals even more vividly the functional basis of spatial organization in most African communities, as can be seen in the following description:

> the dwelling of each Mossi kin group has the appearance of a small walled village. . . . The individual dwellings are constructed in such a way—the wall of each house or courtyard being contiguous to that of the nearest neighbour as to form a circular wall whose exterior is closed at all but two points. The dwelling of each kin group has a small exit and a large open entrance way just within which is located a thatch-covered sun shelter (Zande) where the men of the lineage gather to rest, to work at small crafts, and to talk. Guests are received, gossip exchanged and social and ceremonial obligations discussed in its shade. Here also, the men of the lineage take their meals, brought out to them from the kitchens of their wives. . . . A few paces away is the grinding platform (here) where the women gather to prepare the grain for their families meals. . . . Each woman has her assigned place at this platform where she keeps her pestle and where she stations herself at dawn and again at dusk to grind her millet and learn the news of the day.

Thus, we see that spatial arrangement of houses in Zambian villages has a meaning that transcends the needs and wants of individual households; it is a microcosm of the pattern of social organization of the entire tribe of which the village is a part.

Village Leadership

It has already been shown that Zambian rural communities are organized around a senior kinsman—the village headman—who is a common element among all rural communities in Zambia. Village leadership operates within a hereditary framework, and the individual village headman holds power in trust. As such, he not only performs administrative functions, he is also a symbol of the group's unity and solidarity since, he provides the focal point of all relationships. Numerous case studies of community development work in rural areas of

Zambia have revealed the role of the village leadership in the success of projects that require wide participation. Nonparticipation of, or rejection by, the village headman has more often than not led to the failure of community projects.

Kinship Networks

To fully understand the pattern of social organization in rural Zambia, and indeed in many other rural African communities, one must see it in terms of kinship. Kinship is a communal bond that binds the past, present, and future generations together. It is a web of relationships within which individual members stand in particular social relations to each other; and it is this bond which is the main governing social force. Young (1937:55) aptly observed this phenomenon in the following words:

> The communal bond operates to prevent any self-separating individualistic development. The individual is in some way something more than a human unit; he, or she, is inseparable from those who were there before and, equally inseparable from those who are to come after.

Looking a little closer at its functions, the institution of kinship in Zambia could be likened to a "comprehensive social insurance scheme" in which the individual member finds not only broad-based companionship but also social arrangements which demand mutual aid and reciprocal obligations. The whole system is supported by a complex of relationships that are carefully woven into logical systems that have meaning for, and are understood by, all. Each individual member of the kinship is taught through social education to find his rightful place. He occupies a position of security since tradition demands that an individual appeal to his seniors and command his subordinates in times of trouble. By the rules of kinship, both categories of kinsmen are obligated to respond.

The overall importance of kinship, for our purposes, can be summed up by stressing the importance of the principle of comradeship. This tenet requires that individuals in a particular family group, village, or tribe live not only with, but for each other. In this way, their lives are meaningfully intertwined. It is this principle that is invoked in demanding participation in intra- and intergroup/village cooperative activities such as work, parties, ceremonies, and celebrations.

Urban Social Systems

In order to complete the picture of Zambian society, we must now turn to an analysis of the urban scene, since Zambian society is a mixture of both rural and urban features. In analyzing the pattern of social organization in the urban situation, we will still be interested in patterns of residence, kinship networks, and the nature of social relations.

As has already been indicated, urbanism is a relatively new phenomenon in Zambia. It began after the discovery of copper and with industrial development in the 1920s. Most of the present large urban centers are post-World War II developments (Kay, 1968). Prior to that time most Zambians came to work in the towns as seasonal migrant laborers who ultimately returned to their villages which remained as the focus of life.

The main floodgates of urbanization were opened by the attainment of independence in 1964. This was the time when the towns experienced unprecedented urban growth, with most towns increasing their populations by 50%-80% in the first five years of independence. During this period nearly 2.5% of the population migrated from rural to urban areas.

The significant feature of urbanization was the change in the people's attitudes toward the towns. In preindependence days, restrictive policies barred Zambians from adopting towns as their homes. But, after independence, Zambians were free to choose their home. With the introduction of home ownership, Site and Service, and Squatter Upgrading Schemes, more and more Zambians began establishing homes in the towns.

Even today, with the coming of some measure of permanence, towns are still foreign to the majority of Zambian town dwellers, particularly because rules of residence are drastically different from those in the rural areas. Whereas in a village community one lives among a community of relatives, qualifications for belonging to a particular urban residential area are based mainly on economic factors. This leads to a situation where people may be grouped into a "community" because they belong to the same economic stratum but who otherwise have little else in common. For people who, only yesterday, were integral members of kin-based village communities and who still belong to these communities at heart, the urban grouping is an artificial aggregation rather than a community. They live as individuals and survive on what they as individuals or members of a nuclear family can provide. Ultimately, when all else has failed, they must turn to "impersonal" institutions with foreign rules and regulations of eligibility.

In response to this situation most urban Zambians have tended to live in two worlds: they are physically in town, but their lives are governed by their tribal customs and traditions. One might say they have not gone a full cycle of acculturation and initiation into urban living. Powdermaker (1962) once observed the fact that some residents of the copper mines would go to church on Sunday morning and conduct or participate in traditional rituals and ceremonies in the evening. This pattern of adaptive behavior, which incorporates urbanism and traditionalism, is what Nyirenda (1975) refers to as "cultural dualism."

It must be emphasized that because of this free flow of interaction between town and country, the emergent urban social systems found in Zambia and in many other African countries are nothing more than functional compromises between Western urbanism and traditional African patterns of social organization (Banton, 1957; Bascom, 1955; Little, 1957; Lloyd, 1953; Nyirenda, 1975).

In all these efforts to merge town and country into one social system, the individual participants have relied on tribe and kinship as basic institutions within which to develop the new urban social network. These traditional institutions perform two basic functions for the Zambian urban dwellers: first, they provide him with the means through which he may gain help from others in times of need or when misfortune strikes; and second, they provide him with the only identifiable means for the preservation of his family, kinship and tribal, or ethnic identity. They are his "survival kit" in a strange and sometimes cruel urban world. Through them, the individual is able to develop multifunctional personal links with other individuals mutually bound by the same institutions.

In concluding this section, we would like to stress the fact, borne out by the above analyses, that Zambian society is a society in transition, where both rural and urban patterns of social organization are slowly being merged into one widening social field. This conclusion has important implications for the social planners and those responsible for the provision of social services. No static model of social service provision will adequately cater to the needs of this changing society.

CONVENTIONAL SOCIAL WORK PATTERNS

The provision of social services in Zambia is primarily a government responsibility. The Department of Social Welfare within the Ministry of Labour and Social Services emphasizes a casework program in five areas: general welfare, family and child welfare, corrections, research and training, and public relations. General welfare takes the form of rations, clothing, accommodation, rent payment, and travel assistance. Public assistance is the largest part of this service, although it is not supported by an act of Parliament, as is the case with other statutory services.

The service also includes places of safety for temporary accommodation of destitutes, homes for the aged, and supportive services to the handicapped. Family and child welfare includes helping where there is either matrimonial conflict or motherless children. Also included, but declining in use, are institutional care for children (committed under Juvenile Ordinance or Orphans Act) and the supervision of adoptions. Delinquency and correctional services include: probation, after-care service, provision of an approved school, a remand home, and a probation hostel.

In rural areas, there is limited activity by the Department of Social Welfare, which provides some services listed above; but most activity comes from the Department of Community Development. This department promotes self-help projects such as group-housing projects, and the building of community halls, schools, clinics, footbridges, and so on. Women's clubs are a major part of these services. Traditionally, they focused on knitting, sewing, and cookery. However, after 1971, they began to emphasize more economic activities such as the growing of maize and vegetables, poultry rearing, and small village industries such as pottery and basketry. The adult literacy program, which now stresses "functional literacy" (an attempt at linking literacy and agricultural productivity), has been reasonably successful.

Community development in urban areas is the responsibility of the local government authorities. Most community development centers offer adult literacy, preschools, women's clubs, recreation clubs, site and service schemes, and casework services. These services are usually given in coordination with other services provided by other departments of local government authorities such as housing and health care. In mining communities, the responsible company takes the role of the local authority in providing social services for their employees and their families. These include housing, health, training, and recreational facilities.

There has been some limited activity by voluntary organizations, including churches. Services provided by these organizations include recreational and training facilities (such as those provided by the YMCA, Scouts, and Girl Guides), health facilities (such as those provided by missions and Zambia helpers), and child welfare. Many problems face these organizations, but the major ones seem to include indigenization of the membership, organized funding, and coordination of programs with those offered by other organizations, including government agencies. With such an "impressive" group of services in a country, why should there be concern? Basically, it is because of the lack of relevance of the services to the real needs of the people. A brief look at the historical roots of these programs will show that it would have been very difficult for them to be anything but irrelevant.

The Department of Social Welfare models its program on a British system. This is not surprising since in the colonial administration the early social welfare officers were mostly British and were merely implementing the only system that they knew. A good example of this wholesale importation of a foreign system is the Juvenile Ordinance (1953) which is a word for word copy of the British act operative at that time. Despite the fact that the application of the act was initially limited to the railroads and to a predominantly European community, today there is too little similarity between a copperbelt town in Zambia and Manchester or Birmingham in the U.K. to justify the importation of their Juvenile Act.

The community development programs can perhaps claim to be somewhat less "imported." (Many countries in the developed world are only now looking at the possibilities of community development as it has emerged in the developing countries.) There has been, no doubt, some international influence, such as through U.N. advisors. But with its origins in Britain's mass education program, the service itself suffers mainly from the use of an approach that is basically a paternalistic, colonial one. Programs tend to be static, unchanging, and very dependant on staff for their implementation. There seems to be little room allowed for regional differences.

Irrelevancy can also be seen in the fact that the present services do not fit with the goals and values of the people; they do not fit the pattern of life of the service users. For example, child welfare programs such as foster homes and adoption are usually rejected. Such means are completely foreign to Zambian social values regarding the care of children. Rather, the extended family often plays an important role in the general welfare of children, especially in time of crisis. Although it is true that in the modern Zambian situation there is an undermining of the role of the extended family, many old values still remain as discussed earlier in this paper. Evidently then, the requirement is for a service that will not conflict with the existing social values of the community while simultaneously meeting the needs not fulfilled by a disintegrating extended family system. Some kind of "community-formed" extended family might be possibly an answer.

It is important to note that relevancy to people also would include relevancy to their political and philosophical environment. The present dichotomy between political issues and development issues would be replaced by a cooperation in which political leaders would support social services and even lend their authority to ensure popular involvement and government commitment. Similarly, political structures already quite well-developed would be used for the benefit of meeting social problems. Furthermore, the present practice of involving people by asking (or in fact commanding) them to provide the labor would change. Instead they would be involved in need identification and solution planning. Recognition of goals at the early stages would mean altered directions for many programs. Solution planning would reflect major communal values and in particular the prevailing philosophy of humanism, which supports a communal approach to problem-solving. Such solutions would "fit" both people and their problems—they would be relevant.

EMERGING COMMUNAL PATTERNS

The social service institutions may be out of synchronization with the social system, thereby leaving many people's needs unmet and promoting underutilized services. But this is not the whole story. There is evidence that various types of primary groupings have been, and still are, maintaining responsible service to persons within their scope and are even taking on new responsibilities. These include the traditional family or community level groups as well as others organized on a more functional basis. The Zambia Council for Social

Development, in its capacity as a funding agency for self-help projects, has tabulated success in terms of completed community self-help projects. The input of the council (financial and advisory) may have been, in part, responsible for these successes, but the groupings themselves seem to have been a significant factor.

Village Productivity Committee

There has been some spontaneous initiation of such groups. However, the experience of social work students in rural areas has shown that with adequate input of manpower to provide leadership, information, and to stimulate interest and enthusiasm much can be achieved through village groupings, such as the Village Productivity Committee. In one instance, a group of students worked in a resettlement area for subsistence farmers. Initially, there was resistance to any kind of development because the resettlement had not been voluntary but the result of a government defense installation which had necessitated the move of a number of villagers. In addition to the compulsory resettlement, a discrepancy between the villagers' perception of government promises of services and those actually provided caused considerable hostility. A major issue concerned the lack of an adequate water supply for the raising of cattle, an important source of income. The Department of Rural Development had sunk some wells nearby, but they were not suitable for cattle. What was required was a trench leading to a holding reservoir. The student involved worked through the Village Productivity Committee (VPC). There was resistance at first, but the worker persevered; and finally the VPC saw the advantage of the action. They mobilized the village, and very soon a trench was being dug. In this case the functional nature of the project seemed to be the key to overcoming the people's hostility. Also the VPC structure itself was familiar enough (actually the VPC is only a modified headman's council of elders) so that it did not require any extra input for its establishment.

"Functionality," however, is not necessarily defined in terms personal to the participants (although it may be). There seems to be such a thing as communal functionality. This was seen in another situation involving a VPC. This VPC recognized the problem of several old people in the village who were without adequate housing and were too old to build their own. The VPC mobilized all the village members to contribute to the house building according to their ages and sex. To some extent the provision for adequate housing was seen in terms of village pride. But it also reflected the principle of reciprocal obligations; and since the VPC was a structure related to traditional patterns of social organization, it was able to encourage application of the traditional principle.

In small villages, however, there have been problems in the establishment of VPCs. In order to achieve the 20 household minimum, as stipulated by the Registration and Development of Villages Act, several have had to combine into one, which has raised problems. These problems may be related to questions concerning leadership and village autonomy. Whether a merger is successful or not seems to depend on the nature of the merger and its purpose. For instance, in one resettlement area several villages joined together to build a dip tank. The villagers, from their own experience, were aware that economically a dip tank was not feasible for one village and thus joined in to complete the task. Since the economic necessity was evident and real, a merger was achieved but only to facilitate communal effort—leadership positions were virtually untouched or perhaps even enhanced.

Similarly, the Ward Development Council can be justified as functionally necessary for those activities which are economically realistic only for the total ward and for those planning and resource allocation activities which need a more total approach. The Ward Development Council also performs the function of bringing together the village representatives (two from each VPC) and the symbol of the political structure (the councillor who is the chairman). This kind of linkage is vital if there is to be cooperation in development.

In the urban areas service delivery structures are modified, but the basic principles are the same. The example that follows will illustrate this.

The Problem-Focused Approach: The Squatter Upgrading Scheme

The Squatter Upgrading Site and Service Project is a joint venture between the World Bank and the Lusaka City Council to combat the problem of urban housing which has plagued Zambia during the past few decades. The project reflects a major policy change not only in the nature of services provided but, more importantly, in the manner and structure in which the services are provided. Without going into the details of the project, an attempt will be made to describe how the services are organized in order to ensure that they reach the majority of the potential recipients in a meaningful way. So far the Squatter Upgrading Project has proved very successful as an alternative to the conventional "urban renewal" approaches to the solution of problems of urban housing.

The project is located in the City Council of Lusaka, the country's capital city. Operationally, the project unit exists as a department within the city council set up. In turn, the project unit consists of several specialized sections which are organized into a field team. It is the field team that spearheads the planning and execution of specific project operations. The social services section, which is the section of particular interest to us, is one of the sections represented by the field team.

The community development team of workers (which is an integral part of the social services section of the project) acts as an advance party paving the way for the rest of the teams. It not only lays down the foundations of the service but also provides the framework in which the community views and receives the service. As an "advance party" for the project teams, community development workers ensure that the operative principles, which underlie the success of the project, are adequately communicated to the community. These principles can be summarized as follows:

(1) Initiative must come from the people.

(2) Maximization of effective participation by the community people.

(3) Social and physical change should, as far as is possible, reflect the existing organismic structure of the people.

The project's belief in these principles is transmitted to the people through the approaches used in introducing and delivering the service (squatter upgrading) to the people. The service consists of a number of stages and at each of these stages, community development workers play particular roles to ensure that the above-mentioned principles are adhered to and that the people in the community see themselves as planners as well as consumers.

In the first stage (briefing), community development workers ensure that the community is adequately informed about the project. The process of "informing" starts with meetings with the community leadership. Once the leadership "buys" the idea, it is easier to reach the rest of the residents who tend to be less suspicious of the project. With the people and their leaders "committed" to the idea that the project is their own, a way is paved for other service units, such as engineering and finance, to come in.

An equally important phase in the life of the project is that of a physical planning of the layout of the residential areas in need of upgrading. Although the initial plan of the suggested improvements comes from the physical planners, the final decision lies with the residents. These decisions are based on what is functional and makes sense to the residents. For example, in planning road layout, a number of principles are used:

(1) As far as possible, only empty spaces should be used. This cuts down on the number of existing buildings that would need to be pulled down in order to give way to the roads.

(2) Use of existing roads or paths that may be functional or have symbolic meaning to the residents.

Obviously, adherence to these principles means that some of the basic rules in physical planning have to be broken. For example, a decision may be taken to build a road that meanders, following a familiar foot path and avoiding homes and other buildings of symbolic meaning, instead of building a straight road that is economical and makes engineering sense.

In helping the residents to make a meaningful contribution to the planning process, the planning team combines explanations and interpretations of map work and so forth with tours of the areas in order to connect what appears on paper with what exists in reality. This is what is referred to as "walking on the plan." This approach is particularly important when it is considered that the majority of the residents have little or no formal education and are therefore unable to interpret drawings and maps.

Once the layout has been accepted and work has started on decongesting the area, providing basic amenities, and so on, the community development team moves to the next phase of helping the residents form into sections consisting of a specified number of households patterned after the existing political party boundaries. Each section has a leader who occupies a similar rank in the party. These sections then become viable communities through which basic social services are provided, both by the project unit and also on a self-help basis.

Two very important features emerge from the service structure described above. First, the residents play a meaningful role in planning the services. Second, the residents are organized in such a way that they are easily accessible not only to the basic service of improving the squatter settlements but also to other follow-up and continuing services that are later provided in the area.

CONCLUSIONS

Adequate social service delivery demands the involvement of people both as users of the service (to avoid wastage) and as planners (to ensure relevancy). This can best be effected by the use of structures that reflect the "already existing organismic structure" of the people.

There is some degree of formality required in these modern times. Thus, the Village Productivity Committee (VPC) is a formal structure established by the Registration and Development of Villages Act 1971 and is part of a larger development structure which includes development committees at ward, district, and provincial levels. Urban settings require even more formalized organizational structures. But the modification that these structures represent is limited by the two principles of minimum conflict and maximum functionality. It is these limitations which enable the people to identify with the structure and commit themselves to the programs.

However, if the structure itself is relevant, its functioning is more likely to be relevant. A primary grouping is so closely related to the extended family that it is very much "people oriented," and the VPC, as a structure, is socially relevant because of its close link to the village or extended family. It reflects very closely the traditional village decision-making structure. Modified structures such as the urban delivery systems often seem to put emphasis on the involvement of the political groupings in the community, but the need for social relevance is not obviated. Rather, the political organizers have seemingly recognized the principle of minimum conflict in change, and as a result many a section leader or branch chairman takes a role strikingly similar to that of a village headman. Social relevance is evidenced also in the principles of operation which are practiced. In the new systems, as in the traditional pattern, characteristics such as respect for age and appeal to authority in decision-making (which are deemed necessary to take a leadership role) are virtually the same. The two above principles are evident in the formation and maintenance of these structures and in their various problem-solving activities—another demonstration of the link between structure and function.

The potential of such structures for service delivery are manifold. In dealing with village level problems, VPCs have been very effective. They have identified problem parameters, planned a solution, and carried it out; and they have channelled information regarding priority of needs up to the higher bodies for more relevant decision-making in planning and policymaking.

The next small step beyond planning is participation in policymaking. Since implementation always has to be at the lowest level and since it is an accepted fact that "people perform better in projects they have assisted in setting up" (Bregha, 1973:3), it is essential that there be purposeful two-way communication and adequate feedback channels between the VPC and the higher levels.

Most likely the participation process would have to be entered upon gradually to allow public and government administrators to get used to the idea. A pattern that might be followed would be similar to that presented by Bregha (1973:18-26). He suggested that the steps move from information sharing, through consultation and planning to actual transfer of authority. He regarded the last step as particularly useful where there was an element of "self-help or mutual aid" which is certainly an ingredient in the service system of a developing country. In the Canadian situation, Bregha (1973) called for the rejuvenation of voluntary associations, but in the case of developing countries he suggested that existent community groups must be recognized and used constructively, as they strive to meet their own needs, if they are to survive. This survival per se is not a primary goal but, rather, is viewed as important, since these groups which are meaningful face-to-face associations are the most appropriate groups to be involved in the process of participation.

Thus, we have existent structure, with its noted potential and relevance, but its success is not yet assured. In order to operate successfully, the structure itself needs to be supported. The described experience with the social work student involvement with Village Productivity Committees and Ward Development Committees shows that community groups can work with the support of a development worker. Such a worker would take the roles of resource person, advocate, and educator. As the latter, his aim would be to see the group be able to deal with its own problems and crises by using its own members, and, having dealt with these organizational problems, to actually go on to develop its own community (Brooks, 1974:38). But such an approach demands an input of manpower, time, interest, and the setting of a definite priority on the encouragement of community structures. Furthermore, there would need to be an allocation of resources to secure the manpower and the supporting services, but allocation of resources, in a time of shortage, is a difficult requirement. Yet, in the long run, we would be conserving resources. By spending now on social development staff to stimulate the growth and useful performance of community structure, we would be ensuring a more relevant and wise allocation of resources for future services and thus avoid waste or inappropriate allocation of resources.

However, an adequately functioning delivery system will be useless unless such a system fits into the administrative structure of the social services. These groups have to have definite responsibilities with the appropriate links to and from the governmental body. Obviously, there cannot be "total accessibility," as this "would lead to a system's overload and possible collapse of the structure under stress," but "no accessibility means very much a secret rule of the few over the many." Therefore, a "degree of accessibility and the mechanisms for making" use of it are very important (Bregha, 1973:10). A useful model that might be followed is that of professional service providers.

In conclusion, we feel that a social delivery system based on the emerging communal patterns can produce relevant, meaningful help to people in need—provided their potential is recognized and that they are given the necessary support. This is the path to true involvement.

REFERENCES

BANTON, M. (1957). West African city: A study of tribal life in Freetown. London: Oxford University Press.

BASCOM, W. (1955). "Urbanization among the Yoruba." American Journal of Sociology, 60:5.

BREGHA, F. (1973). Public participation in planning, policy and programme. Ontario: Ministry of Culture and Recreation.

BROOKS, E.E. (1974). "Village productivity committees and social development in Zambia." International Social Work, 17(1):38.

CLIFFORD, W. (1966). A primer of social casework in Africa. Nairobi: Oxford University Press.

De JONGH, J. (1969). "Western social work and Afro-Asian values." International Social Work, 12:4.

FORDER, A. (1966). Social casework and administration. London: Faber and Faber.

GLUCKMAN, M., MITCHELL, J.C. and BARNES, J.A. (1949). "The village headman in British Central Africa." Africa, 19(2):7.

HAMMOND, P. (1959). "Economic change and Mossi acculturation." In W. Bascom and M. Henskovits (eds.), African cultures. Chicago: University of Chicago Press.

KAY, G. (1967). Social aspects of village regrouping in Zambia. Lusaka: University of Zambia, Institute for African Studies.

——— (1968). "The towns of Zambia." In R.W. Steel and R. Lawton (eds.), Liverpool essays in geography, a jubilee collection.

LITTLE, K. (1957). "The role of voluntary associations in West African urbanization." American Anthropology, 59:4

LLOYD, P. (1953). "Craft organization in Yoruba towns." Africa, 23:4.

MAQUET, J. (1972). Africanity the cultural unity of black Africa. London: Oxford University Press.

MUKUNDARAO, K. (1969). "Social work in India: Indigenous cultural bases and the process of modernization." International Social Work, 12:3.

NYIRENDA, V.G. (1975). "Social change and social policy in a developing country: The Zambia case." D.S.W. dissertation. Los Angeles: University of California.

POWDERMAKER, H. (1962). Copper town: Changing Africa. New York: Harper and Row.

YOUNG, T.C. (1937). African ways and wisdom: A contribution to understanding. London: The United Society for Christian Literature.

10

THE VISIBILITY OF A
COMMUNITY MENTAL HEALTH CENTER:
ISRAEL

URI AVIRAM
DANIEL BRACHOTT

The Community Mental Health Center (CMHC) in Jaffa, Israel, was established in 1970 and was modeled after the centers in the United States. The establishment of the center was part of the great upsurge of community health and welfare programs which occurred, especially in the U.S.A., during the 1960s. Great hopes were embodied in the community centers. They were viewed as vehicles for social change, through the active and meaningful involvement of the community and the provision of comprehensive services. These community health and welfare programs have been widely criticized. The criticism is based mainly on the fact that many programs were initiated more on the basis of discontent with what existed than on the basis of the proven effectiveness of the new procedures (Carstairs, 1968). Many of the social experiments of the sixties continue to operate without being properly assessed as to whether they actually do what they are intended to. However, it now seems that we have passed the stage of ideology and rhetoric of social necessity and have entered the era of evaluation and accountability.

Program evaluation has become an urgent necessity. It should help policy decision makers, program planners, and administrators to monitor systematically

AUTHORS' NOTE: *Research was supported in part by the Trust Fund for the Development of Psychiatric Services in Israel, a joint program of the Israel Ministry of Health and the Joint Distribution Committee. The authors would like to acknowledge the contribution of D. Davidson, in earlier stages of the project, and the assistance of A. Ron and H. Ozeri, in conducting the field study. They are most grateful to S.L. Kark, J.H. Abramson, and I. Levav, who read an earlier draft of the paper and made useful suggestions. Thanks also to M. Scherman for her assistance in the preparation of the final draft.*

their services, to improve operations, and to plan new services (Rossi and Williams 1972). It should serve as the mechanism by which the public, through its representatives in various governmental bodies and other voluntary organizations, reach decisions about the distribution of public resources to social programs. Furthermore, evaluation provides means for professionals and service providers to be accountable to their communities, clients, and colleagues.

In relation to program evaluation, the mental health service system has not been much different from other social services. The mental health "third revolution" (Hobbs, 1964) has been reflected by the establishment of many community mental health centers supported by large sums of public funds (Feldman, 1973). In spite of the fact that policymakers and program administrators have been continuously urged to evaluate programs, and although public funding for new programs has often been made contingent on the inclusion of an evaluation compotent, evaluation of community mental health programs has been sparse (Zubin, 1968). Mental health professionals were granted vast sums of money during the 1960s with the implicit understanding that new programs, expanded training, and new systems of service delivery would greatly reduce mental health problems in the population. Some decry community mental health as only one in a perpetual series of movements in the mental health field compounded of high expectations that fail to achieve their goals (cf. Roberts et al., 1969). A recent Nader report lambastes the U.S. National Institute of Mental Health for the lack of a rigorous accountability system (Chu and Trotter, 1974).

There is reason to believe that soon we will witness more evaluative research of community mental health centers. Resource scarcity, greatly increased competition for funds among different programs, recognition of unfulfilled promises, and the increased insistence of funding agencies and legislators that allocation of funds be based on documented evidence of the effectiveness of social programs will, no doubt, lead to an emphasis on evaluative research.

Mental health professionals and administrators of mental health programs are faced with the imminent danger that the lack of good professional evaluative research will allow decisions, based on financial-economic criteria, to be forced upon them by outside nonprofessional authorities (Ellsworth, 1975). This danger may provide the needed incentive for organizations to launch evaluative research (Wildavsky, 1972).

The dearth of good program evaluation of mental health services has been related not only to the lack of incentives to the mental health organization and to the threat which the organizations usually see in evaluative research, but also to the complexity and cost of such research and the lack of training in epidemiology and evaluation research of most clinicians heading community mental health centers. These same clinicians, however, in many instances, must decide to do the evaluative research (Beigel, 1974). It is not uncommon among community mental health professionals and administrators to refrain from much needed evaluative research because of the real or imaginary conditions of complexity, the cost of such research, and the lack of training to do it.

It is the purpose of this paper to describe a method of evaluation of certain aspects of a community mental health center program which is simple, inexpensive, and useful for the administrators monitoring their program as well as for the outside authority evaluating the progress of the program and whether its objectives are being met.

It has been observed that program evaluation proved expensive when related to the effectiveness of the total program. Such evaluation could not start before the program had been given adequate time to achieve its stated objectives (Weiss, 1974). By the time evaluation was possible and could be financed, the program could have spent large sums of money, might have failed, or might have become entrenched to such an extent that no evaluative research could overcome the vested interest in it. What seems to be necessary are methods for evaluation of community mental health programs which can be performed early enough to affect the program as it is being shaped. Such evaluation can provide important information to administrators of the program as well as a sense of its effectiveness to the funding authorities, before they invest too much of their resources.

Carol Weiss (1974) distinguishes between three types of decisions which may benefit from different kinds of evaluation programs: policy decisions, strategic decisions, and tactical decisions. It seems that community mental health centers can benefit much from evaluative research which relates to one or several facets of the program and provides important information for administrators making strategic and tactical decisions. Such evaluation is probably less threatening to the organization because it does not evaluate the effectiveness of the total program but rather relates to some aspects of the program with the main purpose of improving it. An internal ongoing evaluation may meet the need for agency accountability, relieve pressures upon administrators by demand for evaluation, and provide them with a useful tool for management of the center and a basis for program improvement once accountability is met.

Three types of studies of mental health services have been described: (1) studies of structure; (2) studies of process; (3) studies of outcome (Zusman and Rieff, 1969; Fox and Rappaport, 1972). It has been recognized that the final evaluation of the effectiveness of any program can be achieved only if outcome studies are conducted. However, such studies have often been of limited utility to program planners and administrators and have not always been feasible (Aviram and Kirk, 1974). In many instances, especially during the early stages of a program, its effectiveness often can be discerned through examination of the program's context and its operational processes (Smith, 1974). Thus, studies of structure, which consist of attempts to describe the dimension and organization of services, and studies of processes, which focus on the procedures of the delivery system, are more feasible at the early stages of the program. These studies provide important feedback for the program administrators as well as an indication to the outside authority whether the program is meeting its objectives.

Evaluating the Community Visibility of the CMHC

A prime goal of the community mental health center is its community-directed activity. The provision of comprehensive and continuous mental health care appears as a goal of the CMHC in community mental health centers legislation as well as in established programs. The desired objective is to reduce the incidence of mental illness and its severity, to reduce hospitalization, to provide services at the community level, and, on the whole, to improve social functioning in the community (Beigel and Levenson, 1972). Evaluating the impact on the community of these efforts must be one of the most relevant types of evaluation research of the community mental health center. Outcome studies of such efforts are contingent on the development of reliable social indicators and valid measures (Bloom, 1968; Dohrenwend and Dohrenwend, 1965). Usually, they require large scale epidemiological studies that are costly, time consuming, and can be conducted only after the program has been in operation for several years. However, other types of studies can provide important feedback on the impact of the community programs, at an earlier stage of the program and at a much lower cost.

The community mental health center has always been thought of as a catalyst for the development of all types of community services impinging on the mental health of the population. The main techniques for this development have been consultation and education. It has been thought that prevention of mental illness would be enhanced through the provision of mental health consultation and education programs for professionals engaged in providing a variety of human services and for various care-giver groups in the population (Beigel and Levenson, 1972). These services, for instance, were included among the first five essential services the provision of which was a prerequisite for federal funding (U.S. Public Health, 1964). It is inconceivable that a well functioning CMHC not have relationships with various community agencies which may affect the provision of mental health services to the population. In order for the CMHC to prevent mental illness and to provide crisis intervention and other types of direct services, it has to be known to the various health, welfare, and educational services in the community. The effectiveness of the CMHC may be assessed by the level of knowledge of its functions and the extent of its use by the various community agencies. In this sense, one of the measures of accountability and program effectiveness of a CMHC is related to its community impact. The community impact can be assessed by answering the following questions:

(1) What is the level of community awareness of the existence of the CMHC?

(2) What is the level of knowledge in the various community agencies of the specific functions of the CMHC, in terms of its direct and indirect community services?

(3) What is the extent of its use by the different community agencies?

The answers to these questions will provide vital information about the "visibility" of the CMHC in the community. Evaluation of the visibility of the CMHC may provide the program administrator with important feedback about the impact of the CMHC on the community and specify areas where changes and more efforts on the part of the CMHC are needed. The aim of this paper is to describe this method of evaluation for the CMHC, especially in its early stages, and to suggest how such an effort at evaluation may be useful.

The Setting

The Community Mental Health Center in Jaffa was the first such center in Israel. It was established as an experimental center consistent with the reorganization plan for mental health services (Tramer, 1975). The proposed plan called for the provision of five essential services to the community: (1) full hospitalization; (2) partial hospitalization; (3) outpatient care; (4) emergency care; and (5) mental health consultation and education.

A survey published by the CMHC in Jaffa in 1973 provided the following information about the area. The catchment area of the center included in 1973 a population of 85,000, with a high incidence of psychiatric disorders. The area includes all of Jaffa and a section of south Tel-Aviv, which are sections of the city of Tel Aviv-Jaffa. This catchment area is characterized by its poverty and other social problems. The adverse economic conditions in this area are reflected by the fact that this catchment area contributes 50% of the persons and families receiving welfare assistance in the city although it comprises only 25% of the population of the city. One of the most striking features of the catchment area is its heterogeneity. It is composed of a population of immigrants, including a majority from the North African Magreb as well as many from Bulgaria and Rumania. About 10% of the population in the area are Arabs of which 55% are Moslems and 45% are Christians (Community Mental Health Center, Jaffa, 1973).

Five years after the CMHC was established it was composed of units providing supportive, indirect, and auxiliary services necessary for the operation of the center. The direct services units included: (1) outpatient—adult unit; (2) outpatient—children and adolescent unit; (3) outpatient—geriatric unit; (4) day hospital; (5) follow up (posthospitalization) unit; (6) rehabilitation unit. The supportive and indirect services units were: (1) administration and maintenance;

(2) research and evaluation; (3) community organization; (4) pharmacology. Inpatient services were provided by a special ward of a state hospital located in a nearby city. This hospital also provided emergency services beyond regular center working time (evenings, nights, and holidays).

At the end of 1975, the actual filled positions were 62, 50 of which were professionals. The center's staff has grown considerably since it was established. Since the middle of 1973, the staff of the center has increased by almost 40% (Brachott et al., 1976).

The CMHC Community Services

In the original proposed plan of the Jaffa CMHC (Israel, Mental Health Services, 1970), community services were given paramount importance. It was suggested that mental health education and consultation should be directed toward community "care-givers"—agencies and people that come in direct contact with the population of the catchment area. The plan stated clearly that the efficacy of the CMHC program would be assessed by evaluating the provision and effect of such services. In the original plan, it was proposed that in order to achieve these objectives at least 20% of the staff's work should be devoted to consultation and educational services.

During the first years of the operation of the CMHC neither was the time ripe nor was a valid and inexpensive method available for evaluating the outcome of community services. However, assessment of the level of CMHC community services and their impact on the community was both feasable and desirable. By a relatively simple and inexpensive method it was possible to measure the amount of time devoted by CMHC workers to community services and to assess the impact of such services by evaluating the visibility of the CMHC in the community, i.e., the awareness of the existence and specific functions of the center by the various community care-giver agencies, and their perception of the level and extent of use of the CMHC services. It was felt that such evaluation could meet accountability demands and at the same time provide useful feedback to the CMHC program administrator. It could allow him to see the extent to which the CMHC meets its proposed community objectives, both in total terms and by specific types of agencies and types of service. Such information can be useful for strategic and tactical decisions as the CMHC program is being shaped. Program monitoring and ongoing changes at early stages of the development of the CMHC may save the CMHC from failure, harsh assessment at later stages, and a threat to the total program.

METHOD

Identifying the Community Agencies

All community health, educational, and welfare agencies operating within the catchment area of the center were identified. Identification was effected through the use of: (1) existing lists of community agencies in the possession of the center; (2) information provided by the central offices of national and municipal educational and health services (e.g., Information about schools in the area was gathered from the city education department and from the city psychological services. The regional health administration provided lists of health care clinics as well as mother and child health clinics); (3) information about existing agencies, validated and supplemented through interviews with community workers who were knowledgeable about the community.

The community agencies which were identified included all known service agencies operating within the community as specified by the boundaries of the catchment area of the community mental health center. Since the catchment area of the center did not always correspond to service areas of other agencies in the community, the list of agencies also included those outside the area that provided services to more than half of the catchment area of the center.

The final list included all 12 health clinics, both of curative and preventive nature; all 24 educational institutions—elementary schools, high schools, and special schools; and 10 different kinds of social services which included three welfare agencies, and community organization departments of a public housing project, adult and juvenile probation agencies, the general and youth divisions of the local police, the employment agency, and the municipal psychological services.

The Community Mental Health Center Visibility Index

A semi-structured interview was conducted with the heads of the agencies, and with at least one member of the staff. Four variables were chosen as indices for the level of CMHC visibility in the community. Three variables were related to community awareness of the CMHC and knowledge of its functions. One variable was related to the extent of use of CMHC services.

The aforementioned variables were combined to form the CMHC Visibility Index. Based on the information gathered in the interviews, each agency was rated on a five-dimension scale:

(1) general awareness of the existence of the CMHC;

(2) knowledge about specific functions and types of services provided by the center;

(3) awareness and knowledge of the community approach of the center;

(4) a low level of contacts and use of the CMHC's services by the agency;

(5) an intensive use of the CMHC's variety of services.

A limited number of referrals to or contacts with CMHC at some point in time would mean a limited use, whereas a continuous relationship between the CMHC and the agency reflected an intensive use. A general knowledge that the CMHC existed in the area would be rated positively on the first dimension of the scale. In order to be rated positively on the second dimension of the scale, the interviewee should have known at least half of the CMHC direct services. An awareness of the CMHC's goals to provide consultation and education and other types of community services beyond the direct treatment services would be scored positively on the community awareness dimension of the scale.

Each agency was assessed by two interviewers. If the interviewees of each agency presented contradictory answers on each of the dimensions, a third agency worker was to be chosen. This procedure, however, was not necessary because those employees interviewed responded nearly identically. The interviewers assessed the data and rated the agencies on the Visibility Index. When assessment on any of the dimensions was positive, a value of one was assigned to the agency for that specific dimension. A negative assessment of the agency on any of the dimensions was valued zero. The Visibility Index score consisted of the sum of the agency's score on the five dimensions and had a range of from zero to five. For example, an agency with a score of zero was one which was assessed negatively on the five dimensions. An agency with a score of five was one which was assessed positively on the five dimensions, i.e., as being aware of the CMHC's existence, having knowledge of the CMHC's specific functions, and being aware of the CMHC community approach. This agency was also assessed as one having intensive contacts with and a high level of use for the CMHC. It is apparent that part of the scale had a Guttman scale characteristic (Stouffer, 1950). A value of one on the second dimension, i.e., knowledge of specific functions of the CMHC, meant receipt of a value of one on the first dimension related to general awareness of the existence of the center. The same is true of the relationship between the fourth and fifth dimension: a positive score on the intensive use dimension correlated with a positive score on the fourth dimension which related to limited level of use.

One should be aware that the five dimensions might be weighted differently by various experts. In view of the lack of empirical research on the relative importance of each dimension and in relation to the goals of this limited evaluation, the same weight was assigned to all the dimensions composing the Visibility Index.

The scores were calculated for each agency, as well as for the total group of agencies or subgroup of agencies. The sum of the scores of the agencies belonging to each of the groups—educational agencies, health agencies, and social services—rated in proportion to the number of agencies in each group, provided the "visibility" score of the CMHC for that group of agencies. Scores were also summarized separately for each dimension. This allowed the assessment of the level of visibility by dimension, by subgroup and by group of agencies. For example, a proportion of the positive scores of the total number of preventive health services on the knowledge of specific functions of the CMHC provided the CMHC "visibility" score for that type of dimension and for that subgroup of health services.

In addition to the procedure which led to the quantified rating of the CMHC relationship with the agencies, summaries were written on each agency. These summaries included information about specific problems and areas of concern of the agencies in relation to the CMHC and the mental health needs of the community.

Interviews

The interviews were conducted by two social workers. The interviewers tried to create a relaxed atmosphere during the interview. They did not specify their focal interest in the CMHC but rather indicated their general interest in assessing the types, needs, and extent of mental health services in the area. They emphasized that the objectives of the study were not to evaluate the specific service but rather to assess the psychiatric services provided to the community. In order to receive information along the five dimensions, the interviewers asked the interviewees if they knew at all about the existence of the CMHC in the area. If the reply was positive, they probed deeper to learn what was known and how the interviewee had heard about the CMHC. They also asked about any cooperation between the agency and the CMHC and if the CMHC provided any services to the interviewee's agency. A positive reply on that question was followed with a question related to the type of service provided by the CMHC (e.g., direct treatment, consultation, interagency cooperation, and education).

As the interview proceeded, questions were asked about the specific use of the CMHC by the agency, referrals, type and extent of services used, and level of cooperative arrangements between the CMHC and the agency. The interviewees were asked to assess the mental health needs of the area. They were asked to describe how they handle the mental health needs of any of their clients and if and how they used the services of the CMHC. A case description of a suicide attempt (for health agencies) or a student's emotional difficulties (for educational agencies) was presented to interviewees in order to assess their awareness of the CMHC and concepts about the types and usefulness of the center's services.

The evaluation of the CMHC was supplemented by a three month time allocation study that was designed to measure the amount of time spent by workers on community work activities.

Table 1: Awareness and Use of the Community Mental Health Center by Different Community Agencies: Percentage of Educational, Health and Social Services which were Aware of and Used the Services of the CMHC

(N = 48)

	Awareness			Use		
	General, Unspeci-fied	Functional, Specific	Awareness of Community Approach	Some Con-tacts	Intens-ive Contact	Average of Scores
Educational Services (N=24)	92	46	21	50	0	42
Health Services (N=14)	100	92	21	86	43	69
Social Services (N=10)	90	70	60	80	10	62
All Services (N=48)	94	69	34	72	18	57

FINDINGS

The Visibility of the CMHC

The summary of findings (Table 1) indicated that the educational services were lowest on the average of all visibility index scores with 42%, compared with 69% for the health services, which were highest. The average of the scores of the social services was 62%. However, when we look at the total scores of the three types of services on each of the dimensions, we realize the great difference between the agencies. While all three types scored high on general awareness of the center, educational and health services were much lower than social services on awareness of the community approach of the CMHC (21% versus 60%). Educational services were much lower on awareness of the specific functions of the CMHC than the other two types of services (46% versus 92% for health services and 70% for social services).

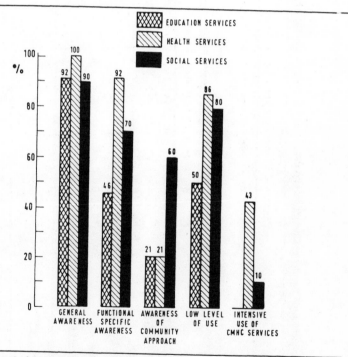

Figure 1: Level of Community Mental Health Center Visibility by Awareness and Use by Three-types of Community Agencies (in percents)

Table 2: Awareness and Use of the Community Mental Health Center by Educational Services in the Catchment Area (N = 24)

| A g e n c y | Awareness | | | | | | | | Use | | | | | | Average Scores |
| | General | | Functional Specific | | Awareness about Community Approach | | Some contacts | | Intensive contacts | | | | | | |
	#	%	#	%	#	%	#	%	#	%	%
Educational Services											
(N = 24)	22	92	11	46	5	21	12	50	0	0	42
A. Elementary Schools											
(N = 16)	14	87	6	37	2	12	8	44	0	0	38
B. High Schools											
(N = 3)	3	100	3	100	1	33	2	66	0	0	60
C. Special Schools											
(N = 5)	5	100	2	40	2	40	2	40	0	0	44

Health services used the CMHC more extensively than did the other two types of services (86% had some contacts with the center). Intensive use of the center was made by 43% of the health services, compared with no intensive use by the educational services and only 10% of the social services. While only 50% of the educational services in the community had some contacts with the CMHC, 80% of the social services had that level of contacts with the center.

Total scores for all services indicate that only 18% of the services in the area showed intensive use of the center. However, more than 70% had established some level of use of the CMHC services. While most of the services in the community were generally aware of the existence of the center, less than 70% had specific knowledge of the CMHC functions and only 34% were aware of its community approach (Table 1).

Tables 2, 3, and 4 provide specific information on each of the five dimensions by agency subtypes.[1] Among the educational services, the high schools and the special schools rated higher on awareness of the CMHC's community approach than the elementary schools (33% and 40% versus 12%). The high schools' average scores were higher than the average scores of the other two subtypes of educational services. While the average score on the Visibility Index for the high schools was 60%, the score for the special schools was 44%, and 38% for the elementary schools. When we look at the average scores for the different types of health services we see that the preventive services rated higher than the curative services (84% versus 65%). Preventive health services made much more intensive use of the CMHC services than the curative services (80% versus 25%). Among the curative health services, only two out of six health clinics made intensive use of the CMHC services. The two hospitals reported only limited use of the CMHC.

The several preventive health services did not receive similar scores. While three of the four mother and child clinics scored 80% or above, one clinic had scores of 40%, indicating no contacts whatsoever with the CMHC. The First Aid Emergency Service in the community made no use of the CMHC. Its score of 20% was the result of a positive score on the general awareness dimension only.

The welfare and probation agencies scored higher than the other types of social services. Only one welfare agency had intensive contacts with the CMHC. No other social service agency used the CMHC services intensively. The only social service which was not aware at all of the existence of the CMHC was the employment agency. All the other types of agencies, except the community organization department of the public housing service, had some contacts with the CMHC above and beyond their awareness of its existence. All five agencies of the welfare and probation types and the youth division of the police were aware of the community approach of the CMHC.

Table 3: Awareness, and use of the Community Mental Health Center by Health Services in the Catchment Area (N = 14)

Agency	Awareness						Use				Average Scores
	General, Unspecified		Functional, specific		Awareness about community approach		Some contacts		Intensive contacts		
	#	%	#	%	#	%	#	%	#	%	
Health Services (Total)											
A. Curative (total)	14	100	13	92	3	21	12	86	6	43	69
a. Hospitals	8	100	8	100	0	0	8	100	2	25	65
# 1	2	100	2	100	0	0	2	100	0	0	60
# 2	1		1		-		1		-		60
b. Health Clinics	6	100	6	100	0	0	6	100	2	33	67
# 1	1		1		-		1		-		60
# 2	1		1		-		1		-		60
# 3	1		1		-		1		1		80
# 4	1		1		-		1		1		80
# 5	1		1		-		1		-		60
# 6	1		1		-		1		-		60
B. Preventive (total)	5	100	5	100	3	60	4	80	4	80	84
a. Mother & Child clinics	4	100	4	100	2	50	3	75	3	75	80
# 1	1		1		-		1		1		80
# 2	1		1		1		1		1		100
# 3	1		1		1		1		1		100
# 4	1		1		-		-		-		40
b. Municipal Public Health Center	1	100	1		1		1		1		100
C. First Aid Emergency Service	1	100	-	0	-	0	-	0	-	0	20

[170]

Major Concerns of Various Community Services

In addition to the information which was quantified on the visibility scale, interviews sought some qualitative data which might reflect the major concerns of various types of community services vis-à-vis the CMHC.

Educational services expressed their need for more educational consultation services from the CMHC. Interviews with personnel of the educational services in the community indicated a need for lectures about mental health problems of school children, problems of the retarded child, drug problems, and so on. Those agencies requested services which would enhance the capacity of teachers to deal with problem children. They also stressed the need for new programs that would be geared toward strengthening the parent's natural support and interactional potential with their children.

Another area of major concern to the educational agencies was related to the low level of coordination between services which deal with mental health problems in the community. The interviewees felt that the CMHC had to take a central role in enhancing better cooperation between various agencies which, in one way or another, deal, or could deal, with mental health problems. Some agencies wanted to have a representative of the CMHC on their staff providing consultation and mental health education to staff and students. Most of the agencies felt that the CMHC did not do enough to inform the community about its function and specific services.

Most of the interviewees of the health agencies also felt that the CMHC did an inadequate job of publicizing its function and specific services. The curative type of health services wanted specific help in providing direct treatment services to patients with mental health problems. It seems that their major concern was to relieve their burden of such patients. However, some interviewees recognized the potential of the CMHC in providing consultation to primary health care providers in order to improve their capacity to deliver services.

While only a few of the interviewees of the curative type services wanted more preventive and community services from the CMHC, that was the major request of the interviewees of the mother and child health clinics. The preventive health services were dissatisfied with the level of preventive mental health activities of the CMHC and requested more educational and consultation services from the CMHC.

The concerns of the social services varied. Probation services expressed a need for emergency diagnostic services from the CMHC. The social welfare agencies wanted better coordination between the CMHC and the welfare agency, in order to improve referrals of welfare clients to the CMHC. These agencies felt that the CMHC did not do enough reaching out. All the social service agencies wanted to see the CMHC more involved in communitywide prevention and mental health education programs; however, this lack was not the major concern of most of these services.

Table 4: Awareness and Use of the Community Mental Health Center by Social Services in the Catchment Area (N = 10)

Agency	Awareness								Use				Average Scores
	General, unspecified		Functional, specific		Awareness about community approach		Some contacts		Intensive contacts		
	#	%	#	%	#	%	#	%	#	%	
Social Services (Total)	9	90	7	70	6	60	8	80	1	10	62
A. Welfare Agencies	3	100	3	100	3	100	3	100	1	33	87
B. Public Housing-Community work	1	100	0	0	0	0	0	0	0	0	20
C. Probation Services	2	100	2	100	2	100	2	100	0	0	80
D. Educational-Psychological Services	1	100	1	100	0	0	1	100	0	0	60
E. Police	2	100	1	50	1	50	2	100	0	0	60
F. Employment Agency	0	0	0	0	0	0	0	0	0	0	0

Time Allocation Study

The time study of workers' activities indicated that the average time that each CMHC worker spent on consultation, education, and other community work (not directly related to individual cases) was only 4%. This figure means that the average worker spent only about one hour and a half per week on community work. Comparison of allocation of time by profession and by units indicated that psychologists spent more time on consultation and education than any other profession. They spent 6% of their time providing consultation and education to institutions in the community, compared with 3% of social workers time spent on such activities. Psychiatrists and nurses were not involved in such community activities. The unit most involved in consultation and education was the children's outpatient unit. Time allocated by workers of this unit to community activities amounted to 10% of their time spent at work compared with 4% for the geriatic unit and 2% for the adults' outpatient and follow-up units.

DISCUSSION

The study and the method presented were aimed at evaluating the extent of the awareness and use of CMHC by various community agencies. One should be aware that the method which has been described could not provide an answer regarding the extent of the center's effectiveness; nor did it attempt to do so. In order to evaluate the efficacy of the CMHC program an outcome study was necessary. Such studies are contingent on the development of reliable indicators and require large scale epidemiological research.

In the original plan of the CMHC, community services, mental health consultation, and education were given paramount importance. This study attempted to measure the efforts invested by the CMHC in community services and to assess their impact in terms of the level of awareness and use of the CMHC services by the community.

Findings indicate the need for changes in the CMHC program in order to achieve the purpose of the center. The visibility of the CMHC is relatively high in view of the limited amount of time spent by the staff of the center on community activities. The 4% average time spent per worker is alarmingly low in view of the stated objectives of the CMHC which proposed that 20% of working time be allocated to consultation and mental health education. One possible explanation for this figure may be related to the lack of knowledge of the CMHC staff in delivery of consultation and education services. The CMHC community services requires the mastery of knowledge and skills not included in the traditional training programs of the various professions which compose the CMHC staff. A special in-service training program for the CMHC is indicated.

The CMHC administrators must devise a training program that will help change patterns of service delivery of present staff and provide them with new knowledge and skills for assessment of community mental health needs. In order to advance the functioning of care-givers in the community, the program must promote agency involvement in mental health education and consultation efforts.

Promotion of the CMHC efforts should be based on differential assessment of results, type of agencies, type and extent of awareness, and use of CMHC programs by these agencies. Findings indicate that, while most of the community agencies were aware of the CMHC's existence, their level of knowledge of its specific functions and the extent of use of the CMHC by community agencies varied a great deal.

Awareness of the community approach of the CMHC was greatest among the community-oriented agencies, such as the mother and child clinics, while far less among those delivering curative or other types of services to individuals as, for instance, the health clinics, hospitals, housing, and all educational services. This may indicate that knowledge and use of the CMHC reflected the agencies' orientation and their efforts to obtain mental health resources for their clients, rather than reflecting the concerted efforts of the CMHC. With respect to the educational services, the relatively low level of knowledge about the CMHC and especially about its community approach may indeed reflect the fact that the CMHC did not invest enough efforts in approaching these agencies. This fact should cause concern to the CMHC even more than the finding that the extent of use of the CMHC by the educational services was low. Educational services are one of the key care-giver organizations in the community and they should have been one of the primary targets of the CMHC community efforts. The center should also enhance its effort at consultation and education with hospitals in the area and especially with health clinics which provide primary health care. It is within the scope of the CMHC mission to promote the capacity of primary health care providers to deal with mental health problems and not only to accept referrals from them. Health clinic staff interviewees expressed very specifically their desire for more consultative and mental health educational services from the center. The desire for more consultation and mental health education was indeed shared by most agencies. The CMHC must expand its program of public relations, mental health education, and community work, especially with noncommunity-oriented agencies. The CMHC workers will, no doubt, need appropriate training for the task which awaits them.

SUMMARY

There is an urgent need for evaluative research in the community mental health centers program. Evaluation should meet accountability requirements as well as provide information for mental health planning and community mental health programs administration. A most appropriate concern of the community mental health program is its impact on the community. A simple, inexpensive method for evaluating aspects of CMHC impact on the community is presented.

A CMHC Visibility Index was developed to measure the level of awareness of the existence and functions of the CMHC, and the extent of use of its services by community agencies. The index was applied in an exploratory survey of community agencies operating in a catchment area of a CMHC in Israel. Information was analyzed by type of agency, by level of awareness, and by extent of use of CMHC services by community agencies. The community study was supplemented by a time allocation survey for type of services provided by center workers.

Findings indicate that most of the agencies in the community were aware of the CMHC's existence. However, they varied in level of awareness and extent of use of the CMHC services. Knowledge about the community approach of the center was relatively low, especially among the noncommunity-oriented agencies. This may be a result of the very little time spent by the CMHC workers on consultation and mental health education, as indicated by the time allocation survey. These findings are reinforced by the request of most community agencies for more consultation and education from the CMHC.

Research results call for efforts by the CMHC to provide community-oriented services, concentrating especially on community educational institutions and primary health care providers as well as on other community care-giver institutions. This will require a larger investment of workers' time on consultation and education, supported by intensive in-service training of CMHC workers to provide them with knowledge and skills necessary for delivery of community services.

The Visibility Index may provide important information to CMHC administrators upon which to base their strategic decisionmaking regarding the development of the center's program. This type of evaluation is based on a simple, inexpensive method which can lead to the assessment of an important aspect of the CMHC program at an early stage in its development and meet both accountability requirements and information needs for further planning and shaping of the CMHC program.

NOTE

1. Information can be presented even more specifically, i.e., by individual agency. This level of specificity may serve the needs of the administrator of the CMHC who wants to identify areas of concern for each agency. Information in Table 3 is thus presented.

REFERENCES

AVIRAM, U., and KIRK, S.A. (1974). Achieving accountability in community mental health programs: A proposed method. Journal of Mental Health Administration, 3(1):31-40.
BEIGEL, A. (1974). Evaluation on a shoestring. Pp. 51-101 in W.A. Hargreaves et al. (eds.),

Resource materials for community mental health program evaluation, Part I. San Francisco: National Institute of Mental Health. (mimeo)

BEIGEL, A., and LEVENSON, A.I. (eds., 1972). The community mental health center. New York: Basic Books.

BLOOM, B.L. (1968). The evaluation of primary prevention programs. In L.M. Roberts, N.S. Greenfield, and M.H. Miller (eds.), Comprehensive mental health. Madison: University of Wisconsin Press.

BRACHOTT, D., AVIRAM, U., and DAVIDSON, D. (1976). The Yaffo Community Mental Health Center. A report submitted to the Trust Fund for the Development of Psychiatric Services in Israel (Israel Ministry of Health and Joint Distribution Committee–Israel). (mimeo)

CARSTAIRS, G.M. (1968). Problems of evaluative research. In R. Williams and L. Ozarin (eds.), Community mental health: An international perspective. San Francisco: Jossey Bass.

CHU, F., and TROTTER, S. (1974). The madness establishment. New York: Grossman.

Community Mental Health Center, Jaffa (1973). Population description bulletin no. 1 (August). Israel Ministry of Health, Mental Health Services. Jaffa: Author.

DOHRENWEND, B.P., and DOHRENWENT, B.S. (1965). The problem of validity in field studies of psychological disorder. Journal of Abnormal Psychology, 70:52-69.

ELLSWORTH, R.D. (1975). Consumer feedback in measuring the effectiveness of mental health programs. Pp. 239-274 in M. Guttentag and E.L. Struening (eds.), Handbook of Evaluative Research. Beverly Hills, Calif.: Sage.

FELDMAN, S. (ed., 1973). The administration of mental health services. Springfield, Ill.: Charles C Thomas.

FOX, P.D., and RAPPAPORT, M. (1972). Some approaches to evaluating community mental health services. Archives of General Psychiatry, 26 (February):172-178.

HOBBS, N. (1964). Mental health third revolution. American Journal of Orthopsychiatry, 34:822-833.

Israel, Mental Health Services of the Ministry of Health (1970). "Proposed Comprehensive Community Mental Health Center in Jaffa: Outline of the Program." Jerusalem: Ministry of Health, Mental Health Services. (mimeo)

ROBERTS, L.M., HALLECK, S.L., LOEB, M.B. (eds., 1969). Community psychiatry. Garden City, N.Y.: Anchor.

ROSSI, P.H., and WILLIAMS, W. (eds., 1972). Evaluating social programs. New York: Seminar Press.

SMITH, J.J. (1974). Manual of principles and methods for program evaluation. Pp. 102-158 in W.A. Hargreaves, C.C. Attkinson, M.H. McIntyre, and L.M. Siegel (eds.), Resource materials for community mental health program evaluation, Part I. San Francisco: National Institute of Mental Health. (mimeo)

STOUFFER, S.A. et al. (1950). Measurement and prediction. Studies in social psychology in World War II (Vol. IV). Princeton, N.J.: Princeton University Press.

TRAMER, L. (1975). A proposal for reorganization of the mental health services system–A comprehensive, integrated plan. Public Health, 18(4):1-12 (in Hebrew).

U.S. Public Health Service (1964). Regulations. Community Mental Health Centers Act of 1963, Title II, Public Law 99-164. Washington, D.C.: Federal Register Office.

WEISS, C.H. (1974). Alternative models of program evaluation. Social Work, 19(6):675-681.

WILDAVSKY, A. (1972). The self evaluating organization. Public Administration Review, 32(September-October).

ZUBIN, J. (1968). The function of the assessment center in community mental health. In L. Roberts et al. (eds.), Comprehensive mental health. Madison: University of Wisconsin Press.

ZUSMAN, J., and REIFF, E.R. (1969). Evaluation of the quality of mental health services. Archives of General Psychiatry, 20(March):352-357.

11

NEIGHBORHOOD DELIVERY AND NATIONAL POLICY IN ENGLAND

PETER WESTLAND

BACKGROUND TO A NEW SYSTEM

Following the publication in 1968 of the Report of the Committee on Local Authority Social Services (later known as the "Seebohm Report" after the Committee Chairman, Lord Seebohm), extensive documentation emerged (Morris, 1974; Glennerster, 1975) discussing the changes in the structure, philosophical issues, and development of the personal social services.

This paper attempts to describe some important aspects of change from the point of view of those involved in the creation of the restructured service and to identify the advantages and some of the problems in service delivery. The question of success or failure of the new system is quite complex due to many variables which have changed between 1966 and 1970 when the analysis and legislation were first prepared. Shortcomings attributed to the reorganization itself are also reflections of the inability of services to deal with a largely unanticipated increase in demand generated by additional social legislation arising from shifts in political perceptions of need and in changes of policy in related fields. Thus, originally conceived in a relatively uncoordinated manner, the personal social services have had to assume unanticipated additional responsibilities. Some failures and successes must also be considered attributable to causes outside the reorganization such as changes in attitude toward those who need the social services and the general state of the economy with its high unemployment and inflation. Therefore, the most pertinent issue now is whether the social services are sufficiently durable, adaptable, and sensitive to respond to changing demands, attitudes, and economic realities.

LOCAL AUTHORITY SOCIAL SERVICES BEFORE 1971

In 1971, 174 Local Authority Social Services Departments were set up in England and Wales, but there was the major reorganization of local government in 1974 reducing the number to 116. The populations serviced by these local government units ranged from 1,000,000 to 160,000. Glennerster (1973) and Morris (1974) describe in some detail the structure and nature of local government units.

Prior to April 1971, the personal social services were located in separate departments within each local authority. Personal social services were provided by health departments, children's departments, and welfare departments, each with independent chief officers and independent controlling political committees. There were very few authorities in which any semblance of corporate management or planning had developed and only a few in which attempts had been made to coordinate the social services under the leadership of Medical Officers of Health. Any effort to coordinate was seen as an attempt to subjugate. Not surprisingly, little real progress was made. The Medical Officer of Health was responsible for mental health and mental handicap services, day nurseries for the under-fives, and some of the social service functions. The Chief Welfare Officer was responsible for the elderly (unless they happened also to be mentally ill), the physically handicapped, the homeless, and (often) the pre- and postnatal welfare of unmarried mothers. The Children's Officer was responsible for residential care of children, preventive work with families, adoption, and for some work with delinquents and children who had come to the attention of juvenile courts because of their failure to attend school. The Education Officer was (and in most places still is) in charge of education welfare—a service which offers social work to families whose children have school difficulties and which provides some specialist social work via child guidance clinics. Also some child guidance facilities were provided by the nonlocal authority part of the health service. The probation service, which was separately administered, was responsible for most juvenile and adult offenders. Typically, these services were somewhat fragmented.

A family unfortunate enough to be homeless, with a mentally handicapped child, another child in care, and with others with school attendance problems, could have the dubious privilege of being visited by four social workers from different departments of the council—some of them from different sections within the same department. Thus, while the individual social workers might have expressed and felt a concern for a whole family or the whole individual, they were prevented, by the administrative structure in which they worked from translating such concern into effective action.

None of the departments was large enough to justify significant expenditure on research into the social needs and problems of the area which they served, and the inevitable problems of interdepartmental collaboration in large bureaucracies effectively prevented any breakthrough in this field. In urban areas few of the departments were large enough to staff a decentralized service, and, consequently, those who needed help had to be prepared to visit the often forbidding town or city hall. Furthermore, a great deal of knowledge of the social services was needed by both client and referring agent to select the "appropriate" department to deal with a particular problem.

There were, of course, features of the pre-1971 structure that could be turned to advantage by imaginative and forceful chief officers; moreover there existed a certain comfort of familiarity for other professionals outside the service. The astute Children's Officer could, in the battle for resources, outstrip the not so astute Chief Welfare Officer. The Chief Welfare Officer arguing for services for the elderly (who have not only needs but votes) could often put in a more popular appeal for staff or money than could the Medical Officer of Health for his mental health services. But the overall result was a situation of lopsided services within local authorities and a rather more interventionist role on the part of the central government. The latter guaranteed, in theory, that minimum standards in child care were established, but in health and welfare there were no such effective outside influences.

The Recommendations of The Seebohm Committee

The Seebohm Committee reported in 1968; legislation followed in 1970; the new departments were set up in 1971. The speed of this timetable for very major organizational change is probably unprecedented, but there were political and professional pressures which contributed to the speed of implementation. With regard to the latter, social services personnel especially felt that the services were established enough to be taken unequivocally from the control of the medical profession. That the medical profession did not entirely share this view is not surprising, and the fact of interdependence of health and social services provides a continuing theme which willl be examined in more detail later.

There were several explicit assumptions in the recommendations of the Seebohm Committee which are fundamental to any review of the impact of reorganization. For detailed study it is necessary to turn to the report itself, but for this analysis two are particularly pertinent.

First, the committee recommended not only major structural changes in the organization of social services but, as importantly, a shift in philosophy. It envisaged a more radical, interventionist, and egalitarian philosophy which would eradicate the last trace of Poor Law thinking which the National Assistance Act of 1948 had, despite its intention, signally failed to do. The Seebohm Report (Paragraph 2) captured the essence of this.

> We recommend a new Local Authority Department, providing a community based and family oriented service which will be available to all. The new Department will, we believe, reach far beyond the discovering and rescue of social casualties; it will enable the greatest possible number of

individuals to act reciprocally, giving a receiving service for the well being of the whole community.

A second key feature of the Seebohm Report, which was essential to the objectives, was the recommended pattern of organization at field level. It was envisaged that social workers would be organized into local units serving populations of 50,000 to 100,000. Basing estimates on national availability of social workers, it was anticipated that each team would be staffed by teams of 10 to 12. It was also anticipated that such area teams would serve as focal points for the community, providing a service which was accessible, acceptable, and comprehensible. It was also anticipated that this model of organization would facilitate a partnership between voluntary and statutory organizations operating within a particular local area.

In reviewing progress, Seebohm (1974) stated that these were "brave words and ambitious objectives," but in retrospect felt that they were neither to be regretted nor regarded as impossibly romantic or unattainable. He acknowledged, however, that progress would be slow initially and perhaps accelerate with the passage of time. However, with the passage of time, it has been demonstrated that progress has been slower than the optimists envisaged and that success has been uneven both in relation to geographical distribution and in different rates of development of services for certain vulnerable groups. These disappointments, however, are attributable more to resource and political considerations than to fundamental shortcomings in the structural reforms of the service. How far the philosophy is attainable remains to be seen.

Establishment of Social Services Departments

A single department was established which, in actuality, did not quite achieve the structural integration that had been envisaged. Seebohm had recommended the inclusion under one department of the following: services provided by children's departments; those welfare services provided under the National Assistance Act, 1948; the education welfare and child guidance services; the personal social services provided by health departments (for the mentally ill, mentally handicapped and certain other services including home helps and day nurseries); and various social welfare services of some housing departments. In fact, the social work service in child guidance and the education welfare service remain unintegrated in most parts of the country, and there is a varying pattern of "welfare" support to housing departments. Social workers in hospitals were not integrated until 1974 when the National Health Service was reorganized. In Scotland, the Probation and After Care Service became part of the newly created departments; in England and Wales it did not. For a detailed analysis of the new pattern, see Glennerster (1975) who, with the exception of registration of child-minders (the responsibility of social services departments), provides a comprehensive table.

The legislation of 1970 posed several administrative, organizational, and professional problems of considerable dimensions. One major difficulty concerned the question of specialization; although Seebohm had argued for the abandonment of specialisms based on administrative categories, the report did not suggest that specialization in itself was to be abandoned. Indeed, it urged that new ways of working with special groups should be encouraged. Thus, a general feeling existed in social work that the Seebohm reorganization required staff to take on mixed caseloads. The attempts by social workers to experiment and to take on previously unfamiliar work led to confusion both within social services departments and among the departments and agencies which had to deal with them. Particular problems especially arose in those authorities where services were handled by staff of mixed qualifications. Staff with professional qualifications who took on work formerly dealt with by an unqualified service found that they dealt with problems less quickly—a problem exacerbated by unfamiliarity with the legislation. Unqualified workers, on the other hand, required much more supervision in mental health work, particularly with families that involved the children's legislation.

The question of role definition of social workers is still not fully resolved. But the key issue now is not whether there should be specialization, but to define the specialisms; to recognize that the emerging specialisms are not the same as those that existed prior to 1971 (which had been determined often by legislative, administrative, and historical accidents); and to define the specific clients requiring a particular method or skill.

Other problems also had to be faced in 1971. Anxious to follow the spirit of the Seebohm Report and decentralize services, most departments, even in dense urban areas, opened area offices with area teams; not surprisingly, this usually meant an increase in staff. Two main difficulties arose. One was the organizational issue of providing a sound administrative support for decentralized services which often in the past had been dominated by a central administration. Second, and more worrying, however, was the need to promote into supervisory positions not only experienced workers but also, because of the rapid rate of expansion, many who were insufficiently experienced.

A contributory factor to this problem lay in the wide variation, depending upon statutory responsibilities, of the supervision patterns of formerly separate departments. For example, the children's department required a fairly high ratio of professional supervisory staff (sometimes one to five or one to six), while in mental health departments a somewhat lower ratio was required. And in welfare departments, where often the work was more routinized, one supervisor for 10 to 11 workers was not unusual. Thus, the immediate effects of reorganization were both positive and negative. On the one hand, there was the attempt to improve standards. On the other hand, because of the low overall proportion of trained staff, there was a direct loss, through promotion to supervisory positions from the front line of those whom the service could least afford to lose.

This negative aspect would have been overcome within two years had it not been for a third and most significant change which outstripped the organizational and professional problems in the speed of its momentum and the sheer size of its impact—the explosion of demand. This demand was created partly by the policy of establishing local teams who were accessible to the public but even more significantly by the publicity given to the social services by the unexpectedly expansionist social policy of the then Conservative government. Ironically, the social services personnel were unprepared for the success of their own campaigns which were adopted as policy by the government, highly publicized but, alas, underresourced. The 1971 legislation had been passed on the premise that no additional expenditure would be required, and, although few actually believed in this, it made the fight for resources rather more difficult in the first critical years.

CONCURRENT SOCIAL REFORMS

Social reform in England has a recent history of piecemeal ad hoc responses to newly identified problems. There is a tendency for clusters of reforms to be introduced together in a contagious rash of social legislation. Therefore, there is a mutual interdependence and interrelationship of the personal social services, and any appraisal of the development of such services requires an evaluation of the impact of the other related changes.

Services For the Chronically Sick and Disabled

The Chronically Sick and Disabled Persons Act (1970) reflected the spirit of the Seebohm Report in that it gave local authorities the duty to seek out those in need and provide them with services rather than waiting for the individual to find his way to the source of possible help. These services included anything which could improve the comfort and convenience of the handicapped in their own homes as well as general services such as day centers, home helps, holidays, and subsidized travel. The act also listed specified services which must be provided if the need were ascertained such as: the supply of physical aids to daily living; physical adaptations to the structure of the client's home (widening doorways, provisions of ramps, installation of specially adapted facilities in bathrooms and kitchens, etc.); provision of telephones, televisions, and so forth.

The act was introduced to the new local authority departments with a great deal of publicity and exhortation, thus hoping to speed up its implementation. Despite a government sponsored pilot scheme (Harris, 1971) for surveying particular areas and identifying the handicapped and their needs as an aid to local authorities, the new act posed great problems for the recently formed social services departments, few of which yet had built up research and intelligence facilities or had accurate existing registers of those actually in need of services. Furthermore, the new law did not make it mandatory for individuals to be registered before receiving services, since it was assumed that some would object to being included on a formal register. There was, therefore, not only the problem for each social services department of gaining some idea of the extent and nature of the problem within its own boundaries but also of allocating sufficient resources.

Local authorities responded in a variety of ways. Some engaged voluntary organizations to leaflet every household within its area, inviting the handicapped to contact their local area office. This method tended to provide a response which completely exceeded the capacity of the authority (either in personnel or allocated financial resources) to deal with it. Others responded by advertising in newspapers and by poster—which produced a proportionally lower response. A few, refusing to be harried by publicity, set up complex 10% surveys, then set aside money and, in some cases, created special teams to ensure the implementation of the act. But, however they approached the problem, social services departments were overwhelmed by the response at the same time they were attempting to restructure and integrate all the services for which they were responsible. The demand, public pressure, and the unpreparedness of the local authorities was such that social workers, skilled and experienced in work with the mentally ill and other groups, found that they spent much of their time with bathmats and toilet seats under one arm and a copy of the Chronically Sick and Disabled Persons Act under the other! Between 1972 and 1973 the numbers of handicapped people on local authority registers almost doubled—from 300,000 to 578,000. This needs to be compared, however, with estimates of one and a quarter million severely handicapped people in Britain.

Several interesting developments have grown out of this particular social problem. It has accelerated the definition of tasks performed by different kinds of social service workers. Much of the practical assistance given to the chronically sick can be delivered by social work assistants, and there has been a marked growth in the proportion of such assistants within area teams. Furthermore, social services departments have begun to employ an increasing number of occupational therapists and develop these services in the community where virtually none had existed before. This latter development has not been without its problems in determining appropriate roles for occupational therapists who have traditionally worked in hospitals. It has also created manpower problems for the health service which has found that local authorities have recruited many from the hospitals. The legislation has stimulated the publication by many authorities of guides for the disabled, indicating what services are available, how to get them, and what buildings, shops, offices, cinemas, public lavatories, and so on are accessible to the disabled. Also, local authority planning departments now exercise much influence over new buildings to which the disabled have access by insisting on adequate provision for the disabled. And, finally, the voluntary sector has been brought into play via a distinct and important role both locally and nationally. Provision for the disabled is one in which active partnership with voluntary organizations is encouraged; local authorities are encouraged to consider co-option of at least one disabled person on the social services committee.

Controversial issues have developed, too, as a result of the act. One concerns the wide variation in practice between local authorities. It is the subject of much public debate locally and nationally, encouraged by the publication of various sets of annual statistics which indicate the performance of all local authorities in this field. As an example, an extract (Table 1), taken from a series of replies in Hansard (27th January, 1976), indicates wide regional variations. However, this statistical information is not yet sufficiently sophisticated to permit valid comparisons between local authorities, as there are widely differing practices in relation to assessing the client's financial contribution to the service given. Thus, a high provider (numerically) could appear as a low spender because the gross expenditure is offset by a much higher level of contribution from the client. Furthermore, it is important to note that the controversy usually centers on the relative showing of local authorities, rather than by intensive debate about what *should* be done and whether greater priority should be given to different vulnerable groups. There is an emerging concern, however, that a significant part of the personal social services input is, in effect, a supplementary income maintenance system. This is particularly true of the provision of telephones, televisions, and the heavy subsidies given to those disabled who use the local public transport system.

Services for Children

Delinquency

The transition for independent local authority children's departments (which were integrated with other social services) was complicated by the nearly simultaneous implementation of legislation which had been passed, but not implemented, two years earlier. The Children and Young Persons Act, 1969, was the culmination of a lengthy controversy about the treatment of delinquents. Essentially, the legislation confirmed a trend which had been developing in the former children's departments toward greater involvement with children who had committed offenses or who had failed to attend school regularly. Previously, the probation service and home office had played a much larger part in the treatment of young offenders. The latter was at the central government level and had direct control of the juvenile residential institutions called approved schools. The new legislation not only transferred these responsibilities to local authority social services departments but also introduced fundamental conceptual changes in the law relating to juveniles. The act was to be implemented in stages and has not yet been fully introduced. It has, however, been the subject of continuing and fierce public debate growing out of a complex history to these new developments and some fundamental assumptions about the nature of delinquency.

In 1964, in a politically influential report, Longford argued that the children of working-class parents were more likely than middle-class children to be apprehended by the police and more likely to be subjected to the processes of the law, to appear before courts and, consequentially, be stigmatized by this process. Such stigmatization was likely to confirm delinquent patterns. Simultaneously, there was growing discontent with the lack of success of the system of treatment of delinquents. The "success" rate of the approved schools, even by the most generous assessment, remained stubbornly at no more than 33%. The third stream of influence came from the child care field itself which suggested that delinquents were no different from other "deprived" children and that delinquency was characterized by identifiable deprivations in childhood. If this theory were correct, then an approach which compensated for the deprivations more likely would be successful. Further, they believed that decisions about the type of care and treatment needed by delinquents should be made by social workers, psychiatrists, and other professionals and not by the courts.

The new legislation embodied these ideas. The juvenile courts now no longer could commit children directly to the approved schools, and the supervision of young offenders was transferred from the probation service to social services departments. The approved schools were to come under the control or influence of local authorities and were to change their name to community homes (with education on the premises), thus integrating them with the general child care residential system. However, despite the optimisim of the new legislation, the actual transition has been marked by many difficulties which, in the interests of space, will be only touched upon in this paper.

The former children's department was not well equipped itself to absorb these new tasks. The newly created social services departments, in the throes of reorganization and struggling with overwhelming demands in other fields, were even less well equipped at the time of transfer. Further complicating the transition was a coincidental significant increase in the incidence of juvenile crime. Although this rise was the continuation of a trend which had been predicted, it gave considerable opportunities for lay magistrates and judges (who had been unenthusiastic about the loss of their power) ample evidence to attack the social services departments for their inability to stem the tide of delinquency and to yearn for the former model of treatment and methods of well defined supervision (challenged by Davies, 1969) as previously carried out by the probation service. Meanwhile, existing staff in the former approved schools were either grossly lacking in numbers and/or in the expertise required by the new

Table 1.

	Assistance With Adaptations Number of Households Assisted Per 1,000 Pop.			Expenditure Per 1,000 Pop.	
	72/3	73/4	74/5	72/3	74/5
National Average	0.62	0.85	0.89	£22.5	£57
London Area	0.99	1.34	1.49	£31.8	£90
N.W. England	0.69	0.80	0.92	£35.6	£96
Southern England	0.31	0.88	0.74	£15.5	£32
South West England	0.49	0.75	0.65	£14.3	£33

system. The results were a crisis in confidence among staff and often inappropriate placements for children who needed to be in special residential care. Many were placed in ordinary community homes for children where it was discovered that delinquents usually did need special care and attention, and if they got it, it was often to the detriment of other children in care. There were well-publicized incidents throughout the country. Some children with seriously delinquent histories could not be placed in residential care and were returned to their own homes only to continue their delinquent behavior. Reappearance of these children in court left the magistrates frustrated because they were able only to recommit the child to the care of the local authority, often roundly criticizing the social services department in the process.

In response to these severe problems there was increasing pressure for the legislation to be revoked or amended. So far, the government has resisted efforts for any major reversion to the status quo ante, arguing that the reorganization of the social services and the lack of resources to implement the legislation effectively does not undermine the principles on which the legislation was based. Moreover, it is now evident that, four years later, after the implementation of the most significant parts of the act, social services departments are beginning to come to grips with some of the major problems.

The specialist community homes for delinquents have slowly begun to reemerge as child care establishments. Better staffed and with more effective links with the communities from which children come, their impact on delinquent and difficult children has yet to be evaluated. Potentially of greater importance, however, has been the emergence of intermediate treatment. The Children and Young Persons Act, 1969, made provision for local authorities to develop treatment in the community for children who had been placed under their supervision as a result of delinquency or failure to attend school. Acting upon provisions of the Children and Young Persons Act, 1969, local authorities have been moving away from the traditional casework approach of working individually with children and their families, toward the establishment of day treatment centers in the areas in which the children live. Children can be required to participate in such schemes which attempt to involve the families and the local community. After a tentative start, education authorities are beginning to participate in these projects. Some education authorities are helping to finance them, sending teachers to participate in the programs and, above all, to recognize that it is better to take some form of education to places, which delinquent children and school dropouts are prepared to attend, than simply to pursue them by legal means and force them to attend schools which they have already rejected or from which they have invited rejection by their behavior. Some schemes are experimenting with employment of new careerists from backgrounds similar to those of the delinquents. Hazel and Cox (1976) have described a scheme providing foster care for delinquents and this model is being adopted elsewhere.

These new initiatives could have been under the aegis of the former children's departments, but it is unlikely that they would have begun to attract resources in competition with other, more popular causes. Finally, it is significant that services for delinquent children have emerged as one of the priorities within social services departments.

Nonaccidental Injury to Children

The emergence of child abuse has influenced both the development of new services and the priority given to different client groups. Estimates indicate that the prevalence of nonaccidental injury in the United Kingdom may be as high as 4,600 every year—which may mean 700 deaths every year. The primary responsibility for initiating legal action to protect children who have come to the attention of any agency (including health and education) rests with the social services department. The social worker has to decide whether the case requires reference to a juvenile court which has authority, when warranted, to commit the child to the care of the local authority or make an order placing the child under the supervision of a social worker. The social worker also decides on the degree of continued parental involvement and to monitor effective support when the child remains at home. If the parents wish to have the child returned to their care at some point, the social worker must decide whether to oppose such an application in the juvenile court.

The interrelationship between the health services, education, police, voluntary organizations, the juvenile courts, and the social services departments is exceptionally complicated; and it is the responsibility of the social services department to do all in its power to ensure that this communication and action network is coordinated, well-informed, and relevantly active in ensuring the protection of children at risk. This is a far from easy task, and the social services department has come under critical scrutiny from the press and the public on several occasions. One widely publicized case, that of Maria Colwell, who at the age of seven was killed by her stepfather in April 1973, led to the establishment by the secretary of state of a committee of enquiry. Their report in 1974 was highly critical of the activities of two social services departments and of a voluntary organization. The report indicated that:

> many of the mistakes made by individuals were either the result of, or were contributed to by, inefficient systems operating in several different fields, notably training, administration, planning, liaison and supervision. It is at the middle and higher levels that this case has clearly shown to us that a great deal of rethinking about child care is overdue.

At the same time, the Department of Health and Social Security (DHSS) issued a circular urging social services and health authorities to set up area review committees composed of representatives from all the agencies within their localities. These committees were to guide and coordinate policies for dealing with children at risk of nonaccidental injury and to initiate and coordinate training programs. They were also to ensure that detailed written procedures were to be devised and adopted by all agencies. Within a year, most social services departments had adopted detailed integrated procedures for use by hospitals, schools, the police, voluntary organizations, and the social services departments. Social workers within the social services departments explicitly became the key figures in the network of communication and action, and the DHSS continued issuing further guidelines. At one point they even reiterated the need to establish registers of children at risk and suggested ways of establishing such registers. This idea, however, raised questions regarding criteria for selection and the imperilment of innocent families.

Interestingly, as a result of the social services departments' vigorous response to the problems of children at risk, the department has begun to come under opposite attack from that which it had formerly received. Particularly, since the numbers of these children comprise a much smaller proportion of the caseload than the chronically sick and disabled and delinquents, it has been argued that social services departments have overreacted. The press now has begun to criticize social services departments for taking legal action too quickly and vigorously in relation to children who, it is felt, have been wrongly identified as at risk. Doctors have complained about being asked to attend too many case conferences. Howells (1974) has argued that the proliferation of communication networks and case conferences is actually counterproductive. Jordan (1977) feels that the Seebohm ideal of a more participating community-based open service has not been realized. He has suggested that there has been a change in attitude by social workers and managers of social services departments, characterized by a greater suspicion of parents and greater defensiveness—the result being a distancing and stigmatizing effect for families who are in need of social work help. All of these criticisms suggest two important changes within the social services department. One is that there has been a significant response by social workers to the problem of children at risk of nonaccidental injury. Second, the social services departments have not yet achieved the finely tuned balance between watchfulness (required by their duty to protect the lives of children) and nonstigmatizing availability and openness (required if families are to be encouraged to seek the kind of help which the new departments were created to provide).

DEVELOPMENTS IN OTHER SERVICES

The Mentally Ill

Twenty years ago, in 1957, the report of the Royal Commission on the Law Relating to Mental Illness and Mental Deficiency reviewed the progress that had been made in the treatment of the mentally ill. The legislation which followed, the Mental Health Act, 1959, introduced the concept of community care for patients who had hitherto spent most of their adult lives in psychiatric institutions. The idea was based on the belief that the large psychiatric hospitals gradually would be scaled down as community services were vastly expanded. The health service would be based primarily in local district hospitals, and the local authorities would provide social work support in the community, day centers, and such residential facilities as might be required. This policy was developed in further reports, and in 1975 a major white paper, "Better Services for the Mentally Ill," reiterated the fundamental principles, while stressing the long-range comprehensive nature of the goals.

Prior to 1971, a few local authorities had made serious attempts to build up services for former patients of psychiatric hospitals. This mental health expertise was one of the first casualties of reorganization. Skilled and experienced social workers were pulled away to meet the demand for supervision and improvement of many services as discussed in the first part of this paper. Psychiatric social workers were particularly in demand and there is little doubt that existing social work services for the mentally ill were seriously diluted over the first two or three years after reorganization.

The population of psychiatric hospitals has declined (at a rate of 3% p.a.), but admission figures have continued to climb due to an ever-rising proportion of readmissions. Knight (1977) and other commentators have argued that this is a reflection of the failure of the community-based health and social services to offer sufficient resources to support these patients. Others have argued social work, day care, and residential facilities cannot expect to have significant impact on admission rates (although their availability should have an affect on the length of stay in hospitals). The growth of psychiatric units within district hospitals has been slower than the closing-out of beds in large psychiatric hospitals, and there are still very many health authorities with no inpatient units within the local district hospitals. As recently as 1974, there were 31 local authorities which provided no residential accomodation, and 63 had no day care facilities. The position has improved since then, but there still remains serious and extensive shortfalls in the provision of facilities to meet the basic guidelines issued by the Department of Health and Social Security in 1972.

There are many reasons for the lack of priority afforded to the development of services for the mentally ill. One is the unavoidable preoccupation at the local level with development of other services which are often the beneficiaries of clear and unambiguous statutory responsibilities. The legislation affecting children and the chronically sick and disabled places specific duties on local authorities. For the elderly, the manifest increase in demand arising purely from demographic changes makes it necessary for resources to be allocated to services for this group. However, for the mentally ill, the local authority has only a general responsibility for providing services; and the cost of supporting the mentally ill falls across a broad spectrum of providers—the penal system, families of the mentally ill, and voluntary organizations struggling to care for the single homeless.

Against this background of grindingly slow development of services for the mentally ill, there have been some positive developments which have created the opportunity for the introduction of new schemes at the local level. In 1976, conscious of the pressures put on to social services departments, the Department of Health and Social Security introduced a joint financing scheme which set aside £8,000,000 in 1976-1977 and £21,000,000 in 1977-1978 from the health services budget. This money was to be available to local authorities to develop programs which will give relief to the health service. Local authorities would have to pay a rising proportion of the cost until they assume responsibility for the full cost within three to five years. Each area was allocated a portion of the £8,000,000. The area health authority, together with the matching local authority, were invited to plan and introduce projects to improve services for the vulnerable, high priority groups such as the mentally ill, mentally handicapped, and the elderly.

This scheme received much criticism on its introduction on the grounds that, if the local authorities did participate in the project, it would, in effect, take up all the growth allowed to them in the next few years. A possible consequence would be that other nonhealth related services would get less than a fair share of growth. Critics felt that the central government was regarding the personal social services as an adjunct to the hard pressed health service—a very sensitive issue both professionally and politically. Notwithstanding these reservations, however, it appears that local authorities, in conjunction with local health services, have been using the money to introduce projects in the field of mental health. Day centers, residential facilities, and social worker posts have been financed in areas in which such services were relatively undeveloped. Such developments have been encouraged further by voluntary organizations working in the mental health field; and these organizations have increasingly adopted a pressure group role in addition to sponsoring projects themselves.

The Mentally Handicapped

In the provision of basic services, very similar considerations apply to services for the mentally handicapped as for the mentally ill. The Department of Health and Social Security White Paper, "Better Services for the Mentally Handicapped" (1971), set targets for the personal social services, and these services have fared relatively better than the mentally ill in the expansion of facilities in the community. This may be partially attributable to the existence at the local level of effective pressure groups of parents of mentally handicapped children. These parents have sought to ensure that some provision is made often in partnership between the social services department and the specialist voluntary organization. The development of facilities for the mentally handicapped is one field in which local initiatives from the community have had considerable influence. It is also a field of work in which the role of social services is unambiguously supportive. Therefore, it does not raise the conflicts which arise in other areas including mental health.

Services for the Elderly

The most significant factor in the development of services for the elderly is the impact of demographic trends. The services actually provided are described by Glennerster (1975). National projections estimate that by 1991 there will be 10,000,000 people over pensionable age (60 for women, 65 for men). This will be one in six of the population. More importantly, however, there will be a 25% increase in the number of people aged 75+ in the 10 year period 1975-1985. The over 75s need five times as many services (as expressed in expenditure terms) as the 64-75 age group, and the implications for the personal social services are considerable. At the present time, about one-third of health and social services expenditure is devoted to the care and treatment of the elderly. McCreadie (1975) calculated that if places in residential care are to be provided for the elderly in the same proportion to the population at risk, as between 1951 and 1966, the number of places will have to be more than doubled over the 15 years, 1973-1988. These potential needs have to be seen in the context of the proportion of personal social services expenditure devoted to the elderly which in 1972-1973 was 42%. Also, since the elderly are not distributed evenly across the country, the distribution of health and personal social services is uneven; and there is little to suggest that supply varies according to need or demand. The report of the Resource Allocation Working Party (1976) demonstrated that the distribution of hospital resources is poorly related to need, and there is a new government policy to begin to redistribute health service resources to areas with the greatest need. However, the personal social services are not, despite continually increasing provision, able to cope adequately with current demands, and the limitation in total growth rate over the next few years presages a growing gap between supply and demand.

For social services departments, there is not only the local demographic reality to face but also the critical influence of other services. A serious shortfall in hospital and community nursing facilities throws additional burdens onto the social services. Similarly, the provision of special sheltered housing for the elderly is the responsibility of local authorities which, outside London, are on a different tier of local government and subject to separate political control. But, the pattern of provision of sheltered housing does not reflect the prevalence of the elderly, despite the widely recognized fact that the provision of sheltered housing at a sufficiently early stage diminishes the subsequent calls on social and health services. On the positive side of services for the elderly, there is a strong tradition of voluntary service. Recent government initiatives have given great emphasis to good neighbor schemes and the need to strengthen the voluntary sector. Finally, there has been a restatement of the general aim of policy. Now the emphasis is on helping the elderly maintain maximum independence in their own homes for as long as possible; developing domiciliary services; and promoting a more active approach to the treatment of the elderly in hospitals.

REORGANIZATION OF THE NATIONAL HEALTH SERVICE

Significance for the Personal Social Services

In 1974, the National Health Service was reorganized (Taylor, 1977). The reorganization integrated the community health services (health visitors district nurses), the hospital services, and, to a lesser degree, the general practitioner service (family doctor). At the local level the service is based on districts which are centered around district general hospitals. These hospitals include all the health services in the district and serve a population of 100,000 to 500,000. Two or more districts are embraced in an area organization, leading to a total of 90 area health authorities and 14 regional health authorities which are responsible for allocation of resources and planning of services.

An attempt was made also to draw boundaries at district or area levels which would be coterminous with local authority social service boundaries to facilitate joint planning and close coordination. In practice, however, this idea was not able to be carried out fully due to the physical location of district general hospitals and their catchment areas. Yet, despite the limitations, the reorganization of health services has created a unique opportunity for the joint planning of health and social services. Health districts were advised to set up health care planning teams at district level. These teams were required to include social workers and other representatives of the "matching" social services.

There are many encouraging and positive features about this new system. For the first time, the interdependent sectors of the health service are required to plan together their future activities. Equally, for the first time, there is a recognition that social services activities and plans are crucially affected by health service provision and that the availability and nature of community based social services is vital to changes in health service policy. It gives each service, at a local level as well, a direct opportunity to influence the other's policies. Financially, there are advantages to both the health and the social services, as a result of the introduction of joint financing. Joint financing (although implemented at the local level in respect to locally conceived schemes) is, in effect, a method of transferring central government funds to local authorities with a precisely defined set of objectives. Without this scheme, it is unlikely that local authorities would be able to develop adequate services since they would remain dependent upon the lesser revenues raised by local taxation.

From the patient's standpoint, hospitals have come to be regarded as caring effectively about a wide range of problems. The "hospital" can now prescribe appropriate services, rather than refer patients elsewhere at a time when they are least able to cope with complexities. This has also led to better integrated medical and social care, although most social services departments have moved cautiously to introduce reforms within hospital social work departments. One problem which has arisen from the new system must be mentioned briefly due to its significance. With regard to the definition of responsibility for the residential care and treatment of the elderly, there have been many problems, particularly at the local level. Under provided health districts have tended to look to social services to compensate for the lack of long stay facilities for chronic geriatric patients whose needs are largely for nursing rather than medical care. Social services have perceived their role as providing care for those who are not in need of substantial nursing attention. Added to the differences in role perception is the dramatic increase in average age of residents in local authority homes for the elderly. Between 1966 and 1977 the number of residents aged 85 and over has risen by 50% compared with an increase in the residential population of only 26%. The increasing frailty and mental confusion among these residents has considerable and serious implications for the staffing of such homes. Some health care planning teams are beginning to face the issue, and it is hoped that in the future jointly operated facilities will be developed to cater to those who need health and social care.

For social services departments, a further significant feature of the reorganization of the health service was the transfer to them of responsibility for social workers in hospitals. These social workers had been unaffected by the social services reorganization following the Seebohm Report and had been directly employed by the hospitals. Local authorities, therefore, had inherited a bewildering mixture of social work provision in 1974. The transfer, however, was accompanied by some controversy with opposition from a minority of hospital social workers and some doctors. But after a slow beginning, hospital-based social workers are extending their identification from the patient in the hospital to the wider responsibilities for the patient and his family. Furthermore, direct access to community services and the authority to prescribe domiciliary, day, and residential care has helped hospital social workers to become more broadly effective. In those hospitals which previously had no direct social work support, social workers are now being made available from the community-based area teams.

PLANNING AND PRIORITIES IN THE PERSONAL SOCIAL SERVICES

Before 1971, there had been little attempt at sophisticated forward planning within the personal social services. It was unusual for an authority to plan more than three years ahead and, because of the serious shortfall in all provisions, there was a tendency for forward planning simply to adopt an incremental approach. The distribution of responsibility among three departments for different aspects of the social services and the lack of a corporate approach within local authorities impeded attempts at assessment and planning of service needs. Another influential feature was the laissez-faire approach to central government. With the exception of certain children's services, guidance was issued spasmodically with little effort to monitor its effects and even less to intervene in the affairs of those authorities which chose to ignore the advice.

In 1971-1972, however, the government instructed local authorities to produce Ten-Year Forward Plans for Social Services and required very detailed submissions about intentions. It set national average targets for general guidance, and the forward plans were based on the economic assumption that the personal social services would receive an increase in revenue of about 10% per annum in real terms. By the time the plans were produced the resource assumptions had withered under the attack of inflation and the deteriorating general economic situation. The resource assumptions continued to plummet in succeeding years—to 8.5% in 1972 and 7% in 1973—and by 1976-1977 the forecast growth rate had dropped to 2% for social services (in the context of no growth at all for all other local authority services). More recently still it has dropped to 1.8%. It is forecast that this decrease will cease by 1980-1981. In reality, the explosion of demand and the encouragement of the early planning forecasts generated expenditure beyond the forecast levels. From 1970-1971 to 1971-1972, the expenditure growth rate was 15% in real terms; in the succeeding year 14%, and in 1972-1973 it was 12%. More recently, government measures have ensured that the disparity of forecasts and performance has been greatly reduced, and by the end of 1977 the two are likely to coincide.

The dramatic change from a high to virtually no growth rate has demanded a major revision of plans and has forced the social services locally and nationally to concentrate on priorities and develop increasingly sophisticated planning and control mechanisms. But central government has had to face the hostility and pressure from local authority politicians; and senior bureaucrats are now facing the hostility and resistance of social workers and other local authority staff as they reluctantly begin to accept the economic realities of government policies. Increasingly, the government has sought to intervene in setting priorities for limited expansion and has begun to tackle the difficult question of transfer of resources between existing services. A major step toward this came from the Department of Health and Social Security (1976) with a consultative document outlining the future priorities for health and social services. The DHSS clearly recommended that any growth should be devoted to the elderly, the mentally ill, the mentally handicapped, and services for children and families with children. It proposed differential growth rates ranging from 3.2% to 1.8%. It accepted, however, that the differential growth rates would not be mirrored necessarily in each locality because of differing levels of needs and provision. It further suggested that expansion should be within domiciliary and fieldwork services at the expense of residential care. This document was notable also for attempting an integrated approach to health and social services planning and for stressing the modest transfer of financial resources from health to social services.

Application of Priorities to Local Service Delivery

Algie and Miller (1976) have suggested that there are four dimensions to the establishment of social services priorities and that no definition of priorities is valid unless it encompasses all. They are objectives, client needs, service types, and logistics.

In accepting the relevance of this analysis, social service departments have had to begin to adopt a radically different approach to the determination of priorities. Conventional approaches—simple political policy and administrative instructions—are neither satisfactory as a means of determining priorities nor acceptable to those who have to implement them. There are as yet, however, no really successful examples of reconciliation and integration of the views of social workers (who actually make the immediate choices between those who can and cannot receive services) and the views of senior managers (who attempt to set the guidelines within which these choices are made). The latter set guidelines consciously (through lists of tasks in priority order) or less consciously by allocating resources to certain facilities.

Workload Management and Priorities

In an attempt to follow a more scientific approach to workload management, some social services department workloads are being determined by the allocation of "involvement units" to different types of cases. A case which requires frequent face-to-face contact may be given five units, whereas a case needing contact only once in three months may be given one unit. In one week, a social worker can conduct 15 to 20 face-to-face interviews with clients for whom he has ongoing responsibility (not including intake or new referral work). Each social worker is individually assessed as having the capacity to cope with a fixed number of units. Cases can be allocated with quite accurate expectations of the social worker's likely input. For the system to work, however, it requires frequent reviews of current cases so that they may be reclassified or closed according to progress. Also, this system does not help to determine priorities but actually complicates the question. The more sophisticated the system, the more factors (about social worker, client, and resources) need to be known; and such assessment demands greater initial input to make the necessary comprehensive evaluation.

PRELIMINARY EVALUATION OF THE ACHIEVEMENTS OF SOCIAL SERVICES DEPARTMENTS

Many attempts have been made to establish criteria for evaluating service delivery systems (e.g., Kahn, 1976; United Nations European Seminar Report, 1977). The following features are usually included in such attempts:

(1) Are the services accessible and responsive to local needs?

(2) Are users treated with respect and are they satisfied?

(3) Are real services being delivered effectively and efficiently?

(4) Are users offered a stable and continuous relationship when they need it?

(5) Are users allowed some choice between potential sources of help?

It is possible to draw some tentative conclusions about the English system.

Are Services Accessible and Responsive to Local Needs?

As discussed in this paper earlier, Seebohm envisaged the creation of area teams serving populations of 50,000 to 100,000 with a staff of 10 to 12 social workers plus other administrative, professional, and ancillary staff. These area teams are the doors to service through which most users pass, however brief their contact with a social worker. Since 1974, the hospital social work department has become another point of entry. However, it has become clear that the number of social workers originally allocated was a gross underestimate for all, save the rural areas with thinly scattered populations. In urban areas, teams with 20 to 30 social workers plus 10 to 20 others (assistants, trainees, occupational therapists, community workers, and administrators) for a population of 40,000 to 50,000 are not uncommon. Yet creation of area teams and the development of community group work has undoubtedly provided accessibility and drawn in many who both receive and give services. At this time, the most successful inner urban model appears to be the small team covering a population of no more than 15,000 with social workers, community workers, and others becoming involved in a wide range of community activities. Most social services departments, however, have established larger area offices to cover larger populations of the size recommended by Seebohm. They are usually comprised of one group of social workers dealing with intake and short-term work and two or more other groups of workers dealing with clients who required longer term contact. This is an efficient system because it enables intake social workers to develop a general expertise in assessment and diagnosis and frees other social workers for long term work. Furthermore, the intake system provides a small identifiable group of workers who become known to referring agencies. The disadvantage of this system, however, is that groups within the area team generally do not have responsibility for a small enough geographical area to make much headway on the development of or involvement in a network of community groups. These groups, no doubt, could offer complementary services *and* assist in identifying problems and issues which are peculiar to that locality. The problem of accessibility has diminished with the introduction of both of these models. In the larger model, however, detailed knowledge of the community has to be sacrificed in the interests of a somewhat more effective service for individual clients and improved cooperation with referring agencies.

Are Users Treated with Respect and Are They Satisfied?

There has been considerable debate about the effectiveness of the new departments in diminishing the stigmatizing effect of seeking help from the social services. Undoubtedly, the role of social workers as protectors of life, particularly in relation to children, has had an effect on public expectation of the social services. For some clients, this has meant that the authority inherent in some aspects of the social worker's role is perceived more directly. For the social worker, there is a real dilemma in view of the statutory responsibility which he carries. There is less evidence than Jordan (1977) has suggested that this problem has created a widespread mistrust of the social services among those who need help. Glampson and Goldberg (1976) indicated that users of the social services in 1975 were better informed about the functions (of social services departments) and more satisfied with the services they received than in 1972. There were, however, specific complaints concerning the social worker or the service given. There were also frequent comments about the immaturity of the worker but not about lack of sympathy or empathy. A study of service delivery (Social Work Service, 1975) did reveal that "privacy for clients and workers was scarce—poor waiting accommodation and lack of space for confidential interviewing were noted in some offices." This problem is not a new feature of local services but an indication that their ideals and intentions are not yet matched by the available facilities.

Are Real Services Being Delivered
Effectively and Efficiently?

There is considerable evidence to support the view that the reorganized social services departments have improved and expanded real services to those in need. The evidence is partly in the annual statistics produced by the Department of Health and Social Security which measure the quantitative increases in services in recent years. The combination of national policy and increased power of the social services at the local level have ensured that the expansion of these services has exceeded that of others. In addition, the recent deceleration in rate of growth in social services has been smaller than in others. Furthermore, the large departments have been able to effectively deploy a wider range of management and organizational skills, and there is a continuous reappraisal of the efficiency of the services. The effectiveness of domiciliary and day care services is more accessible to measurement than some activities and there is increasing interest in the cost effectiveness of alternative services with similar objectives.

There are, however, no universally acceptable definitions of social worker's tasks nor of definitions of output within social services departments. The tentative indications of growing client satisfaction are strongest in areas in which the social worker acts as doorkeeper to practical services, but more sophisticated criteria are being explored. An unusual feature of the social services departments has been their eagerness to experiment with new ways of tackling problems and taking risk. Finally, with regard to shortfall in service provision, it is more a reflection of the explosion of demand and the national economic situation than to structural shortcomings in local social service organization.

Are Users Offered a Continuous and Stable Relationship When They Need It?

The social services departments have not yet achieved the capacity to offer stability and continuity of personal relationships for those clients who need this kind of help. Several reasons are accountable:

(1) Reorganization led to much movement, upwards and sideways, among social workers.

(2) The high turnover rate of staff (although in less populated areas more stability has been achieved).

(3) The expansion of the social services and the development of training facilities, which has brought increasing numbers of young trained staff into social work and thrown wave after wave of new recruits into the front line (Passchendaele Policy), particularly in urban areas.

(4) The stress of work has led to a high loss of staff. On the other hand, in the recent past the development of in-service staff training programs the increasing professionalization of supervision and the introduction of techniques for determining and managing the social worker's work load have combined with the deceleration of the expansion program to inject a growing stability of personnel within departments.

Are Users Allowed Some Choice Between Potential Sources of Help?

The creation of multipurpose social services departments was thought by some to be inviting the problem of monolithic monopolistic structures in which the users would increasingly face the choice of accepting the offered service or receiving none at all. Nevertheless, there remains a strong and growing voluntary movement in almost all the fields in which the social services are active. Yet the voluntary organizations find themselves in a vulnerable position due to their dependence upon the central and local government for financial assistance. Also the economic recession has led to a decline in funding by charitable trusts. These voluntary services, however, are not universally available, their quality is variable, and they do not provide the comprehensive range of services which the local authorities are required to provide. Many potential clients do have some choice between statutory and voluntary agencies, and there are still significant areas of personal social services which are controlled by statutory agencies other than the social services departments. However, significantly, the advocates of state service and state intervention have moved well from the poor-law concept of minimal services for the poor, and the social services departments are attempting to achieve universally acceptable standards.

CONCLUSION

It is apparent that the integrated social services at local level in England stop short of total integration of all personal social services. The local authorities are heavily dependent upon legislation, support, direction, and exhortation from central government. Nevertheless, there is a range of discretion within the methods of delivering service and, with some exceptions, the amount and type of service and its distribution between different identifiable groups. The total expenditure of local government is being brought under central control more effectively than hitherto, but local authorities have a good deal of freedom to distribute their total resources between all of the different services under their control. The new departments have, undoubtedly, proved successful in attracting more resources, and their organization is becoming more sophisticated.

The earlier problems for social workers of developing new skills and adapting the old ones are being overcome, but in their place new difficulties of reconciling the apparently conflicting responsibilities of the social services departments are being experienced. The departments have supportive, therapeutic, gatekeeping, social control, and community development responsibilities. It is not yet clear whether professional methods can overcome the difficulties arising from these sometimes conflicting tasks in such a way as to fully evoke the confidence of those who need to use the services.

Finally, it is apparent that the new social services organization cannot, on its own, achieve an optimum balance between supply and expectation. As the services have grown, they have been outstripped in every field by demand which has been generated by many different factors. The gap is never likely to be closed, for expectations are always rising. There is a danger that the integrated social services may be discredited because of their inevitable failure to keep pace with demand. Their existence has thrown this social phenomenon into sharp relief. Thus, while the lag is created by a range of social, structural, economic, and political forces, it is the social services department which provides the visible sign of society's failure to solve some of its major social problems. Yet the present system of organizing services in England is better than its predecessors. Any further changes in structure need to be contemplated in the context of the interrelationship of social, political, and economic factors which are outside the control of the service providers.

REFERENCES

ALGIE, M., and MILLER, M. (1976). "Popping their question." Health and Social Services Journal, 86(December).

Better Services for the Mentally Ill (1975). Cmnd. 6233. London: HMSO.

Better Services for the Mentally Handicapped (1971). Cmnd. 4683. London: HMSO.

Committee of Enquiry into the Care and Supervision Provided in Relation to Maria Colwell (1974). Report. London: HMSO.

Committee on Local Authority and Allied Personal Social Services (1968). Report Cmnd. 3703. London: HMSO.

DAVIES, M. (1969). Probationers in their social environment. London: HMSO.

Department of Health and Social Security (1976). Priorities for health and social services in England. London: HMSO.

GLAMPSON, A., and GOLDBERG, E.M. (1976). "The consumer's viewpoint." Social Work Today, 8(6).

GLENNERSTER, H. (1975). "Social services in Great Britain." Pp. 69-111 in D. Thursz and J.L. Vigilante (eds.), Meeting human needs: An overview of nine countries. Beverly Hills, Calif.: Sage.

HARRIS, A. (1971). Handicapped and impaired in Great Britain. London: HMSO.

HAZEL, N., and COX, C. (1976). "The special family placement project in Kent." Social Work Service, 12.

HOWELLS, J. (1974). Remember Maria. London: Butterworths.

JORDAN, W. (1977). "A service with a human face." Community Care, (April):24-27.

KAHN, A.J. (1976). "Service delivery at the neighbourhood level: Experience, theory and fads." Social Service Review, 50(1).

KNIGHT, L. (1977). "Still the Cinderella." Community Care, (April):47-49.

LONGFORD, Lord (1964). "Crime, a challenge to us all." Report of the Labour Party's Study Group. London: Labour Party.

McCREADIE, C. (1975). "Personal social services." In R. Klein (ed.), Inflation and priorities. London: Centre for Studies in Social Policy.

MORRIS, B. (1974). Towards a caring society. New York: Columbia University Press.

Resource Allocation Working Party (1976). Report. "Sharing resources for health in England. London: Department of Health and Social Security.

SEEBOHM, Lord (1974). Unpublished paper delivered to the Community Service Society, New York.

Social Work Service (1975). June 1975. London: Department of Health and Social Security.

TAYLOR, D. (1977). "The re-organised National Health Service." Paper no. 58. London: Office of Health Economics.

United Nations (1977). European Seminar Report on Integrated Approaches to Social Services at the Local Level. Geneva: U.N. Division of Social Affairs.

12

SOCIAL ACTION AND SERVICES AT THE
NEIGHBORHOOD LEVEL: GREAT BRITAIN

HOWARD A. PALLEY

One of the contemporary dilemmas of social reform is determining the appropriate relative role of national (and local) bureaucracies vis-à-vis local community and neighborhood representatives in the area of general social service delivery and related social welfare provision (Marris and Rein, 1973:285-287). This essay will, first of all, briefly review the structure of local social service delivery and the role of various participants in the delivery of such services in Great Britain. Also, this essay will review some national-local and neighborhood linkages in this social service delivery system. More specifically, this paper will present a case study of an innovative neighborhood focused social service project, the British Community Development Project (CDP)—a largely nationally funded "neighborhood-based experiment aimed at finding new ways of meeting the needs of people" (Community Development Project Working Group, 1974:162).

Prior to a further indication of the direction of this essay, it is important to offer a definition of the general or personal social services. The American social welfare analyst Alfred Kahn defines general social services as "programs that protect or restore family life, help individuals cope with external or internalized problems, enhance development and facilitate access through information, guidance, advocacy, and concrete help of several kinds" (Kahn, 1973:19). Such services are referred to in Great Britain as "personal social services" (Committee on Local Authority and Allied Personal Social Services: 1968). This essay will emphasize consideration of such personal social services although it will also offer some observations on related social welfare provision, such as educational provision, and impact of employment needs on poverty areas.

LOCAL AUTHORITY AND SOCIAL
SERVICE DELIVERY

Public expenditures in the United Kingdom by local authorities for personal social services totaled about £622 million in 1974-1975. (For England and Wales, the cost of personal social services for 1974-1975 was estimated as accounting for 13 3/4% of total government expenditures for health and personal social services [Department of Health and Social Security, 1975:88].) Most of the £622 million was raised by localities—only 8.2% of this amount was funded by a subsidy of the national government.

National policy for such social services is vague in Great Britain. Traditionally, local authorities have the responsibility of providing social work clinical services, residential care services, day care services and support services for the homebound. Such services are aimed at persons in needy categories: children and their families, the elderly, the mentally ill, the mentally retarded, and the physically handicapped. As such services are often delivered on a neighborhood basis, they constitute neighborhood services. As the Director of Social Services of London's Kensington-Chelsea area has noted, "The role of the personal services is to meet special social and personal needs with special skills—needs of neighborhoods and communities, as well as of the individuals and families" (Utting, 1975:453).

The structure of such neighborhood-based social service delivery reflects the fact that the United Kingdom is a unitary state. Thus, local authorities and, indeed, all public agencies are creatures of the national Parliament, with powers and duties established by parliamentary statute. In the event that local government is not considered to be performing according to its statutory obligations, the national government may undertake such functions directly.

Glennerster (1975:70) has compiled the following list of agencies which are concerned nationally with social services:

(1) The Home Secretary, who is concerned with the Police Service, the Prison Service, the treatment of offenders, the Probation and After Care Service, and who has certain responsibilities for a small programme of community development;

(2) The Secretary of State for Health and Social Services, who is responsible for the National Health Service, the whole of social insurance and supplementary benefits, and personal social services;

(3) The Secretary of State for Education and Science; and finally,

(4) The Secretary of State for the Environment, who oversees local government and housing, town and country planning, and transport.

As has been noted, it is the local authorities in the United Kingdom who are charged with primary operating responsibilities for personal social service programs. The functions of local government in urban areas are conducted by elected metropolitan county councils. Within the metropolitan counties there are metropolitan districts. Elected district councils are responsible for providing education, housing, and personal social services.[1] Outside urban regions in England and Wales, county councils are directly responsible for such functions as planning important highways, police and fire services, education and personal social services (but not public housing). The Local Authority Social Services Act of 1970 mandated that appropriate local authorities (county and metropolitan district councils) appoint both a director of social services and a social services committee for localities in England and Wales. The directors of social services are responsible to the local social service committees and the local authorities for the operation of the local social service programs.

Except for services administered nationally, such as the National Health Service and the Supplementary Benefits Program, or the experimental Community Development Project of the Home Office, most social welfare programs are funded primarily out of local revenues. Local councils utilize, as a basic source of revenue for local programs, a "rate" or local property tax. This tax generally meets about half of such councils' expenditures. Nationally, a "rate support grant" based on a complex formula, including the number of children and elderly in a local area, is provided to local areas to supplement the revenue raised by local councils. Such revenue sources provided for a wide range of local activities, such as education, police, and fire services. The personal social services must therefore compete with these other local activities for both local resources and limited available national resources. Furthermore, local authority personal social service departments differ greatly in needs, resources, and applicable programs producing what Bleddyn Davies terms "territorial injustice" or regional inequities (Davies et al., 1972:122). The need for specific assistance for "depressed areas" with special needs and particularly higher social service needs has led to demands for "positive discrimination" to assist such depressed areas with disproportionately poor, and often socially disorganized, populations (Committee of Inquiry, 1976:233-234; National Community Development Project, 1976:25). In response to such demands the Community Development Project was established as a national program which facilitates provision of services discriminating positively in favor of selected poor neighborhoods.

THE BRITISH NATIONAL COMMUNITY
DEVELOPMENT PROJECT: AN OVERVIEW

The British Community Development Project is a small pilot project aimed at both involving poor residents of localities in decisions involving neighborhood service delivery and in improving the quality and quantity of such local services. The program was initiated in 1970 with the cost of all local projects borne largely (75%) by the national Home Office and partly (25%) by participating local authorities.

Initially the Community Development Project (CDP) was based on the assumption that the problems of local slums or "disadvantaged sectors" could be alleviated by improved field coordination of personal social services, and the mobilization of self-help and mutual aid by local communities. CDPs were established in local neighborhoods with great deprivation. Local authority groups were utilized to identify needs, promote improved coordination and accessibility of services in the selected areas, and foster both increased community involvement and improved communication between local communities and local services. Related research activities were located in local universities or polytechnics.

Local CDP projects were placed in neighborhoods with populations of between 10,000 to 20,000 persons. Such placement was in "disadvantaged areas" of cities and small towns. While such placement was initiated by the Home Office, local CDP programs were only established where the local authority accepted a Home Office invitation.

The extent of sustained local implementation of CDP projects beyond the five-year pilot project period was to be dependent on the level of resources available to the locality for providing services. Such neighborhood services are, as noted earlier, ordinarily and primarily funded locally—and as poor areas are generally areas of both declining industry and declining revenues, as well as increasing demand for services, such limited resources handicapped local authorities seeking to provide services for the disadvantaged in CDP areas.[2]

By 1975, Community Development Project officials would cast doubt on an initial project emphasis on the ability of the CDP to achieve a goal of substantially alleviating poverty in selected poor neighborhoods through local social action and the rehabilitation of poor individuals (National Community Development Project, 1975:1-3). In a report termed a Forward Plan, they express pessimism about the ability of the CDP to make more than a small dent in alleviating problems of "poverty and urban decline"—which are viewed as problems of the political-economic system. The Forward Plan notes that by 1975 officials in the Community Development Projects

> have challenged accounts of their areas based on social pathology. Poverty is seen as a consequence of fundamental inequalities in our present political and economic system. The conditions which working class people experience are a consequence of these inequalities. Improved coordination of existing social and welfare services can at best make only a marginal impact. The projects' experience has led them largely to discount the value of attempting to influence policy and promote technical strategies for change in isolation from the development of working class action. By this we do not mean vague schemes for "participation" and "involvement" in policy formation but rather the deliberate attempt to provide information

and resources so that groups can formulate their own demands and press directly for change. [National Community Development Project, 1975:1]

This approach reflected the belief that poverty in CDP areas was a product of the presence of an "underclass" of poor whose clout in the political system was not equal to that of either real estate developers, large industrial enterprises (such as Hills Plastics), commercial enterprises (such as the DeVere Hotel group) or city planners whose overall concerns with development in poverty areas did not reflect the social costs of such developments (Benington, 1975).

Under the CDP program, 12 local projects were established in Great Britain. In 1970, the projects were initiated in Coventry, Tynemouth, Oldham, and Glamorgan. In 1971, additional projects were announced for the West Riding area of Yorkshire, the London Borough of Newham, the burgh of Paisley in Scotland, the county of Cumberland and the city of New Castle upon Tyne. An additional project was also instituted for the City of Birmingham. By October 1972, all of the projects were underway. With all phases of the program in full operation the program reached an expenditure level of three-fourths of a million in 1974. (As of 1976, seven local projects were no longer in operation, the remaining ongoing projects were within the following localities: New Castle upon Tyne [Benwell], Birmingham [Saltley], Oldham [Clarksfield], North Tyneside [Percy and Trinity], and Paisley [Ferguslie Park].)

Procedurally, the local projects are related to the Home Office through a consultative council; also data on the CDPs is collected for the Home Office through a central information and intelligence unit.

Formally, however, local projects fall under the authority of local government authorities. Controversy over the degree to which such control should be exercised by local authorities or by neighborhood-based organizations aided by community workers is illustrated by a dispute in the Batley CDP. Batley is a textile town in Yorkshire with a population of 42,000. Structurally, in terms of local government structure, nine Batley local councillors sit on the Kirklees Metropolitan District Council. In Batley, a dispute arose in 1974 as to the control of the local social service information center known as the Advice Centre for the Town (ACT). Batley CDP workers requested a grant from the Kirklees Metropolitan District Council of £8,000 in order to operate ACT. The councillors offered £6,000 with the condition that three local councillors be placed on the ACT management board—which, at that time, consisted of 12 representatives of the local tenants' association. This outraged local community workers who appealed to the Home Office, which in turn backed up the local authorities. In a July 16, 1974, letter to a local member of Parliament, Home Secretary Roy Jenkins noted that "social action [funds] are intended for programmes of experimental action that the local team considers appropriate to the needs and circumstances of its area and that its employing local authority is prepared to approve. It is within the discretion of the local authority to decide what schemes to support; the Home Office has no power of direction" (Edgington, 1974:612). Similar debates regarding "community control" and the related arguments regarding the level of community protest accompnaying CDP projects arose with respect to Southwark, Coventry, and Liverpool CDPs. These disputes mirrored the earlier conflicts regarding community action and the authority of local government authorities which had characterized the early phase of the American "War on Poverty."

In the view of some commentators (Guthrie, 1970; Corina, 1976) some conflict between community workers and local governmental officials was inevitable but, if accompanied by understanding on both sides, it could help local residents in securing the meeting of educational, housing, employment, recreation, and general social service needs. As Guthrie notes:

> Local authorities, with or without reorganization, must be prepared to meet the double challenge of apathy on the one hand and unconventional political activity on the other. Community workers . . . will be able to help in the process of interpreting policies to people and of interpreting people's feelings to the [local government] authority. Conversely, those who choose to effect social change outside of conventional channels of local democracy must be ready to understand not only the tangible problems of a local authority in maintaining the essential services, but also the less tangible factors local authorities have to live with. For both sides a conflict of opinion is not merely an obstacle to social change or an improper interference with statutory powers; it is the essential weapon of democracy, which in some places has been too long gathering rust. [Guthrie, 1970:18]

Generally, the CDPs were involved in a broad range of neighborhood innovations designed to improve neighborhood services. Among the overall achievements of the program were the bringing together of residents to discuss local problems; the establishment of advice and information centers (such as Batley's Advice Centre for the Town), and the strengthening of previously existing centers, aimed at facilitating communication between local residents and service agencies; projects aimed at improved environmental surroundings, and improved recreational facilities. Other projects include community centers, language teaching schools for immigrants, nursery and child day care centers, training of child care workers, social service provision for the elderly, summer holiday programs for deprived children, and programs to assist maltreated women.

THE NATURE OF TWELVE CDP AREAS

Projects and services varied with respect to the nature of the "risk" groups found in particular CDP areas. Thus, it is important to review the age composition and distribution within particular areas (see Table 1). Ten of the 12

CDP areas experienced population decline between 1961 and 1971. (The exceptions were the CDP areas of Batley and Cleator Moor.) The Saltley area had 23% more children under 5 years of age in 1971 than in 1961, despite an 11% loss of population. In all areas but Vauxhall, the proportion of population aged 0-4 years was higher than the national average. Except for Newington, Benwell, and Hillfields, there also was a higher proportion of the population in the 5-19 age group.

While the proportion of population aged 65 or more was not greater in most areas than the national average, six areas had a high proportion of households consisting of an elderly person living alone. A compositional pattern indicating high risk of poverty is illustrated by Saltley, in which "there are almost two separate age distributions, with the white population typically elderly without young family, and young immigrants with families of pre-school or infant age" (Community Development Project Working Group, 1974:166). The predicament of project areas is aptly illustrated by the 1975 *Forward Plan* comment on the plight of Saltley: "in the last 20 years many local factories have closed; local skilled labour has followed new investment in jobs and housing on the connurbation's suburban fringe. Saltley is left now with fewer and poorer paid local jobs, an increasing number of unskilled and immigrant workers—the latter coping with specific bureaucratic and political restrictions—and a fast deteriorating housing stock milked by a combination of financial and property institutions" (National Community Development Project, 1975:15).

CDP areas were characterized generally by high unemployment levels, high concentrations of semi- and unskilled workers, difficulties relating to transportation to areas with better employment opportunities, and the lack of success of policies seeking to attract new industry to high unemployment areas. In all project areas unemployment was above the national average. In the Liverpool and Paisley CDP areas, the rate of unemployment was four to five times higher than that of the nation as a whole; in the Newcastle and Tynemouth CDP areas, unemployment was over three times the national unemployment rate; in the Newham, Cumberland, and Glamorgan CDP areas, the rate of unemployment was double—or more than double—the national rate (Community Development Project Working Group, 1974:167).

THE CDPs AND NEIGHBORHOOD SERVICES

Education

One of the key areas of neighborhood service provision under the CDPs relates to the field of education. Educational activities were defined in the report of the Community Development Project Working Group (1974:178) as follows:

Table 1: Age structure of the population of the 12 CDP areas, compared with that of the whole of Great Britain, April 1971

| CDP areas[a] | Percentage of persons present on census night in each of the following age groups: | | | | | | Percentage of present private households consisting of one pensionable person |
	0-4 %	5-19 %	20-44 %	45-64 %	65+ %	all no.	%
London boroughs							
Canning Town (Newham)	9	25	30	25	11	42,369 (100%)	12
Newington (Southwark)	9	20	33	26	11	13,595 (100%)	13
Other cities							
Saltley (Birmingham)	11	25	32	23	9	13,869 (100%)	11
Vauxhall (Liverpool)	7	29	28	24	11	14,073 (100%)	12
Hillfields (Coventry)	10	22	33	24	11	16,531 (100%)	14
Benwell (Newcastle)	11	22	33	21	13	14,449 (100%)	15
Towns							
Clarksfield (Oldham)	9	24	28	25	14	25,280 (100%)	17
Ferguslie Park (Paisley)	13	34	29	15	8	12,260 (100%)	9
Percy and Trinity (Tynemouth)	11	27	30	21	11	16,120 (100%)	14
Batley (West Riding)	10	24	31	23	13	42,004 (100%)	15
Small towns/rural areas							
Cleator Moor (Cumberland)	9	27	31	23	11	11,215 (100%)	11
Glyncorrwg (Glamorgan)	9	28	30	23	11	8,647 (100%)	9
Great Britain[b]	8	23	32	24	13	538,027[c] (100%)	12

a. Census 1971 Small Area Statistics (Ward Library), Tables 4, 6, 7 and 18.
b. Census 1971 Great Britain: Summary Tables (1% Sample). London, HMSO, 1973, Tables 1 and 23. Includes figures for England, Wales and Scotland.
c. A 1% sample cited in Community Development Project Working Group, "The British National Community Development Project, 1969-1974." *Community Development Journal*, 9(October, 1974), 166.

(a) Conventional education development: improving and extending facilities, introduction of new equipment, development of pre-school provision, more teaching resources. The assumption is that the system could be effective but needs more resources to work.

(b) Community education: particularly developing home-school links, the need for a curriculum relevant to inner-city areas, and the idea of the "community school." The aim is to change relationships between school and community and develop "constructive discontent" which will encourage a critical stance among children towards their environment. The assumption is that this can best be done by working through schools.

(c) Emphasis on work outside schools, on informal adult education, dealing with real-life situations—problems of work, unemployment or rent with groups not already involved in the educational process. The aim is to stimulate knowledge and awareness, and encourage pressure for change among those directly affected. The assumption is that this can be done by working through schools.

Educational activity projects undertaken under the CDP program vary from area to area. Conventional educational programs and community educational programs were undertaken in Liverpool, Coventry, Southwark, Glamorgan, and Batley. (Such educational programs often sought to employ a variety of teaching methods including outside speakers, taped interviews by students, small group discussions, and task-oriented projects [Lees, 1975:124].) The Southwark Project included child-minder training and preschool visiting services utilizing public and voluntary resources for children under five years of age. It included provision of a home/school officer for work with the families of school age children. The CDP in Glamorgan helped establish a parents' forum, playgroups, and recreational activities and initiated the formation of a community resource center. The CDP program generally has fostered more linkages between teachers, pupils, parents, and the local neighborhoods. Indeed, in Coventry and Canning Town, the community education program has contributed to the creation of political and professional pressure advocating compensatory educational programs for these disadvantaged areas.

With respect to the issue of political and social action education within the framework of educational progamming the 1975 Forward Plan report of the Canning Town CDP noted that:

Informal discussions have been held with local teachers and others who are concerned with the failure of schooling to do more that is relevant to the life of the wider community and to provide greater social and political awareness as well as the basic skills which must be a pre-condition to the realisations of notions of involvement, participation and successful community action. It is hoped that the series of meetings may lend either to an experimental community and political education programme or to the secondment of a teacher to research and prepare such a programme. [National Community Development Project, 1975:35]

While this statement indicates the goal orientation of community workers, it also indicates the preliminary nature of operationalized efforts in this area of community education. Furthermore, by grouping "political education" with the need for compensatory skill programs, the activities of community workers in this CDP probably increased the difficulty of securing "positive discrimination" in terms of meeting the skill needs of children from low-income families.

In addition to the provision of educational services, CDPs have been focusing on a range of services for particular "risk" groups within the local population. Services to three such "risk" groups—the elderly, youth, and new immigrants (mainly Asians)—will be discussed next.

Services to the Elderly, Youth, and Immigrants

The CDPs in Coventry, Cleator Moor, and Southwark were all involved in projects aimed at providing services for the elderly. Coventry emphasized structuring services for the elderly by allowing for a greater participant role of elderly consumers of social services so that such services would enhance, rather than diminish, the status of this group. The CDP in Cleator Moor was concerned with identifying inadequacies in service programs to meet the needs of the elderly and exploring approaches to involve the elderly in meeting such service needs. Southwark sought both to examine effectiveness of existing traditional services and to initiate new services where needed—such as, the establishment of an employment bureau serving those over 60, the establishment of a visiting service using neighborhood residents, and the fostering of self-help projects.

Programs for youth have been either neighborhood development projects or projects established as part of the education program. They have included the development of recreational facilities, nursery and preschool provision, and summer recreational programs. In some neighborhoods, community workers have successfully organized local neighborhood organizations around the issue of development and organization of playground facilities. For instance, the Canning Town CDP reported the following success in 1975:

Local groups, formed to press for and develop facilities for children, have been supported throughout the Project Area. In the cases of the Big Hill Adventure Playground Association (Cleator Moor) and the Freedom Land Adventure Playground Group (Frizington) the local committees are fully responsible for the development of the playgrounds and for the full-time playleaders seconded to them by CDP. The next year will be one of consolidation of the playgrounds and the local committees and the demonstration of the importance of this area of such provision for children. [National Community Development Project, 1975:35]

With regard to immigrant populations, both the Saltley and Batley areas have been concerned with service delivery essentially to their Indian/Pakistani immigrants. Saltley has developed a project particularly focusing on the processing of applications and problems relating to securing access to information related to immigrant status.

By 1975, as part of its activities, the CDP project in Saltley had developed a newsletter, the *Saltley News,* as a significant vehicle for communication with the Urdu-speaking immigrant community. It proved to be so popular that its focus was redesigned so that it had a greater Birmingham rather than predominantly Saltley focus (National Community Development Project, 1975:20). The CDP project in Batley conducted a survey encompassing both the social and economic needs of the Pakistani and Gujerati communities, as well as the religious-cultural needs of these groups (McGrath, 1975). Coventry had developed a network of language training groups for Asians. Such groups studied basic communication skills and met in homes, temples, schools, and in a factory setting.

Neighborhood Information and Advice

All the CDP experiments have sought to improve the level of relevant social welfare information available to residents. The Community Development Project Working Group has indicated that these approaches have involved these basic activities: "(i) shopfront information centers, either shared with the project officers or as independent resident controlled centers; (ii) work with community groups offering information, advice, technical expertise (e.g., legal, welfare and housing rights), grants and hardware (duplicating facilities, video t.v. equipment); (iii) project news-sheets disseminating information and data, or community newspapers run by local residents with support from CDP" (Community Development Project Working Group, 1974:180).

At Cleator Moor a general information service dealt with a range of issues including bus fares, available housing and welfare benefits; Coventry's CDP provided service emphasis on legal and welfare rights of residents. In the minds of many residents of the Batley CDP, the informal advice center was considered the most desirable means of facilitating eligible local residents' applications for income rebates or allowance subsidies on their rentals (Taylor-Gooby, 1976:45).[3] Another factor which may have affected neighborhood popularity of the advice center in this case is that the Batley Center—the Advice Center for Tenants—was initially controlled by neighborhood residents.

A related move fostered by some CDPs seeking to improve service delivery was the movement to promote integration of services at the local level. Such integration occurred in two CDPs (Liverpool and Paisley) which established community service centers bringing together several local authority services in one common structure. The aim herein was to integrate and coordinate neighborhood service activities and *then to link such services to neighborhood resident-run information services.*

CONCLUSIONS

This paper has attempted to review briefly the essentially local decentralized nature of British neighborhood social service. As such services are essentially funded by local revenues—in areas of economic decline—local officials have difficulty funding adequate services. In addition, linkages between national planning of social services and implementation of neighborhood social service projects are weak. The national government has not exercised authority with respect to the implementation of such local services. To a very great extent, in a nation noted for the degree of authority of the national government, neighborhood social services delivery provides an instance of an area where the authority of local government still holds sway.

The main focus of this paper has been a review of a primarily nationally funded project, the Community Development Project, undertaken by the Home Office to strengthen social welfare service provision in selected neighborhood areas of economic and social deprivation. Among the goals of such projects have been emphasis on provision of services to particular risk groups—children, the aged, and recent immigrants. Among the approaches used have been the development of information and advice centers, organizational development to articulate consumer needs, technical assistance regarding legal advice, and social welfare rights, as well as better coordination of local social service delivery. The projects undertaken fall under the jurisdiction of local government authority. At times, community workers and residents of Community Development Project areas have clashed with respect to issues of "community control" and the appropriate level of local advocacy for the demands of poor residents. Also, many community workers, while viewing neighborhood personal social service activities as helpful to residents, despaired as to the ability of such services to alleviate the poverty of residents without the presence of major national institutional changes.

In spite of the limitatations of the CDP experiment, some successful efforts have been made to consolidate existing neighborhood social services, to develop new social service programs as needs are discovered, to improve communications with potential consumers regarding the social welfare entitlements, and to improve coordination of existing neighborhood services.

NOTES

1. The parliamentary statute governing Scottish personal social services is separate, although similar, to that governing personal social services in England and Wales. One important difference is that Scottish local authorities include probation activities among the personal social services while such activities are not considered personal social services in England and Wales.

2. For example, CDP areas such as Canning Town, North Shields, and Southwark suffered from the decline of port-related industries; Oldham and Batley were characterized by declining textile industries; mining enterprises had shut down in Upper Afan, Cleator

Moor, and Saltley. Benwell and Coventry's Hillfields also experienced industrial decline. With economic decline, skilled workers left the areas, leaving behind concentrations of low-income families, elderly residents and semi- and unskilled workers.

3. Those eligible individuals living in public "council housing" receive rent "rebates"; those renting privately receive a rental "allowance." These amounts are received from the national government.

REFERENCES

BENINGTON, J. (1975). "The flaw in the pluralist heaven: Changing strategies in the Coventry CDP." Pp. 174-187 in R. Lees and G. Smith (eds.), Action-research in community development. London: Routledge and Kegan Paul.

Committee of Inquiry (1976). Report—Local government finance. London: Her Majesty's Stationery Office.

Committee on Local Authority and Allied Personal Services (1968). Report. London: Her Majesty's Stationery Office.

Community Development Project Working Group (1974). "The British National Community Development Project, 1969-1974." Community Development Journal, 9(October):162-185.

CORINA, L. (1976). "Community work and local authority decision making: Potential and problems." Community Development Journal, 11(October):174-184.

DAVIES, B., BARTON, A., and McMILLIAN, I. (1972). Variations in children's services among British urban authorities. London: G. Bell and Sons.

Department of Health and Social Security (1975). Annual Report, 1974. London: Her Majesty's Stationery Office.

EDGINGTON, J. (1974). "The Batley battle." New Society, 29(September 5):611-612.

GLENNERSTER, H. (1975). "Social services in Great Britain: Taking care of people." Pp. 69-111 in D. Thursz and J.L. Vigilante (eds.), Meeting human needs. Beverly Hills, Calif.: Sage.

GUTHRIE, E. (1970). "Local authorities and social change." Pp. 15-18 in A. Lapping (ed.), Fabian Tract 400-Community Action. London: Fabian Society.

KAHN, A.J. (1973). Social policy and social services. New York: Random House.

LEES, R. (1975). "Curriculum development and the community approach." Pp. 123-127 in R. Lees and G. Smith (eds.), Action-research in community development. London: Routledge and Kegan Paul.

MARRIS, P., and REIN, M. (1973). Dilemmas of social reform. Chicago: Aldine.

McGRATH, M. (1975). "Social needs of an immigrant population." Pp. 128-139 in R. Lees and G. Smith (eds.), Action-research in community development. London: Routledge and Kegan Paul.

National Community Development Project (1976). Rates of decline: An unacceptable base of public finance. London: CDP Information and Intelligence Unit.

——— (1975). Forward plan 1975-1976. London: CDP Information and Intelligence Unit.

TAYLOR-GOOBY, P.F. (1976). "Rent benefits and tenants' attitudes: The Batley rent rebate and allowance study." Journal of Social Policy, 5(January):33-48.

UTTING, B. (1975). "Social work: Where people are resources." New Society, 31(February 20):453-456.

13

COMMUNITY WORK IN INDIA:
EVALUATION IN THE HEALTH SECTOR

STAN WEISNER

COMMUNITY WORK EVALUATION:
AN INNOVATIVE APPROACH

In the first volume of this series, Thursz and Vigilante (1975:21) suggested that "perhaps the most significant social service required and used today by both developing and developed countries is community organization." Arthur Dunham's (1968) comprehensive survey found that community work[1] programs and methods are operating in over 60 countries. Therefore, the purpose of this paper is to present a new and practical approach to evaluating a community work program. We will try to assess the impact across 38 villages of community work intervention on a behavioral indicator in one development sector.[2] Although its components are not "new" in and of themselves,[3] together they represent a significant departure from traditional case-by-case "task" and "process" goal assessments. We will attempt to analyze and report the findings of an evaluative study actually carried out in the contest of an ongoing community development program in India. Although fairly specific implications are drawn for community work practice and rural planning strategy in only one development sector (health) and in a rural setting, the approach adopted is viewed as a replicable study design which can be implemented in other cultural contexts and development sectors with the use of comparable evaluative criteria.

More specifically, the approach has at least three distinguishing features. First, it relies on the assumption that community workers as a group, despite the fact that they often view the community as an interrelated system (Ross, 1955; Sanders, 1958), have *differential levels of impact in each field or development sector* in which they are active. Thus, it becomes essential for evaluative purposes that generalist community workers, as well as those active in only one sector, define outcome criteria in terms of discrete areas of people's social and economic lives, i.e., health, agriculture, education, and transportation. In other words, one should be able to determine whether the various activities of the community worker have the same impact on people's health behavior as on their agricultural practices. If not, why not? In which sectors are community workers most effective?

A second component applies the "socio-behavioral" approach suggested by Fellin, Rothman, and others (Fellin et al., 1967; Kunkel, 1970). This approach calls for the development and use of *very specific measureable and observable behavioral indicators to assess change.* Changes in people's behavior, then, become the primary yardstick for measuring success, not the traditional goals of project completion or community participation.

A third dimension involves the issues of selecting the unit of analysis and the methods to be used. In the area of community work evaluation, the most common focus for study has been on the single case—neighborhood, village or regional unit. Often, fascinating action episodes are described in some detail from which a great deal can be learned and applied. Comparative case studies (see Terrell and Weisner, 1976; Das Gupta, 1968) are also frequently used as an efficient and valuable method of inquiry. If, however, the unit of analysis is relatively self-contained and a sufficient number of cases can be isolated for study, the researcher can employ more powerful statistical methods (such as correlation and regression analysis) on a far wider range of community experiences (see, Gilbert and Specht, 1977; Aiken and Alford, 1970).

In the rural Indian context, with somewhat isolated village units organized into regional groupings called development blocks,[4] *a study of the impact of these social service programs and activities across a large number of villages* becomes a very useful avenue for a cross-community survey. While problems of comparability persist, the effects of most of the significant sociodemographic variables can be minimized through the use of purposive sampling techniques and control variables.

Perhaps the most difficult aspect of the type of evaluation effort described above is the chronic problem of data availability. While this might be less problematic in centrally planned economies with more structured information gathering and retrieval systems, it remains a critical concern elsewhere, particularly in the less developed countries. During this study, the author was fortunate enough to be attached to the Government of India's Pilot Research Project in Growth Centers[5] which had collected considerable information between 1971 and 1974 on hundreds of villages in 20 selected blocks throughout the country as part of extensive efforts at developing a workable nationwide rural planning strategy.

Talala Block (Junagadh District) in the southern part of Gujarat, India's westernmost state, was selected as the study site most suited for this investigation (see map in Appendix). Its data base was considered the most reliable by growth center project staff, and its demographic characteristics were typical of most blocks in the project. Its relatively small size (75,000 inhabitants in 49 villages) made additional data collection in the field less difficult for an outside researcher. India's nationwide Community Development Program (started in 1952), as well as a system of primary health care, had been active in the block for over two decades. Thus, Talala Block became the most logical site for an evaluation study of community work in the health sector.

Another major consideration in undertaking a study of this kind involves the selection of the development sector most appropriate for analysis, as well as the specific behavioral criteria which are to be used to assess outcome. Although the setting of behavioral treatment goals at the individual and group level is now commonplace among helping professionals, this has not been the case at the community level. While frequently very useful statistical indicators exist in the areas of economic productivity, public health standards, educational achievement, and so on, they are seldom viewed as possibly being influenced by direct community work intervention. Roland Warren (1966) has tended to view aggregate societal outcomes as "un-planned change" *affecting* individuals and groups.

In this study, utilization levels of public health facilities serve as the central focus of our investigation. Hypotheses are developed which try to explain the variation among the villagers in Talala Block in terms of the utilization behavior at an aggregate and individual level. Various geographic, socioeconomic, and community work factors are tested for their relative power in explaining the dependent variable, utilization. (We will come back to a more specific definition of utilization later on in this paper.)

Utilization analysis is certainly not new in the health field. However, it has generally been applied as a means of identifying groups served or to monitor the impact of a particular program or campaign, and not as a comprehensive evaluative tool in the study of a community intervention method. A question to which utilization analysis can offer some answers was raised almost 20 years ago in India by Dr. M.S. Gore, Dean of the Tata Institute of Social Sciences: "Do we first build and then try to persuade to use? Or persuade first and then provide?" (Government of India, 1957:5). The question has not lost its relevance, nor has it been satisfactorily answered.

One way to approach this question involves an investigation of facilities and services available to user groups and their level of utilization. In the area of health, this kind of "study of the sociology of utilization of innovations and health facilities [was suggested as a] productive area of research" in a conference on Behavioral Research in Health and Extension Education (Government of India, 1957:42). Although utilization of health facilities as a social indicator appears to be a complex, long-range objective, "steps in this direction are needed as part of a general effort to improve the means of evaluating the performance of social systems" (Lieban, 1973:1055).

One important task of the planner is to ensure that there are sufficient resources available at the right place and time to meet consumer demand.[6] For community workers, one key task is to educate and encourage utilization among those people in need of the service provided. The corresponding goal of the planner would entail utilization of services sufficient to satisfy a "diagnosed need" (Bradshaw, 1972). Although other factors will intervene in this three stage process of provision, encouragement, and utilization, utilization can provide a measure which assesses to some extent the efforts of community workers and planners to reach a common goal.[7]

In the following sections of this paper, the various background, theoretical, and procedural elements that made up the body of this study are discussed. First, the methods of data collection and analysis are discussed along with the three groups of hypotheses. The first major section is then devoted to an overview of community work and rural planning methods (based on the concept of growth centers) as they have been developed in India. This somewhat detailed review allows the reader unfamiliar with the Indian experience to place the study itself in a broader framework. The next section is concerned with the issues of rural health in India and health conditions in the block studied. Both these sections highlight community work and other antecedents of utilization behavior tested in the study. In the last section, specific hypotheses are explicated along with a discussion of the empirical findings and their practice implications.

ZEROING IN ON UTILIZATION:
METHODOLOGY AND HYPOTHESES

Methods of Data Collection and Analysis

The data analyzed in this study comes from two main sources. Village survey data from Talala Block in southern Gujarat were collected over a two year period (1971-1973) by the Government of India's Pilot Research Project in Growth Centers. The primary purpose of the project was to test 36 hypotheses formulated to explain the dependent variable in the study—utilization rates by villages of the block primary health center in Talala (the largest town in the block and the block headquarters).

Additional survey data were gathered in the block during subsequent fieldwork. These data focused more directly on the providers and users of the various health services in the block. Intake records at the block primary health center and other local health facilities were examined, the interviews were conducted with a random sample of actual users of the facilities (n = 227); in-depth interviews were conducted with heads of households (n = 31). The sample of household heads came from five selected villages in one region in the block and involved purposive sampling techniques to ensure proportional caste representation from each village. These data, in conjunction with interviews with all government doctors and a sample of community health workers and private medical practitioners active in the block, provided the information used to supplement the growth center project village data. They provided a means for testing out in the field preliminary findings based on analysis of village level data collected by the growth center project field staff.

Standard statistical reporting procedures were used to present descriptive data. The major method of analysis involved the use of correlation (Pearson's r and Yules Q) and regression. In order to explain as much as possible of the variance in our dependent variable, utilization, a series of explanatory variables were operationalized for the village level data (n = 38) and a "best model" developed.[8] These measures served as the social indicators of concepts associated with community work intervention, growth center planning and the socio-economic context.

The basic analytical framework for data analysis involved testing the predictive power of variables within each of these three categories in terms of their relationship to the utilization of the Primary Health Center in Talala Block. The three groups of hypotheses are introduced below and discussed in more depth in the remainder of the paper.

Three Groups of Hypotheses

Spatial/Institutional Factors

Micro-level planners using a growth center planning strategy (discussed in the following section) rely heavily on spatial and institutional factors in making decisions regarding the placement or expansion of a facility or service, so that the total travel distance for all villages being served is minimized. A second major consideration is the degree to which a village has been able to attract and support social and economic institutions. These selected growth potential villages, assuming they do not already have a health facility in their village, should be more likely to be informed of and use other available facilities.

Therefore, assuming that utilization levels of public health facilities are in part a function of physical accessibility, the hypotheses was that *the greater the physical accessibility (or conversely, the shorter the distance) of a village, the greater the likelihood that villagers would be aware of, seek out, and use public health facilities when needed.* A similar relationship was hypothesized for institutional development and utilization—*the greater the institutional development, the greater the utilization.*

Community Work Intervention Factors

The hypothesis in this second category was simply that *more community work intervention and community level activity will promote greater utilization.*

Assuming that utilization levels of public health facilities are at least in part a result of community work intervention and related community activity, increased utilization should be associated with: (1) a greater number of contacts with community workers, (2) stronger and more active village *panchayats* (village councils), and (3) greater numbers of communication linkages outside the village (radios, postal, correspondence, etc.). In other words, community worker visits and the activity level of community worker generated village processes (such as panchayat activities and the source and level of its financial strength) should produce villages more likely to use available public health facilities.

Socioeconomic Factors

There are also a number of socioeconomic conditions which can play an important role in determining utilization levels. For example, numerous studies (Lerner, 1958; Rogers, 1969) have shown that higher socioeconomic status is associated with innovation adoption. McKinlay (1972) and others (Aday and Eichhorn, 1972) have shown this to be the case for health services utilization. Assuming this also held true for the health sector, the hypothesis was that *villages which were wealthier and had a higher social status than other villages in a block would be more likely to be aware of, seek out, and use public health facilities when needed.*

COMMUNITY WORK IN INDIA:
WHERE IT HAS BEEN AND WHERE IT IS GOING

A Brief Overview

Community work as a method of intervention has many historical and theoretical roots in each part of the world. Historically, in India, one finds two major influences. First is the Gandhian influence with its emphasis on village self-help and self-sufficiency. The second stems from the experiments in India in agricultural extension and community education carried out under British rule. The most notable was a "comprehensive and reproducible method of rural regeneration . . . evolved at Etawah by Albert Mayer, which provided the basic pattern for the country-wide scheme of Community Development and National Extension Service" (Pande, 1967:193).

The basic organizational unit for the program since its inception has been the development block. A Block Development Officer coordinates all development efforts and is assisted by a number of catalytic agents and experts in the fields of education, health, agriculture, animal husbandry, village industry, housing, and so on.

A generalist village level worker, who later in many states was assigned a larger number of villages and more specific functions, is the person largely responsible for maintaining a physical presence in each village of government-sponsored programs. Regular visits are made to organize meetings, informal discussion groups, and demonstrations in order to promote villagers' awareness of better methods and techniques available in the various sectors.

Despite some notable exceptions, when particularly skilled community workers or panchayat leaders have made a difference (see Niehoff, 1966; Biddle and Biddle, 1968; Gangrade, 1968), or when physical targets were reached during the 1950s with modest increases in agricultural production, number of community centers, roads built, wells dug, and so on, by and large, it has been found (Dube, 1958; Taylor, 1965) that the basic attitudes and behavior of the people have not been substantially changed.

On a larger national scale, the program has been subjected in recent years to a growing amount of empirically based studies, critical of its inability to promote sustained development efforts (Nair, 1961; Bendix, 1964; Battcharyya, 1970; Hunter, 1970). Politically, it has also lost a great deal of its former popularity. Some (Berreman, 1963; Moore, 1966)[9] have seriously questioned the applicability of the community development model to Indian cultural and political conditions.

Alternative strategies have been explored in various parts of the country to at least ensure an increase in vital agricultural production. Since 1961, for example, a pilot project, the Package Program, financed jointly by the Government of India and the Ford Foundation, has been in operation in 15 districts to determine the effects of and problems involved in intensive agriculture. The focus was shifted away from the individual village to area wide planning of support services, including transportation, storage, and credit.

Although the program in these regions did result in impressive gains in agricultural production, it apparently has had other less favorable long-range political effects (Frankel, 1971). One of the major policy contributions of the program was its emphasis on area-wide planning, even at the district level, and its recognition of the need for a total package of supportive services to supplement the introduction of more modern agricultural techniques. It was this area-wide focus which helped shape the growth center planning strategy of the seventies, although it dealt with all sectors and sought practical methods for planning services in even smaller regional units (Andrade, 1970).

Lessons drawn from India's earlier experiments, its Community Development Program and the Intensive Agricultural Development Program (the "Package Program"), are varied and have led to little consensus as to their implications. Some claim that the community development approach was never really tried and that village energies were never tapped to their fullest potential by the often undertrained and overworked village level worker. Others point to the success of India's Intensive Agricultural Development Program areas and their sharp increases in agricultural productivity during the late sixties, but few claim this approach would either be reproducible in more than a few select areas or that it would be appropriate in other sectors.

As India's Community Development Program moves through its third decade, it will continue to find itself subjected to sharp criticism. Yet, no one realistically foresees its disappearance from the scene. Rather, there is a continuing search for viable alternatives to revitalize its basic structure and methods. The emergence of the growth center planning approach in the 1970s has provided the opportunity for community workers, micro-planners, and development administrators alike to incorporate the best of both strategies. Wanmali (1970:iii) has noted that this approach to rural development will be "instrumental in shedding light on the future role and form of the community development movement."

In many ways the two approaches contrast. The community development approach has traditionally been village based, relying on "felt needs" to be expressed by each village and encouraging the formulation of village "task" goals. Growth center planning, on the other hand, is more concerned with the formulation of regional goals based on an integrated framework. The roles that the village level change-agent and the micro-level planner play in this new framework will be determined only after careful analysis of existing conditions in the health sector, as well as other sectors in which they will jointly be involved. In the following section, we take a look at the methods associated with the growth center approach.

Rural Planning: The Growth Center Approach

For years, the emphasis in Indian rural planning has been on village development, based on the assumption that the village unit could and should meet most basic human needs. Much of this can be traced to the important role of the village in Indian society.[10] In recent years, some (Shah,1974:228) have recognized the concomitant need to "develop the intermediary centers, the market centers, or large-size villages" as opposed to the former village focus of the Community Development Program. In the late sixties, still others (Ghidyal, 1967:12) were calling for "greater attention . . . devoted to intervillage and regional projects that will lead to area development . . . and articulate the village better with the region and the nation."

In 1968, the Ministry of Community Development and Cooperation submitted its proposal for a pilot study of what became the Pilot Research Project in Growth Centers (Council for Social Development and Ford Foundation, 1969). Other public and private organizations were beginning to move in a similar direction (Andrade, 1970; Wanmali, 1970; Gupta, 1971; Sen, 1972; Tamil Nadu Nutrition Project, 1973). Micro-level planning entails many different approaches depending on the context and personnel involved, resources available, and so forth. For the purposes of this study, the focus will be on growth center planning in the health sector and the basic framework and methodology developed by the Growth Center Project.[11]

In pursuing this study in the health sector, elements of both community work and micro-planning are analyzed, and implications are drawn from both strategies. It is hoped in this way that findings can shed light on both strategies—traditional community work and growth center planning, which Ensminger and Loomis (Government of India, 1972b:2) have called the "next logical phase of [India's] Community Development Program."

RURAL HEALTH CARE

India's Public Health Center Scheme

The Indian government's response to the problems of rural health care has relied heavily on its nationwide public health center scheme. Based on the recommendations of the influential Shore Committee Report (Government of India, 1946), a regional network of state-administered primary health centers with subcenters was established after 1952 in order to provide primarily allopathic ("Western") health care to the rural population as part of the Community Development Program (also established in 1952). The objective was to provide an integrated program of preventive and curative health care on a block-wide, regional basis. Within two decades, over 5,200 public health centers were established, with at least one in every community development block (Government of India, 1972a:33).

The centers are primarily outpatient clinics, although most are equipped with 10 to 12 beds. Each is supposed to be staffed by two generalist physicians—one for health and one for family planning—and a supporting staff of nurses, midwives, vaccinators, community health workers, and other paramedical personnel. Additional centers are currently being planned in order to reduce the population dependency ratio for each facility as part of the new "basic minimum needs" program in the current Fifth Five Year Plan. The national goal as stated in the plan will be one primary health center for every 32,000 to 50,000 people, supported by eight to 10 subcenters located in selected villages throughout a block. The major rationale for this expansion is to increase the physical accessibility of the facilities to the more remote villages. It will require almost doubling the current number of public facilities and will require approximately 40% of the entire money allocated for health in the Fifth Plan (Gwatkin, 1974:92).

In addition to the system of Western medicine introduced through the primary health centers, there exists an entire array of alternative sources of curative medical care. Private practitioners, representing a wide assortment of medical transitions, are to be found in practically every region of the country.[12]

According to Health Ministry reports, the nationwide primary health center network sees nearly 200,000,000 patients per year—equivalent to one visit per year by one-third of India's population. Primary health center utilization figures vary dramatically from state to state, although the reasons for this are not clear in view of the supposedly uniform pattern of services throughout the country. An accurate figure on the number of patients being treated by private practitioners is not available, although it is assumed to be much higher. Government licensing regulations for private practitioners are not strictly enforced, particularly outside of the larger cities and towns, and self-regulation has not taken place on a formal basis. Qualifications among practitioners vary greatly. Approximately one-half of the existing primary health centers are staffed with two fully licensed physicians. Almost all the rest have at least one (Government of India, 1972a:33).[13]

Decisions by consumers about seeking health care depend on a number of factors ranging from convenience and necessity to a belief system which is not yet fully understood in terms of its implications for health utilization. While the success of efforts by medical practitioners and supporting personnel to foster better health care hinges to a large extent on their ability to effectively institute preventive measures (such as health education), they must also be able to consistently attract patients in need of curative care.

To accomplish this within the public sector, some advocate the provision of more accessible and better equipped public health facilities in order to increase the number of options available to consumers and thus increase utilization. Others claim that differences between the local "health culture" and the nonindigenous modern medical system are so great that until some degree of "cultural congruence" is attained between the two social systems, efforts at the delivery of modern health services will continue to be frustrated. Those who advocate increased facilities usually cite the need for comprehensive area planning which determines the optimal locations of new facilities on a region by region basis. Those more concerned with the social distance between the rural health centers and their potential patients call for increased intervention at the village level by community health workers and a heightened awareness of the local "health culture" by medical practitioners (Lewis, 1955; Banerji, 1973).

Arguments for more public facilities are based on the assumption that there is currently an unmet need for medical services which cannot be completely satisfied by the private sector. Arguments for increased community intervention at the village level seem to reflect the feeling that the need has not yet been fully recognized among potential users and requires considerable primary health center supported community outreach and education. In either case, however, it has been acknowledged that utilization levels of existing and planned facilities need to be increased. Since many rural primary health centers are not now operating at full capacity, governmental expansion plans have been questioned.

In studying the utilization patterns of one primary health center in Talala Block, we in no way begin to address the dilemmas surrounding the actual role of the primary health center in the overall health delivery system. But we do raise questions which help to identify the determinants of utilization in an effort to improve the effectiveness of health planners and community health workers to facilitate access and use of the primary health center by the villages served. This approach accepts implicitly the fact that the primary health center is still considered the most efficient way, organizationally, to deliver health care to rural villagers and that it will remain the keystone of India's rural health program. While we may be ignoring more pressing concerns about the overall direction and effectiveness of the system as a whole, increased utilization levels would result in existing public facilities being used at a level closer to capacity, in part overcoming the "present well-known underutilization of many rural health centers" (Kakar et al., 1972:1).

The Study Site: Talala Block, Gujarat

As a study site, Talala serves as a typical block, at least in terms of its utilization levels and health conditions. Its current population is 75,000, which is growing at a yearly rate of about 5%. The predominant caste is Patel (60%). Approximately 10% are considered "scheduled castes," primarily Kolis, Harijans, and Siddis.[14]

The two major crops in the area have traditionally been groundnuts and wheat. The net area sown is 57%. About 15% of the cropped area is irrigated, mainly by tubewell. There is no regulated market in Talala Block. Agricultural produce is taken to Veraval, a nearby port town. Although there are no large agro-based industries, there is one small-scale sugar processing plant. Talala town is located on a rail line (which has five stations in the block) and on a state highway (see map in Appendix). Eighteen villages have all-weather roads and 31 have dirt roads which are impassable during the monsoon and a two to three month period thereafter—a period of almost six months.

Twenty-six percent of all adults are literate, a somewhat lower figure than the district figure of 31% and the state figure of 36%. Educational institutions in the block consist of 54 primary schools and four middle or high schools located in Talala and three other smaller villages.

There are 39 established credit cooperatives in the block with only 28 actually functioning. No other forms of cooperatives are to be found, although plans are in operation to develop a cooperative sugar factory in Talala.

As in most community development blocks in the country, Talala has a primary health center in its block headquarters. The center is staffed by two medical officers (one focusing on family planning) and a full cadre of supporting staff, both in the center and stationed throughout the block in villages or in one of the five subhealth centers and dispensaries, or one of the four family planning centers. In addition to these centers, there are two allopathic dispensaries.

There are also at least 25 registered private practitioners providing curative health care. One-half of them are located in Talala town, but make visits to villages when called upon. None of the private practitioners in the block is formally as qualified as the government physicians, although this has in no way detracted from their overall popularity among the villagers in the block.

Interviews with health officials and a search of available statistics shed additional light on some other aspects of health care in the area. First, Talala is fairly typical in its utilization patterns, its level of development, and the kinds of health services available. Second, the kinds of health services utilized range widely between publicly provided facilities and allopathic, ayurvedic (traditional), and homeopathic private practitioners. Third, the range of illnesses is characteristic for rural regions of India, the most commonly treated diseases being chronic fevers, gastro-intestinal disorders, and skin-related problems. Major causes of illness include poor sanitation and water services. Fourth, the utilization rates for the major public health facilities are far below their potential capacity for service to the region, and the short-term trend does not indicate any significant increase in the numbers treated.

Health Care Utilization Models

The discussion which follows introduces some ideas concerning the antecedents of utilization of public services in general and health services in particular. The purpose is to put the specific study of public health care utilization in Gujarat in a wider theoretical perspective. Although the study itself is more limited in scope, it is important to consider this broader framework.

In analyzing the utilization (or demand) of a public good, one faces a dilemma addressed by Buchanan (1968:5):

> Decisions on the demand-supply of public goods are made through political, not market institutions, and there is no analogue to competitive order that eases the analytical task.

This raises serious questions as to the practical values of the utilization measure for market analysis involving public goods. In the context of this study, however, utilization is defined more narrowly as the *actual demand for a particular public good (i.e., curative health services) as measured by the number of users per unit of time.* [15]

An advantage in "borrowing" the concept of utilization of demand from more traditional kinds of economic analysis is its relevance to related public activities in the health sector—community health work and planning. It has been suggested that

> getting individuals to accept and use socially provided benefits in socially preferred ways is a universally valid social objective. Though there is no

sure way to make this occur ... it is entirely possible to increase the likelihood of it occurring (Miller and Pruger, 1975:3-4).

One way to effect this increase in health is to study patterns of utilization in order to better inform community workers and planners operating in the field. By identifying the various factors that affect *at least one observable end product of their efforts,* i.e., public health facility utilization, they can better set priorities and plan activities.

In presenting a case for health services utilization models, Veeder (1975) identifies the major studies involved in the explication of these models. They represent research in the field over the past 20 years. The three most frequently cited models come from Rosenstock (1966), Suchman (1965) and Anderson (1968).[16] A common theme in all three is a commitment to the identification of the most important antecedents of health utilization in order to better understand and improve the delivery of health services. Differences in the models are more in emphasis than in content.

In developing hypotheses which could explain health utilization in this study, similar elements to those found in the Rosenstock, Suchman, and Anderson formulations are tested. Of the three groups of factors in which Veeder (1975:106) found general agreement regarding availability, accessibility, and demography, those involving social group influences are particularly difficult to measure in a study which uses the village as the unit of analysis. Nevertheless, this additional dimension—the "social group" external influence caused by community work intervention—was included and assessed for its relative impact on utilization behavior in the present study.

FACTORS EXPLAINING UTILIZATION:
SOME EMPIRICAL FINDINGS AND THEIR IMPLICATIONS

Overview

In the following section, data is presented which confirms some of our hypotheses and rejects others. The most striking finding is the *weak association between our utilization measure and all community work intervention indicators at both the village and individual level.* Variables which prove to be the best predictors of utilization behavior are *distance,* the *existence of a village cooperative,* and three socioeconomic indicators—*wealth, literacy,* and *caste.* A series of practice implications in the health sector for community work and micro-level planning suggested by these findings is presented in this section.

Findings based on individual data, while generally confirming those based on village data, do not always correspond with findings reported at the aggregate village level. This should be kept in mind in assessing the impact of each of the factors studied. For example, while individual membership in a village credit cooperative does not seem to make a significant difference in reported utilization behavior, the existence of a cooperative in a village does seem to have a slightly positive effect at the aggregate level.

Discussion of Significant Findings

All the specific factors which were originally expected to explain utilization of the primary health center per 100 population (utilization/100) are listed below with their zero-order correlations. An examination of this list would indicate which among all the specific hypotheses showed a moderately strong correlation with utilization/100.[17] The purpose of this approach is to highlight through correlational analysis some of the important variables related to utilization behavior[18] and then draw implications from them for community work and planning in the health sector. Also included in this discussion are the results of regression analysis to find the best single set of predictors of health care utilization in Talala Block. First, geographic and institutional factors associated with the growth center planning strategy are discussed. Then findings related to community work indicators are presented, followed by an analysis of each of the significant socioeconomic variables.

Spatial/Institutional Factors

In this study, the first group of indicators tested attempted to critically assess across villages the impact of physical accessibility and institutional development on the dependent variable utilization/100. Both serve as significant inputs into a growth center planning process. In regard to distance, we hypothesized that *the greater the physical accessibility, the greater the village's utilization/100.*

The inverse relationship between distance and utilization was found to be a moderately strong one, indicating that residents in villages closer to the primary health center did in fact make greater use of its services. Given the poor transportation system in the block, this is not an unexpected finding. Institutional development seemed to make no difference in regard to utilization behavior with the one exception of the cooperative. We consider both of these findings below.

Geography. One of the most commonly accepted explanators of utilization behavior is the physical distance which separates the consumer from the service desired. Decreasing use with increased distance has long been found (Denune, 1927) to hold true for a variety of services, particularly in rural communities. Spatial variables as factors in utilization of medical services have been studied for more than 40 years and have underscored this relationship (Shannon et al., 1969).

Based on village level data, utilization/100 showed a standardized zero-order correlation of −.42 with distance from Talala. To further test this finding, a

Table 1: Zero-order Correlations with Utilization/100
         Population $(r_{UX})^a$

		r_{UX}
I.	Spatial/Institutional Factors	
	A. Geography	
	1. KILOMETER DISTANCE TO PRIMARY HEALTH CENTER	-.42
	2. Transportability index	
	(conveyance - weighted distance)	-.42
	B. Institutional development	
	1. Total number of institutions	-.07
	2. Presence/absence of critical infrastructure	
	a. Middle school	.03
	b. Electricity	-.04
	c. Village level worker headquarters	.06
	d. CREDIT COOPERATIVE	.20
	e. Post Office	.003
	f. Community center	.01
II.	Community Work Intervention Factors	
	A. 1. Village level worker visits/month	.18
	2. Development officer visits/month (Block development	
	officer and village level worker)	.16
	B. Health worker visits/month	.03
	C. Panchayat meetings/year	.15
	D. Panchayat resources/100 population	.10
	E. Panchayat resources-percent of local contributions	-.05
	F. Number of radios/100 population	.24
	G. Number of letters in and out/100 population	-.19
III.	Socio-economic Factors	
	A. Percent of landless households	-.10
	B. 1. Percent of employed male adults	-.07
	2. Labor out-migration	-.13
	C. Wealth indicators	
	1. Percent net area irrigated to net area sown	.26
	2. Percent of area sown more than once	.05
	3. Percent of crops marketed	.09
	4. Average wage	.07
	5. NUMBER OF BICYCLES/100 POPULATION	.59
	6. Number of bullock carts/100 population	.31
	7. Number of bicycles and bullock carts/100 population	.41
	D. Literacy indicators	
	1. PERCENT LITERATE (1971)	
	a. TOTAL POPULATION	.34
	b. Female	.34
	c. Male	.31
	2. Percent increase in literacy rates (1961-71)	
	a. Female	.28
	b. Male	.04
	E. PERCENT SCHEDULED CASTE FAMILIES	-.26
	F. a. Death rate	-.21
	b. Infant mortality rate	-.21
	G. Population size	.08

a. Variables which remained significant at the .05 level in subsequent regression analysis are shown in capital letters. The most reliable indicator with the highest correlation within a common sub-group (spatial measures, number of conveyances and literacy) was selected for further analysis.

similar analysis of utilization of the primary health center was carried out in two other study blocks involved in the growth center project: Thaneswar, in the Punjab, and Ghazipur, in Uttar Pradesh. Thaneswar, a more developed block, and Ghazipur, a less developed block than Talala, both had similar correlations between utilization/100 and distance of −.37 and −.47, respectively. With the single exception of number of bicyles/100, distance was the only factor which was significantly correlated with utilization in all three blocks. When distance was tested in various regression models with other variables, it alone remained significant at the .05 level, explaining 17% of the variance in utilization/100 (R^2 = .17). Since it is a unidimensional, bivariate relationship, it can easily be displayed graphically (see Table 2).

This graph indicates specifically that for every 10 kilometers distance closer a village is to the primary health center, approximately five more people/100 population will attend the primary health center in a given year. Thus, in a village with 2,000 residents, assuming all else constant, there should be an additional 100 visits each year to the primary health center for every 10 kilometers the village lies closer to the primary health center.

The sample of patients interviewed at the health centers mentioned distance as a health care problem in only two of 92 reported difficulties stated by interviewees. However, these were respondents who had arrived already at the center and were in the process of receiving treatment. They also tended to come from nearby villages, and so were less likely to report distance as a serious problem than respondents from a random sample.

The household sample shows a somewhat different pattern. When the respondents were asked specifically about problems related to the location of a local health facility, they overwhelmingly reported distance to be a major problem. Of the 31 households interviewed, 24 of the 25 respondents who mentioned any problem at all mentioned distance as a major problem in utilization.

The distance problem raises the issue of the role of transporation as a mitigating factor in regard to problems of facility location and distance. Certainly, ownership of private, as well as access to public conveyances can play a significant role in explaining differences in utilization behavior both at the village and the individual level.

From the initial analysis of growth center village level data, the number of bicycles and bullock carts/100 population (as indicators of private conveyance

Table 2: Utilization/100 by Kilometer Distance from Talala Primary Health Center

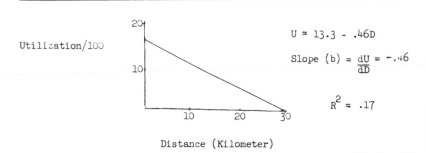

a. The slope (b) is not standardized.

mobility) seemed to be a highly plausible determinent of utilization behavior. It alone explained 34.7% of the variance in utilization/100 and remained significant at the .05 level in models with other variables. Particularly in an area with few hills and other natural obstacles, and where roads are of sufficient quality to allow for easy travel (as is the case in the near vicinity of Talala town), the role of the bicycle and bullock cart was seen as a very important one, both for the individual owner as well as when aggregated for any one village. Subsequent analysis in the field, however, did much to call this initial conjecturing into question. Over half of the health center patients coming from outside travel by foot or use public transportation, and access to private conveyances is more an occasional convenience than a frequently relied upon means of intervillage transporation.[19] (Reference to this measure as a significant indicator of wealth is made later in this section.)

Issues of transportation notwithstanding, geographic distance of a village from a health center clearly serves as one of the strongest predictors of utilization. It seems to act as a powerful spatial and structural feature inhibiting usage of public health facilities—a fact sometimes overlooked by eager outreach workers. This underscores the importance of a growth center planning approach for the health sector and points to the need for decentralizing facilities and making them physically accessible to potential users. For health planners determining placement of public health facilities below the block level, careful consideration will have to be given to the goal of minimizing overall travel distance for all affected villages.

For community workers, the significance of the distance factor should raise questions as to their potential impact in the most remote villages. Even the staunchest Gandhian advocate of village self-sufficiency would not deny the growing need for geographically more accessible modern medical facilities. Clearly, the efforts by community workers to noticeably affect utilization levels are going to continue to be hampered by problems associated with geography and transportation.

In order to maximize future community work intervention efforts in the health sector, priority villages might be selected which are in the "middle range" in terms of their physical proximity from the nearest primary health center. Thus, intervention would be focused on moderately "distant" villages as targets for change, rather than on the closest or most distant villages which would be less likely to benefit from the activities of the community worker.[20]

Institutional Factors. In addition to the spatial dimension, a second vital aspect involves the ranking of villages according to institutional development in order to more readily identify points of potential growth. Villages in which institutional development has been more extensive are assumed to have more dynamism, wealth, attractive physical qualities, and other factors conducive to growth. In planning for the placement of new or enlarged health facilities in rural India, careful allocation decisions are made, based in part, on the relative levels of institutional development among several neighboring villages. Thus, in order to maximize the use of a scarce resource, like a health facility, villages are selected which would attract by their location the greatest number of patients. An hypothesis related to this planning maxim is examined in this study. The hypotheses was that *the greater the overall institutional development of a village (i.e., number of institutions, such as post office, store, school, market, etc.), the greater the utilization/100.*

Another set of hypotheses tested the effect on utilization of the presence in a village of a particular institution. The feeling was that residents of a village which had the advantages of exposure to a particularly useful institution might be more likely to be aware of and use public health facilities more frequently. If any one of the selected institutions did prove to be critical to a higher level of utilization, then this could be seen as a necessary step in the process of institution-building prior to sectoral planning based on anticipated levels of utilization.

In subsequent analysis, our hypothesis regarding the total number of institutions was rejected at the .05 level. With only one execption, the same held true for hypotheses concerned with individual institutions. *The only institution which retained its significance in the regression analysis was the existence of a village credit cooperative.*

Cooperative credit societies potentially play a critical role in the larger rural economy. Although direct benefits come to cultivators and other entrepreneurs in terms of increased access to investable funds, the fact that the societies are so often the only voluntary group or association (other than panchayat and caste associations) in a village gives them special significance.[21] For the village as a whole, the presence of a cooperative can also mean a great deal in terms of sociopolitical and organizational skills learned during and after the formation of the cooperative. Although formal agendas seem to revolve around matters directly related to the extension of credit, the informal airing of more general development problems of the village is very likely to take place, leading to a greater awareness of other social facilities and thus higher utilization. In Warren's (1963) terminology, the village cooperative credit society provides a village unit—"a community"—with an organization which optimally has both strong vertical and horizontal ties.

While on the individual level, membership in a cooperative does not appear to have any influence on utilization behavior, in the absence of other types of voluntary associations at the village level, it does seem to make a difference for the village as a whole. This was confirmed by the Block Extension Officer for Cooperatives in Talala who reported that in villages in which cooperatives were active, health and related issues affecting the village as a whole were often discussed. This in itself could lead to a potentially mobilized community.

Turning to the implications of this finding—the impact of a village cooperative on utilization behavior—although neither a strong one nor one which holds for individual members, illustrates the potential importance in the health sector of the development of voluntary associations in rural village settings. The micro-planner, trying to determine optimal locations for public health facilities, might specifically look for active voluntary associations in assessing potential utilization patterns among villages in an entire block.

For the community worker, the knowledge of the relationship between the presence of a cooperative and higher utilization could be extremely helpful in setting priorities. For instance, rather than pursue activities directly aimed at changing health behavior (like organizing talks, holding meetings, or visiting families—all aimed at raising health awareness and utilization), a more effective policy might be to promote the creation of appropriate voluntary associations (like a village credit cooperative or even a village health cooperative) as an intermediary step to the longer range goal of increased public health facility utilization.

Community Work Intervention Factors

The next group of hypotheses tested a number of indicators of the kinds of village level activity which are performed by or through community workers or panchayats and serve some educative function in the area of health as well as other sectors. The hypotheses generally tested the assumption that *a village with more of any of these factors would tend to have higher utilization levels.* As mentioned previously, all of these hypotheses were, however, rejected at the .05 level of significance.

For the 38 villages included in the sample, the number of visits by extension personnel, frequency of village panchayat meetings, strength (measured in terms of financial resources) of the local panchayat, and number of communication linkages (radios and letters) to the outside world made no difference in determining utilization levels across villages. Although the indicators fail to capture any qualitative dimensions of community work, they give a strong indication that more visits, more meetings, stronger and more active panchayats, and increased communication linkages will *not* necessarily lead to higher utilization levels of public health centers. Given the high level of manpower and resources that have been put into this type of activity in the past, serious questions are raised about the efficacy of these efforts in the health sector. To more accurately assess the meaning of these findings, additional field data concerned with the above indicators is analyzed below. Also a more qualitative discussion of the community worker in Talala Block is presented, which sheds some light on the kind of community worker active in the block. First, let us examine on the individual level the impact on utilization behavior of community health work visits.

A community worker visits a rural, often isolated village for many reasons. In most cases, however, he serves a vital linkage function with the outside world. In the health sector, this tie is particularly valuable since current and proposed government health programs are often discussed along with health education principles, family planning issues, and so forth. In most of India, promoting the residents' awareness of these programs and facilities and advocating their use are also common tasks of the outreach worker (Gandhigram Institute, 1972). Thus, one hypothesis tested in this study examines the relationship between the *quantity* of these visits and public health facility utilization.

Our village data rejected this notion. Weak, though positive correlations of .18 for village level workers, .16 for development officers, and .03 for community health workers were not significant at the .05 level. Additional data from the household sample of the general population of users and nonusers tend to substantiate our findings on the village level. In fact, a fairly strong *negative* relationship was found between community health worker visits and health utilization in the household sample.

Twenty-four out of 31 respondents had been visited by at least one community worker in the past year. The purpose of the visits was often little more than to inquire about malaria symptoms or to give a small pox vaccination or to offer information about family planning if adoption of the practice was desired.

In the health center sample of users, a slight positive relationship was found between those who had been seen by a health visitor, a family planning worker, a vaccinator, or a malaria worker, and those with a higher number of doctor visits.

Note, however, that this data is from a sample of *users,* who are more likely to have a higher utilization rate than the general population and to have been affected by community worker visits.

Table 3: Number of Visits to Doctor Per Family Member Per Year
By Whether a Family Had Been Visited By a Community
Health Worker in the Previous Year (Household Sample)

		Utilization			
		High[a]	Low		
Visited by					
a Community	Yes	10	14	24	
Health Worker	No	4	2	6	
		14	16	30[b]	Q = -.47

a. In the household sample, the mean dividing point is 1.5 doctor visits per household member per year.
b. In the household sample, one respondent "didn't know."

Table 4: Number of Visits to Doctor Per Family Member Per Year
By Whether a Family Had Been Visited By A Community
Health Worker in the Previous Year (Health Center Sample)

		Utilization					
		High[a]	Low				
Visited by	Yes	65	53	118			
a Community							
Health Worker	No	29	40	69			
		94	93	187[b]	Q	=	.25

a. In the health center sample, the mean dividing point is 2.0 doctor visits per household member per year.
b. In the health center sample, 40 of the 227 respondents could not remember.

Health talks and demonstrations by community workers in the village itself can also serve a vital function in promoting health center utilization. Several studies have successfully tried to isolate and measure their impact (note studies by Singh and Sen Gupta, 1965; Roy and Kivlin, 1968; Das Gupta, 1968; Gangrade, 1968; Mehta, 1972). Our findings, however, both on a village and individual level, fail to show a strong relationship between village health talks and utilization. (However, such talks might be considered a more accurate assessment of the *quality* of the extension work than frequency of visits.)

Another avenue through which village residents are informed of and urged to use existing government sources is meetings of village leaders. Village council meetings are often used as a forum for discussion of health and other issues concerning daily life in a particular village. Village leaders can significantly influence an entire village population. The continuing growth and development of strong village councils is also a function of a village outreach worker, and a strong and active village council is one important vehicle for effective community work. The hypothesis was that the following three measures are

Table 5: Number of Visits to Doctor Per Family Member Per Year
By Whether a Person Had Heard a Village Health Talk
(Household Sample)

		Utilization					
		High	Low				
HEARD	Yes	5	9	14			
Village							
Health Talk	No	9	7	16			
		14	16	30	Q	=	-.12

positively related to public health facility utilization: (1) the frequency of panchayat meetings, (2) the financial strength of the panchayat, and (3) the degree to which the panchayat is supported financially by village dues and contributions as opposed to outside financial aid. Each of these hypothesized relationships to health utilization did not, however, hold in this study.

In cross-village multivariate analysis, the two hypotheses regarding village panchayat strength (panchayat resources/100 population and local panchayat resources as a percent of total resources) and health utilization were rejected. Although the zero-order correlation between number of meetings in a village and utilization was as high as .15, it was not a significant factor at the .05 level in the various models generated in regression analysis.

Using the individual as the unit of analysis, the weak, negative relationship between village meeting attendance and utilization is illustrated in Table 6.

Thus, for the village as a whole, as well as for individuals, varying degrees of panchayat meeting attendance do not seem to have made a difference in explaining utilization behavior. Yet, further analysis in the field not captured by our quantitative measures has provided another view regarding the potential influential role some panchayat leaders can play. In this regard, there has been an increasing amount of literature (Mehta, 1972) in the field of rural leadership in any effort involving social change.

In the household sample, analysis revealed that two of the villages studied (Ankolwadi and Bamanasa) were consistently rated highest by block personnel in terms of their constructive response to a series of curative and preventive health programs. A common distinguishing factor in each village which began to emerge was that both had progressive leaders who were engaged in block level activities. In each village one finds two major block level leaders (in Ankolwadi, the president of the block panchayat; in Bamanasa, the vice-president of the block health committee). Both men are clearly strong leaders within their own communities, similar to others found in neighboring villages, but *each also has stong vertical ties outside his village.* [22]

Table 6: Number of Visits to Doctor Per Family Member Per Year
By Whether a Village Meeting Had Been Attended
(Household Sample)

		Utilization			
		High	Low		
Village	Yes	8	11	19	
Meeting	No	6	5	11	
Attendance		14	16	30	Q = -.25

None of these examples is sufficient in itself to warrant any overall generalizations, although they do shed light on a dimension of panchayat influence not found in our original measure.

In recent years, an increasing amount of literature has been written about the relatively untapped resources of telecommunications in the field of rural development. Its role in innovation diffusion has been highlighted as one of the most vital tools in this process. Particularly in the fields of education and agriculture, the introduction on a large scale of the private and community radio has been a giant step toward linking people and transmitting information rapidly.

Studies by Damle (1956), Neurath and Mathur (1959), Kivlin et al. (1968), Shingi et al. (1973), and others have gone a long way toward understanding the optimal conditions and methods for maximizing the benefits of expanded communication facilities in the various sectors.

Although the *role of the radio across villages was not significant in explaining utilization across villages,* [23] *results showed that those individuals who owned a radio did tend to have a higher utilization.* In the household interviews the utilization rates for radio owners was one-half times greater than for nonowners. The relationship between radio ownership and utilization is shown in Table 7.

To summarize, while we may not be surprised to find community work intervention has had only a residual effect on utilization behavior, compared to geographical and institutional factors, as development planners we should remember to study more carefully the relative importance of the role of community workers in each sector before making unwise resource and personnel allocation decisions.

If, as this study shows, community work intervention—in the form of village contacts, health talks, and purposive efforts toward the development of stronger and more autonomous village level organizations—has failed to significantly affect use levels of government health facilities, then either village level intervention methods need to be drastically altered or practice goals changed.

Isolating those factors which do significantly shape desired behavioral goals and then integrating them into practice seems to be a logical first step toward formulating an effective intervention strategy. The following section continues that process based on the significant findings in this study.

Table 7: Number of Visits to Doctor Per Family Member Per Year By Whether Household Owns a Radio (Household Sample)

		Utilization					
		High	Low				
Own Radio	Yes	10	8	18			
	No	3	9	12			
		13	17	30	Q	=	.58

Socioeconomic Factors

In discussing the various approaches to the study of health facility utilization, McKinlay (1972:140) raises serious questions about the advisability and adequacy of relying on any one approach to accurately explain or predict health behavior. For heuristic purposes, he identifies categories which have been used in the past and highlights the importance of the economic and sociodemographic approaches. We will first consider aspects of the economic approach.

Wealth. It has been repeatedly demonstrated that income level is a major determinant of the use of medical services.

> A vast literature exists in the United States which links family and individual income to the utilization of . . . various facilities. [McKinlay, 1972:119]

In a country like Great Britain—a somewhat better parallel to the Indian situation where care is available through the National Health Service—studies by Rein (1969) and Kadushin (1967) have shown these "barriers" to be somewhat reduced. However, even in Great Britain,

> There is no firm evidence that a nationalized, relatively efficient and free health and welfare service has been able to eradicate the variations by social class in the rates of use of certain "freely available" facilities. [McKinlay, 1972:120]

In village India, where class distinctions are intricately woven into the complex social fabric of caste, isolating the income/wealth factor is even more difficult. This study, however, draws from available data those indicators which begin to distinguish economic levels: land ownership, land usage, mean wage levels, and ownership of transportation vehicles. The hypotheses developed for utilization behavior are then based on the general assumption that the larger the financial and capital resources of a particular village and/or its inhabitants, the greater the awareness and use of neighboring health facilities.

Numerous studies conducted in various cultural settings heavily support the tentative assertion in this study that various indicators of wealth are related to higher utilization levels. A general conclusion drawn by Aday and Eichhorn (1972:23) in this regard is that "in the past, the higher the income, the greater was the volume of physician services consumed."

Although three indicators of wealth—i.e., irrigation level, percent of crops marketed, and average wage—are rejected by the data at the .05 level, a less direct, but more reliable measure of wealth—number of bicycles/100 population—was strongly related to utilization.

Thus, the measure of number of bicycles/100 population (dismissed earlier as an inappropriate measure of intervillage mobility) serves as a highly visible indicator of wealth. For the large majority of villagers, a bicycle is considered a luxury. (There are only 500 in the entire block.) One could assume that a higher percent of bicycle ownership in a village would be indicative of a higher disposable income and thus a greater propensity and financial ability to seek public or private medical care whenever needed.

As reported earlier, together with presence/absence of a cooperative, the square of bicycles/100 population explained the most variance in utilization. The bicycle variable when squared reflected a predicted relationship with utilization which is curvilinear in shape. This procedure resulted in the amount of variance explained by the model. The "best model," developed during stepwise regression analysis, includes the continuous variable of number of bicycles/100 population and the dichotomous variable of presence or absence of a cooperative. Together with a wealth indicator (number of bicycles squared), the percentage of variance explained (R^2) went up from .41 to .47 with the addition of the cooperative variable increasing the explanatory power of the model. The regression equation is shown in Table 8 and is displayed graphically.

The presence of a cooperative in a village does tend to increase the utilization of the village as a whole by some incremental amount, although the shape of the curvilinear relationship between utilization/100 and bicycles remains the same. The entire curve shifts upward approximately one unit of utilization for every three additional "bicycle units." As far as wealth is concerned, for every additional "bicycle unit" of wealth, a village will tend to increase its utilization of the primary health center at an increasing rate.

The significance of the wealth factor in the model highlights for microplanners a common dilemma—poorer and lower status villages and individuals

Table 8: Relationship Between Utilization/100 and the Number of Bicycles/100 and Existence of a Village Cooperative ("Best Model")

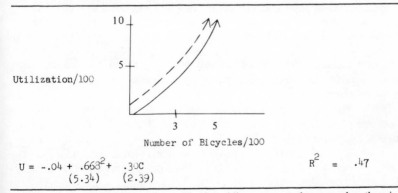

Utilization/100

Number of Bicycles/100

$$U = -.04 + .66B^2 + .30C \qquad R^2 = .47$$
$$\quad\quad\quad (5.34) \quad (2.39)$$

a. The t ratios are shown in parentheses. The dotted line represents the curve when there is a village cooperative (C = 1).

who probably could benefit most from more frequent utilization of curative health services tend to use them the least. In placing facilities and services in the more developed and centrally located settlements, this problem will likely be exacerbated.

For the community worker, intervention techniques could be geared to serve specific income groups and a detailed strategy developed to determine whether the focus should be on low, middle, or high income villages or groups.

Literacy. In turning to the sociodemographic determinants of health behavior, we begin to address a series of factors which, although limited in their explanatory power, are crucial to our understanding of utilization patterns.

While on the surface sociodemographic factors appear to offer quite plausible explanations for utilization behavior, with the exception of age and sex differences, most empirical findings have failed to reveal in much depth why variations exist. Age and sex are important predictors of utilization, primarily because of their close association to morbidity patterns among the very young, the old, and women (due to problems related to obstetrical care).

> The medical sociological literature is replete with examples of the "established" inverse relationship between socio-economic status . . . and illness (and, by extension, utilization behavior). [McKinlay, 1972:121]

Primarily for methodological reasons, however, these findings have recently been challenged by Kadushin (1967) and McBroom (1970). Their studies point out the tendency for lower status persons to overreport and perhaps to express anxiety in more physical terms. Nevertheless, utilization tends to be directly related to higher socioeconomic status.

In the area of education, the literature supports the contention that

> consumption of physicians' services increases as educational level increases, primarily due to the greater use of preventive services by the better educated. [Aday and Eichhorn, 1972:19]

Although literacy rates and educational level are in no way conceptually interchangeable, the same direction of the relationship with utilization is presumed in this study.[24]

In the literature on modernization and innovation adoption, literacy has consistently stood out as a significant explanatory factor in health as well as in other developmental sectors. The ability to read and write at a functional level can open up entirely new vistas for an individual and provides, often for the first time, a powerful tool for shaping a family's own destiny (Freire, 1972; Shingi et al., 1973). Therefore, a postulation for this study was that public health facility utilization would show a significant positive relationship with the literacy level of the village as a whole. Although hypotheses related to the rate of increase in literacy rates did not prove to be significant, of all the socioeconomic measures tested, *the literacy rate for the total population was the best explanator of utilization*[25] (r = .337) and was significant at the .05 level. Individual level data, as shown in Tables 9 and 10, confirm these findings.

Thus, for both the village community and the individual, *whether one is literate does make a difference in whether public health care is sought.*

The important role that literacy plays in determining health behavior is perhaps not as meaningful a finding to the micro-planner as to the community worker. For the community worker, it can serve as a key guide in ordering intervention priorities at both the individual and village level. Thus, instead of focusing on health education in working with families in a village, he might suggest that certain family members pursue literacy training. On the village level, the same general policy could be followed and efforts made to start a literacy club as a means of achieving a number of long-range goals, including increased public health facility utilization.

Caste. Another important sociodemographic predictor of utilization involves ethnicity. Aday and Eichhorn (1972:20) cite Anderson's research and at least a dozen other related empirical studies in concluding that "race predicts the volume of services consumed and . . . these relationships are independent of income differences."

In an Indian setting, where within a single region race is usually not a factor,[26] the question of social status is more likely to be determined by caste membership (and linguistic differences in many areas of the country). As a system of social stratification, caste in many ways can imply a more rigid set of role expectations than the ascribed status of race and the achieved status of class combined. Its impact on Indian society has been, and continues to be, pervasive (Rudolph and Rudolph, 1967).

As a predictor of health utilization, caste is suggested as a major factor independent of interrelated socioeconomic characteristics. It is assumed that members of higher status castes are likely to be offered more respect and better care at local health centers, which could lead to their more frequent use of available services. It is interesting to note the Government of India's efforts in every region of the country to formally identify low status castes as "scheduled" or "backward."

Table 9: Number of Visits to Doctor Per Family Member Per Year By Whether There was a Literate Member in Household (Household Sample)

		High	Low			
Someone in	Yes	12	11	23		
Household	No	3	5	8		
Literate		15	16	31	Q =	.30

Table 10: Number of Visits to Doctor Per Family Member Per Year By Whether There Was a Literate Member in Household

		Utilization			
		High	Low		
Literate	Yes	59	33	92	
Respondent	NO	66	69	135	
		125	102	227	Q = .31

The hypotheses was that *villages which have a higher percentage of scheduled caste families will tend to have lower utilization levels.* Although a more comprehensive look at the influence of caste would have involved a ranking of all castes in the area, this would have involved some highly interpretative background research beyond the scope of this study. Thus, the indicator selected provides only a rough estimate of the "caste factor."

The caste factor was a significant one at both the village and individual levels. From the household sample, Table 11 shows the relationship between caste and utilization.

Measures of caste usually tend to have high intercorrelations with other socioeconomic status indicators. This was the case in our study as well. The relationship, for instance, between literacy rates and caste is fairly strong—across villages, r = .380, among individuals, Q = .47.

Obviously, the problems of literacy, caste, and many other existing socioeconomic conditions cannot be seen in isolation and, as with caste, may subsume many other related factors.

Membership in a scheduled caste does seem to be one key indicator of socioeconomic status and can also serve as a useful guide for the micro-planner in identifying village utilization patterns. Perhaps, therefore, the community health worker needs to develop "caste-specific" intervention methods for promoting public health facility utilization. In other words, given that there are

Table 11: Number of Visits to Doctor Per Family Member Per Year By Whether a Respondent Was a Member of a Scheduled Caste (Household Sample)

		Utilization			
		High	Low		
Caste	Scheduled	3	7	10	
Membership	Non-scheduled	12	9	21	
		15	16	31	Q = -.51

Table 12: Whether a Respondent's Family Is a Member of a Scheduled Caste
By Whether Head of Household Is Literate (Household Sample)

	Non-scheduled Caste	Scheduled Caste		
Literate	17	6	23	
Not Literate	4	4	8	
	21	10	31	Q = .47

differential utilization rates for low and high status castes under current
conditions, a wise idea might be to develop more suitable approaches for each of
the various caste groupings.

THE NEED FOR REPLICATION

What has this study shown and what kinds of issues has it left unexamined?
We have shifted rapidly from a general discussion of the conceptual issues
involved in utilization analysis to a background presentation of specific problems
related to community work and health in India. This process, relying heavily on
a set of empirical findings, provided the structure for an evaluative look at
community work in the health sector.

Summary of Findings

The significant findings show spatial and institutional considerations (distance
and the presence of a credit cooperative) used in the growth center planning
process to be of critical importance in explaining utilization patterns across the
village sample. Socioeconomic factors, such as wealth, literacy, caste, and the
existence of village leadership with vertical ties outside the village are also shown
to be significant determinents of utilization levels across villages. The most
powerful predictive model explaining public health facility utilization included
village wealth levels and the presence of a village cooperative. None of the
measures in the community work intervention group of variables were found to
have a significant measurable impact on utilization. Findings from correlation
and regression analysis of village level data were generally confirmed by the
subsequent analysis of the individual level data from the sample of households
and public health facility users in Talala Block.

Each of these findings provides some initial practice guidelines for more
effective intervention in that they underscore the importance of increasing
physical accessibility to the health centers, raising the general level of literacy

and standard of living and encouraging more indigenous village level associations within the village as effective means of encouraging health care utilization. In short, they suggest ways for community workers to reorder priorities to accomplish at least one task in the health sector.

Limitations of Study

Some attention must also be given to the limitations inherent in this kind of study. First of all, findings are not statistically generalizable to areas outside of Talala Block or to sectors other than health, although implications drawn may have some practical relevance to micro-planners and community workers in health who are active in similar areas in the country. It is assumed, however, that factors which explain utilization of social facilities will tend to vary from one sector to another, and practice implications drawn for community workers and micro-planners will also vary. Therefore, generalizations to those involved in agriculture, education, and so forth are clearly not justified.

Second, the selection of utilization as the dependent variable in itself considerably limits the scope of the investigation to only one aspect of a broad public sector commitment to providing curative *and* preventive health care services. Although utilization analysis is a small slice of a whole complex of goals, it deals with a concrete behavioral outcome common to many community workers. For the micro-planner, it provides a very critical measure of accountability, i.e., whether decisions made in allocating scarce resources lead to efficient utilization levels. In each case, utilization analysis serves the dual function of providing insights into the planning and provision of a social service delivery system.

CONCLUSION

In discussing the future of community work and planning methods in India, Ensminger (1972:32) states:

> we must accept the fact that the beginning point is where the people live and they most certainly live in villages. . . . The role of the village level extension worker as a stimulus to village change must be reaffirmed.

As is suggested by findings in this study, more selective use must be made of community work as the intervention strategy of choice. Use at this time in *all* sectors may not be the most effective allocation of available skilled personnel. Although in some sectors, community work may prove to be an essential intervention tool, in others it may have significantly less impact on changing a target community's behavior than perhaps a carefully planned increase or strategic relocation of a particular service or facility. If a litmus test of community work intervention is observable behavior change, then one way community workers can begin to seriously evaluate their efforts is to identify specific change objectives in the community and their contribution to achieving them.

Social work practitioners at the individual and group level continue to be hard pressed to assess the impact of their intervention (Fischer, 1976). At the community level, the problem of evaluation remains equally difficult involving a complex array of individuals and organizations. Accordingly, evaluators of community work intervention efforts should begin to break down the substantive areas (or sectors) in which they are active; select suitable and measurable indicators by which to monitor change; and assess their impact across discrete community units (i.e., villages, neighborhoods, catchment areas, etc.). By doing this, designs similar to the one used in this study could be replicated in various sectors and in different economic and cultural contexts. Although results initially very likely would be mixed, a pattern would begin to emerge which showed under what conditions community work is the preferred strategy of intervention.

Perhaps with this kind of approach to evaluation—replicated in each sector—one could begin to address the question raised by Goldstein (1973:217): "Given the identification of the particular units in their relationship to the problem or task, what is the most efficient and economic point of intervention?"

This study of utilization behavior in the health sector is only a small step in this overall process. By identifying significant spatial, institutional, and socioeconomic antecedents of utilization behavior, it provides the community worker in Talala Block with a working framework to begin to reassess current tactics and strategies. For those active in other community work programs in other countries, this study serves as a challenge to expand our knowledge base, to examine the strengths and weaknesses of our own intervention efforts, and to learn and apply what we discover in the process.

NOTES

1. The term community work will be used in this paper to connote the activities usually associated with community organization and community development.

2. The term sector is used in this study to describe an aspect of development policy, such as health, agriculture, transportation, education, and so forth.

3. Certainly other excellent models for evaluating community work programs exist (see, for example, Taylor, 1965; Suchman, 1967; Government of India, 1960, 1961; United Nations Research Institute on Social Development, 1970).

4. A development block is an administrative unit created as part of India's Community Development Program. It usually contains 100 to 200 villages with a total population of 100,000 to 200,000. There are usually several blocks within the various districts in each state.

5. The Pilot Research Project in Growth Centers was a five year Government of India sponsored rural planning project partially funded by the Ford Foundation, with technical assistance from the Council for Social Development, to which the author was attached during an internship with the University of California's Berkeley Professional Studies Program in India (1973-1974) at the Delhi School of Social Work, Delhi University.

6. Abernathy and Moore (1971:24) have been quite specific in this regard: "Successful planning, implementation and evaluation of regional health services programs requires a prior understanding of the utilization patterns inherent to a region's population."

7. Although more comprehensive measures of health attitudes and behavior than utilization have been developed and tested, they have not been evaluated in the context of an existing system of available facilities and services. For example, innovation adoption literature has produced several informative studies identifying the characteristics of innovators (see Rogers, 1962, 1969). In the health field, Roy and Kivlin (1968) have developed a composite index of health attitudes and behavior which includes measures of health knowledge, visits to doctors, vaccination and immunication behavior, and so forth. The extent to which they have been useful to actual decision makers in the field has been somewhat limited.

8. Eleven of the 49 villages in the study block were excluded from correlation and regression analysis since they had either their own public health center or residents were using one other than the Primary Health Center in Talala town. To arrive at a "best model," various combinations of independent variables were added in a successive "stepwise" fashion until a model was found which explained the most variance in the dependent variable.

9. Berreman (1963:93), for example, quite explicitly states: "the contemporary rural community in India is simply not structured for democratic egalitarian self-administration." He calls for a reappraisal of the program's ambitious goals.

10. Some studies (Bendix, 1964; Ensminger, 1972) have critically analyzed the decisions made by Nehru and other Indian leaders shortly after Independence to establish a village-oriented, nationwide community development program. The program could have been postponed another 10 to 20 years until the country could gain more experience in community development, train superior staff, gather better and more extensive data, and have at their disposal sufficient resources to invest more efficiently and according to a plan. Ensminger (1972:18) comes to the conclusion that, given the political realities, Nehru could not have made any other decision. He could not deny the demands of the millions in the over 500,000 villages of India.

11. The general method used involves identifying "central places" or "growth centers" by ranking the various settlements in a micro-region (block or district) according to size, institutional development, spatial criteria, direction and flow of people for various goods and services and under unique characteristics of a particular village, and then deciding upon a hierarchical framework of "service centers" (called a General Settlement Plan). The strategy is based to a large degree on the concepts developed by Walter Christaller (1933) who introduced Central Place Theory as it related to wholesale commodity distribution. For a concise summary of the project's overall goals and methodology, see Shah (1974).

12. It is estimated that approximately 250,000 physicians from the *ayurvedic* (traditional Hindu), *Ruani* (traditional Muslim), and homeopathic indigenous traditions practice in the country, 60% of them in rural areas. This compares to an estimate of about 115,000 allopathic physicians, fewer than a third of whom are found in the rural areas (Gwatkin, 1974:80-81).

13. Except for vacancies due to turnover, the State of Gujarat has fully staffed all of its primary health centers.

14. Caste, perhaps the most important delineation of social status, also usually defines the occupational role of its members. There are hundreds of caste and subcaste groups throughout India. In this part of Gujarat, the Patels are considered a relatively high status

caste. They tend to be landed cultivators in this area. Kolis are a lower caste, usually involved in farm labor. Certain castes, like the Kolis and Harijans (untouchables), are designated as "scheduled" by the government, which defines its members as socially and economically "backward" or disadvantaged, and often targets them for special government programs.

15. When the village is the unit of analysis, the actual measure is number of users per village per unit of time. In the household and health center samples, the measure is number of visits to a doctor per family member per unit of time.

16. The Rosenstock model is concerned with the psychological motivational determinants of health services utilization. Suchman presents a more sociologically oriented model for health utilization behavior. The most recent and comprehensive health utilization model has been suggested by Anderson. In a recent research summary, Aday and Eichhorn (1972) catalogue the major indices and correlates of health utilization.

17. Throughout the following section, utilization/100 will refer to the number of persons/100 population of each village who utilized the Talala Primary Health Center in Talala town during 1971. One limitation of the growth center utilization data is that it only reports the number of persons per village who used the primary health center at least once during the year of 1971. Thus, it is not a measure of the number of total trips by the village as a whole.

18. A correlation matrix including all factors significant at the .05 level and used in subsequent regression analysis is shown below:

CORRELATION MATRIX

	U	D	B	L	F	C
Utilization/100	–	–	–	–	–	–
Distance	−.415	–	–	–	–	–
Bicycles/100	.590	−.384	–	–	–	–
Literacy	.342	−.338	.006	–	–	–
Families (scheduled caste)	−.259	.154	−.162	−.380	–	–
Cooperatives	.203	−.085	−.158	.370	−.355	–

19. Respondents in both the household and health center samples reported that public bus and train service during the few months when the roads are open and passable is often of critical importance in being able to travel to health centers.

20. In Talala Block, since 1974, and elsewhere, increasing use is being made of mobile units to provide health care to isolated rural areas.

21. In Talala Block in 1970-1971, there were 39 cooperative credit societies in operation with a total membership of 6,079, representing over 50% of the 11,116 families in the block. The first society began in 1952-1953 with 29 members, growing rapidly in number to 36 cooperatives by 1965-1966 with over 5,000 members.

22. The third example is found in another village (Chitravad) in the northern part of the block. It is the only village in the entire district to have built and staffed its own village-supported health center. Most of its residents are followers of the Aga Khan religious community and have been able to establish a trust fund to financially support the center through the international Aga Khan community. Here again, village leaders have been influential in establishing its health program to a large extent because of higher level organizational ties outside the village.

23. Other measures of communication outside the village were also rejected by the data. The variance of the indicator based on number of newspapers was too small to warrant analysis. (They were rarely available in most of the block.) The degree of outside contact, measured by number of letters in and out of the village, was also found not to be significant at the .05 level.

24. This should particularly hold true when the mean levels of educational attainment are quite low in an area; and having some schooling is, at best, synonymous with the attainment of basic reading and writing skills.

25. Female and male literacy rates showed somewhat lower correlations of .34 and .31, respectively. Each of the three measures were highly intercorrelated.

26. A rare exception to this situation is found in the area of southern Gujarat, where this study was conducted. A small enclave of Siddis—a group of descendents from former African slaves in the region—live in Talala Block and are in the sample studied.

REFERENCES

ABERNATHY, W.J., and MOORE, J.R., Jr. (1971). Regional planning of primary health care services. Stanford, Calif.: Stanford University School of Business.

ADAY, L., and EICHHORN, R.L. (1972). The utilizations of health services: Indices and correlates. Lafayette, Ind.: Purdue University.

AIKEN, M., and ALFORD, R.R. (1970). "Community structure and innovation: The case of public housing." American Political Science Review, (September).

ANDERSON, R. (1968). A behavioral model of families' use of health services. Chicago: University of Chicago. Chicago Center for Health Administrative Services Studies.

ANDRADE, P. (1970). Urban and regional planning in India in the seventies. New Delhi: Ford Foundation.

BANERJI, D. (1973). "Health behavior of rural populations: Impact of rural health services." Economic and Political Weekly, 7(51):2261-2268.

BENDIX, R. (1964). "Public authority in a developing political community: The case of India." Pp. 215-298 in Nation-building and citizenship. New York: John Wiley.

BERREMAN, G. (1963). "Caste and community development." Human Organization, 22(spring).

BHATTACHARYYA, S.N. (1970). Community development: An analysis of the programme in India. Calcutta: Academic Publishers.

BIDDLE, W., and BIDDLE, L. (1968). The community development process: The rediscovery of local initiative. New York: Henry Holt.

BRADSHAW, J. (1972). "The concept of social need." New Society, 496(March 30):640-643.

BUCHANAN, J. (1968). The demand and supply of public goods. Chicago: Rand McNally.

CHRISTALLER, W. (1933). Die Zentralen Orte in Suddeutschland. Jena, Germany: Gustav Fischer Verlag.

Council for Social Development and Ford Foundation (1969). Preliminary report on pilot projects for integrated area development: Two case studies. New Delhi, India.

DAMLE, Y.B. (1956). "Communication of modern ideas and knowledge in Indian villages." Public Opinion Quarterly, 20(spring):257-270.

DAS GUPTA, S. (1968). Social work and social change: A case study in community development. Boston: Extending Horizons Books.

DENUNE, P.P. (1927). "The social and economic relations of the farmer with the towns in Pickaway County, Ohio." Colombus: Ohio State University Bureau of Business.

DUBE, S.C. (1958). India's changing villages: Human factors in community development. London: Routledge and Kegan Paul.

DUNHAM, A. (1968). "Community development—Whither bound?" Social Work Practice, pp. 48-61.

ENSMINGER, D. (1972). Rural India in transition. New Delhi: All India Panchayat Parishad.

FELLIN, P., ROTHMAN, J., and MEYER, H.J. (1967). "Implications of the socio-behavioral approach for community organization practice." In E. Thomas (ed.), The socio-behavioral approach and applications to social work. New York: Council on Social Work Education.

FISCHER, J. (1976). The effectiveness of social casework. Springfield, Ill.: Charles C Thomas.

FRANKEL, F. (1971). India's green revolution. Princeton, N.J.: Princeton University Press.

FREIRE, P. (1972). Pedagogy of the oppressed. New York: Herder and Herder.

Gandhigram Institute (1972). "Work manual for health inspectors." Bulletin of the Gandhigram Institute of Rural Health and Family Planning. India.

GANGRADE, K.D. (1968). "The change agent in community development: India's village level worker." International Review of Community Development, 19-20:309-326.

GHILDYAL, U.C. (1967). Objectives of community development. Hyderabad, India: National Institute of Community Development.

GILBERT, N., and SPECHT, H. (1977). Coordinating social services: An analysis of community organizational and staff characteristics. New York: Praeger.

GOLDSTEIN, H. (1973). Social work practice: A unitary approach. Columbia: University of South Carolina Press.

Government of India (1946). Report on the health survey and development committee. New Delhi: Ministry of Health.

――― (1957). A report on the conference held at New Delhi on September 10-11, 1956, to discuss the social and cultural factors in environmental sanitation in rural India.

――― (1960, 1961). Summary of evaluation study (1954-1960). New Delhi: Planning Commission, Programme Evaluation Organization.

――― (1969). Report of Conference on Review of Behavioral Research in Health and Extension Education. New Delhi, India: (May 19-20).

――― (1972a). Health in India. New Delhi: Ministry of Health and Family Planning, Directorate General of Health Services, Central Health Education Bureau.

――― (1972b). Second progress report on the pilot research project in growth centres. New Delhi: Central Research Cell. Department of Community Development.

GUPTA, R. (1971). The Musahri plan. New Delhi: Association of Voluntary Agencies for Rural Development.

GWATKIN, D. (1974). Health and nutrition in India. New Delhi: Ford Foundation.

HUNTER, G. (1970). The administration of agricultural development: Lessons from India. London: Oxford University Press.

KADUSHIN, C. (1967). "Social class and ill health—The need for further research." Sociological Inquiry, 37(spring):323-332.

KAKAR, D.N., SPRINIVAS, A.K., and PARKER, R.L. (1972). "People's perception of illness and their use of medical care services in Punjab." Paper presented at Seminar on Behavioral Research in Health and Medical Care, sponsored by the International Council of Medical Research, March 15-18, New Delhi.

KIVLIN, J.E., ROY, P., FLIEGEL, F.C. and SEN, L.K. (1968). Communication in India: Experiments in introducing change. Hyderabad: National Institute of Community Development.

KUNKEL, J.H. (1970). Society and economic growth. New York: Oxford University Press.

LERNER, D. (1958). The passing traditional society. Glencoe, Ill.: Free Press.

LEWIS, O. (1955). Village life in northern India: New York: Vintage.

LIEBAN, R.W. (1973). "Medical anthropology." In J.J. Honigman, Anthropology. Chicago: Rand McNally.

McBROOM, W.H. (1970). "Illness, illness behavior, and socioeconomic status." Journal of Health and Social Behavior, 11(December):319-326.

McKINLAY, J.B. (1972). "Some approaches and problems in the study of the use of services—An overview." Journal of Health and Social Behavior, 13(June):115-152.

MEHTA, B.G. (1972). Emerging patterns of rural leadership. New Delhi: Wiley Eastern Private Ltd.

MILLER, L., and PRUGER, R. (1975). "Two activities of social services: Maintenance and people changing." Mimeo (November).

MOORE, B. (1966). "Democracy in Asia: India and the price of peaceful change." Pp. 314-410 in Social origins of dictatorship and democracy. Boston: Beacon.

NAIR, K. (1961). Blossoms in the dust. London: Gerald Duckworth.

NEURATH, P., and MATHUR, J.C. (1959). An Indian experiment in farm radio forum, national union catalogue, 1956-1967. Paris: UNESCO.

NIEHOFF, A.H. (1966). A casebook of social change. Chicago: Aldine.

PANDE, V.P. (1967). Village community projects in India. Bombay: Asia Publishing House.

REIN, M. (1969). "Social class and the utilization of medical care services: A study of British experience under the national health service." Hospitals, 43(July1):43-54.

ROGERS, E.M. (1962). Diffusion of innovations. Glencoe, Ill.: Free Press.

——— (1969). Modernization among peasants: The impact of communication. New York: Holt, Rinehart and Winston.

ROSENSTOCK, I.N. (1966). "Why people use health services?" Health Services Research I, Milbank Memorial Fund Quarterly, 44(July):94-127.

ROSS, M.G. (1955). Community organization theory and principles. New York: Harper and Row.

ROY, P., and KIVLIN, J. (1968). Health innovation and family planning. Hyderabad, India: National Institute of Community Development.

RUDOLPH, L., and RUDOLPH, S.H. (1967). The modernity of tradition: Political development in India. Chicago: University of Chicago Press.

SANDERS, I.T. (1958). "Theories of community development." Rural Sociology, 23(1):1-12.

SEN, L.K. (1972). "A new strategy for community development: Planning for integrated area development and rural growth centres." Pp. 27-36 in L.K. Sen (ed.), Readings on micro-level planning and rural growth. Hyderabad, India: National Institute of Community Development.

SHAH, S.M. (1974). "Growth centers as a strategy for rural development: India's experience." Economic Development and Cultural Change, 22(2):215-228.

SHANNON, G.W., BASHSHUR, R.L., and METZNER, C.A. (1969). "The concept of distance as a factor in accessibility and utilization of health care." Medical Care Review, 26(2).

SHINGI, P.M., FLIEGEL, F., and KIVLIN, J. (1973). "Literacy, alternative links with the larger society and argricultural development." Behavioral Sciences and Community Development, 7(1).

SINGH, K.N., and SEN GUPTA, T. (1965). "Measuring effectiveness of village level workers." Indian Journal of Public Administration, 11(1):42-55.

SUCHMAN, E. (1965). "Social patterns of illness and medical care." Journal of Health and Human Behavior, 6(spring):2-16.

——— (1967). Evaluative research: Principles and practice in public service and social action programs. New York: Russell Sage Foundation.

Tamil Nadu Nutrition Project (1973). Nutrition as a function of public health: Nutrition related morbidity in Tamil Nadu. Madras, India: Sidney M. Cantor.

TAYLOR, C. (1965). India's roots of democracy: A sociological analysis of rural India's experience in planned development since independence. New York: Praeger.

TERRELL, P., and WEISNER, S. (1976). The social impact of revenue sharing. New York: Praeger.

THURSZ, D., and VIGILANTE, J.L. (eds., 1975). Meeting human needs: An overview of nine countries. Beverly Hills, Calif.: Sage.

United Nations Educational, Scientific and Cultural Organization (1959). Measuring results in development projects. Paris.

United Nations Research Institute on Social Development (1970). Contents and measurement of socio-economic development: An empirical inquiry. Report No. 70.10. Geneva.

VEEDER, N. (1975). "Health services utilization models for human services planning." Journal of the American Institute of Planners, 41(2):101-109.

WANMALI, S. (1970). Regional planning for social facilities: An examination of central place concepts and their application, case study of Eastern Maharashtra. Hyderabad, India: National Institute of Community Development.

WARREN, R. (1963). The community in America. Chicago: Rand McNally.

——— (1966). "Community change: Planned or otherwise." Pp. 176-186 in V.M. Sieder (ed.), The rehabilitation agency and community work: A source book for professional training. Washington, D.C.: United States Department of Health, Education and Welfare, Vocational Rehabilitation Administration.

APPENDIX

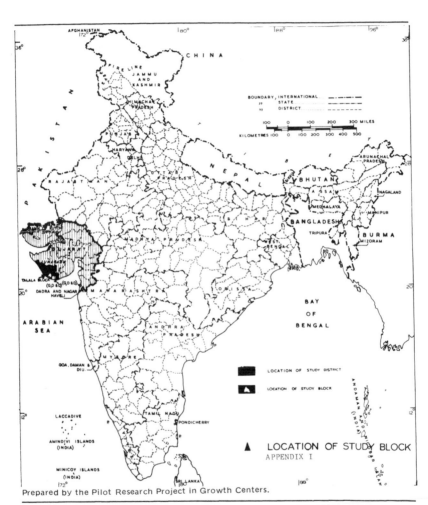

Prepared by the Pilot Research Project in Growth Centers.

Figure 1.

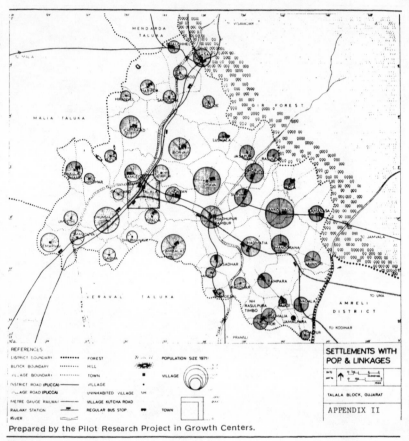

Prepared by the Pilot Research Project in Growth Centers.

Figure 2.

14

SWITZERLAND AS A NEIGHBORHOOD: LOCAL SERVICES DELIVERY

DORIS ENGELMANN

Switzerland represents a rather unique form of societal organization. Thus, in order to obtain any real sense of the nature of local services delivery, we must briefly examine this organization; establish what constitutes a local unit; define the meaning of neighborhood; identify some types of services; and explain who performs them. In this paper a special attempt will be made to convey the spirit and philosophy underlying the services rather than to develop a comprehensive survey.

DEMOGRAPHY, HISTORY, AND ECONOMY

Switzerland's central location has been a major determinant of its historical and political development. It occupies a scant 16,000 square miles in the center of Europe and has a population approaching 6.5 million. It is approximately one-third the size of New York State, and its population is less than that of New York City. Yet it holds within its boundaries an extremely complex society reflecting its Celtic, Roman, and Teutonic religious and linguistic heritages. The language frontiers established in the Middle Ages remain practically unchanged

AUTHOR'S NOTE: *The writer wishes to thank Dr. Mauro Martinoni for facilitating access to the Cantonal Social Service Agency of Ticino and Dr. Emma Morin for providing relevant material on this program. Further assistance in gathering data and reviewing the manuscript was provided by Mr. Hermann Buff, Office of the Permanent Observer of Switzerland to the United Nations.*

to this day, with the predominant language being German (65%), followed by French (18%), Italian (12%), and Romansh (1%).

The origins of the Swiss Confederation date back to 1291, when the freedom of the districts was threatened by the rise of the Habsburg rulers. At this time what became known as the three Forest Cantons (Forest States) entered an eternal pact to help each other in the defense of their respective independence. This oath was strictly one of mutual aid, but it came to represent the core of the current political framework. The importance of this alliance—which defended individuality rather than attempting the unification of its participants—cannot be overstressed. It developed into a particular form of federalism which is difficult even for other democracies to grasp and which permeates every fiber of the country's social fabric.

Nearly six centuries passed before a central government was established and a constitution drafted in 1848. The purpose, however, was not to limit the cantons in favor of the federation, but to declare and protect their sovereignty. They were to be autonomous in all matters except those delegated by them to the federal government. Direct democracy in the form of the referendum, however, made even the powers vested in the central authority ultimately subject to the approval of the Swiss electorate. Since the confederation renounced territorial expansion, its stance with regard to foreign powers became, by necessity, one of neutrality. The federal government was charged with defending this position. (Currently Switzerland maintains an "armed" neutrality for self-defense. While it has no professional army, all able men between ages 20 and 50 are periodically trained and eligible to serve; and military weapons and ammunition are kept by them in their homes.)

Switzerland's geography has been the major determinant of its economic development. There is little physical uniformity in the land-locked web of valleys, rivers, and lakes which radiate from the peaks of the alpine chain spanning the country. Less than one third of the land is suitable for agriculture and living space. The only abundant natural resource is water, now used for the production of hydroelectric power but hardly a base for economic independence. Through ingenuity and hardwork, however, ways have been found of using this energy to develop specialized and precision products from imported raw materials for maximum resale value. The prosperity created by industrialization almost completely replaced the meager pastoral and agricultural existence, and today Switzerland enjoys one of the highest standards of living among industrialized countries.

SOCIAL SERVICES

Development

In keeping with the strong tradition of individualism of the original league, help was expected to ensue from the direct relationship of a person in need to one able to help in his immediate family, work-community, or neighborhood. Social work was defined as the "organized help of the strong for the weak, of the community for the individual" (Steiger, 1948).

The earliest providers of services beyond primary relationships were, as was the case for most preindustrial societies, the various religious organizations. The Reformation sparked a flurry of activities in which religious practices and social work overlapped in the care provided to the sick, the old, the young, and the indigent. Because Swiss practicality placed more weight on concrete tasks than ideologies, religious beliefs often became secondary to humanitarian ideals. The Protestant visiting nurse, a familiar figure of the present, dates back to the 16th century.

Catholic services had a slower development and were based strictly on Christian motivations until the 19th century, when a more active movement gave rise to many religious orders whose endeavors were particularly in the area of education; the hospitals of the Middle Ages endured as "poor houses."

As the Age of Enlightenment brought expansion in so many areas, there was a propagation of humanitarian societies with a religiously and politically neutral foundation. Their purpose was the

promotion, encouragement, and dissemination of all that is good, laudable, and of public value, and which enhances and increases the dignity, well-being and happiness of the citizen, the person, and the community. [Steiger, 1948]

However, regardless of the orientation or denomination of the various organizations, the nature of the services delivered by most was mainly in keeping with the spirit of neutrality in the budding democracy. Services were based more on basic human rights and the principle of self-determination rather than on a particular ideology. Conflicts of interest arose mostly in conjunction with the educational services which were often declined by strongly religious groups.

Organization of Social Planning

The organization of social services has not followed a planned course concerned with basic questions of social development. Rather it has been a residual approach with emphasis concentrated on practical problems and meeting the demands of different circumstances, people, and times. Modern social services still rely largely on voluntary organization. Direct services include both "public" and "private" ones. The distinction, however, is not a hard-and-fast one, for "public" does not necessarily equate with mandatory, or "private" with voluntary. Actually, most public services are provided on a voluntary basis, while many private organizations receive public funds for the provision of mandated (as well as voluntary) services.

In the spirit of democratic federalism and local autonomy, initiative and provision rest almost exclusively with the local level and are entrusted to philanthropic and charitable organizations and to communal authorities. The role of the federal government as a direct provider of services is a minor one compared to many other countries and is limited in most part to foreign aid and emergencies created by wars and natural catastrophes. Because the focus of the central government is not on self-expansion nor the strengthening of its authority but is on facilitating the realization of individual human needs, there is little political motivation to encourage the establishment of social policy for provision of services. This attitude (combined with the particularism described earlier) results in minimal government intervention, the latter taking place only when individual and collective self-help efforts and the provisions of voluntary agencies do not prove sufficient. Nevertheless, while the government abdicates its powers of control, it is still considered financially responsible for the well-being of its people; and many of the cantonal and private services are subsidized with federal funds. Federal and local expenditures for health, education, and welfare are five times larger than the national defense budget. The structure of these federal subsidies is a complex one and reaches all levels, particularly favoring programs based on self-help, rehabilitation, and integration into the mainstream of society.

Because social policy is largely a matter of cantonal competence, there is much variation according to the political as well as economic structure of each of the 25 cantons. Predominantly industrial cantons with their prevalence of city population have many laws regulating the protection of workers, and agrarian cantons have provisions favoring farmers. Through legislation, cantons generally have assumed responsibility for regulating public welfare (poverty), education, and those services falling under the jurisdiction of police authority (minors, guardianship, and correction). Other services differ widely from one canton to another. Local autonomy is paramount in the northeastern regions, where cantonal services are generally limited to supporting municipal and private organizations. In the French-speaking cantons, however, which tend to have a more centralized structure, there is much influence with the provision of cantonally run programs.

On an even more direct level of government within the cantons, there are the local communes which have become increasingly more active and lead to further variation in the delivery of services to their inhabitants, even though the majority of these services are not legally prescribed. There are 3,000 Swiss communes. The commune is the smallest politically independent unit of government. It consists of one or more geographic units, such as villages or towns.

The prevalence of voluntarism has resulted in a dynamic adaptation to the needs of the people but also has led to the duplication of some services and the lack of others. This type of fragmentation has made optimal use of available

resources difficult and accountability nearly impossible. However, these problems generally have been considered as endemic to decentralized federalism and
a price well worth paying for the maintenance of communal independence and
local control and diversified Swiss life. Nonetheless, the need for coordination
has been felt since the beginning of the century, and strictly voluntary efforts
produced some measures of cooperation among agencies. The results were the
formation of well-known nationally active denominational associations such as
the "Swiss Association for Evangelical Charity" (Protestant), "Swiss Caritas
Association" (Catholic), and "Association for Swiss Jewish Welfare Societies";
and several nonsectarian nationally organized private institutions: "Pro
Juventute" (for youth), "Pro Infirmis" (for the handicapped), and "Pro
Senectute" (for the aged). Therefore, even though the central planning boards of
these organizations limit their activity to economic and technical matters
(allowing for diversified local delivery), they represent no small accomplishment
in a country which regards centralization with great suspicion.

Finally, a brief word must be mentioned regarding Swiss social policy and
women. Due to their position of social inferiority and the absence, until this
decade, of woman suffrage, women have been prevented from having any
influence on public policy or occupying positions of leadership and authority.
Thus, while they do constitute the majority of the working force and therefore
can exercise more initiative in the voluntary and private spheres, they still
seldom occupy executive posts. This is a condition which, because of the slow
workings of direct democracy coupled with Swiss conservatism, can be expected
to be a difficult one to eradicate.

Specific Services

Public social services consist mainly of social insurance programs which have
been approved by the people and are federally mandated. But even the area of
centralized programs does not represent a unified entity. The only assistances
which approach universality are the Federal Old Age and Survivors Insurance
(comparable to social security in the United States) and disability insurance,
which benefit every eligible person to the same extent. All persons are eligible
for Old Age and Survivors Insurance, regardless of whether they have been
gainfully employed (and therefore contributed) or not. Persons unable to
function productively because of physical or mental deficit are eligible for
federal disability payments. They are centrally organized and financed but
administered by the social service departments of each canton. Accident
insurance is compulsory for most forms of employment, applies equally to all
cantons, and is managed by a central national agency. Unemployment insurance
was recently accepted by popular vote and became compulsory early in 1977.
Even though it was supported as much for economic reasons as for social
reasons, the adoption of compulsory unemployment insurance is considered by

many to be a turning point in Swiss social policy, representing a move away from individual responsibility and autonomy. Health insurance (although recently prescribed for certain population groups) is based on the self-help principle and is considered a temporary measure. It is therefore decentralized and varies widely. Guidelines and enforcements are delegated to the cantons, many of which pass the responsibility on to the individual communes. The same is true for family allowances, which are prescribed but not uniformly applied. Education is strictly a cantonal matter, with the national government insuring only its compulsory status. Cantons provide medical and dental care through the schools. Health services in general (including mental health) are implemented by private, voluntary, and cantonal or communal institutions. The federal government engages in research and prevention of epidemics. In most cantons, individual communes are responsible for the welfare of indigent citizens. Communes are responsible for their residents, even though they may originate from other cantons or countries. This is evidence of the humanitarian rather than political roots of services in general. The communes are also responsible for protective and correctional youth services.

Social Work as a Profession

The very nature of social work in Switzerland presents organizational and practical problems because it has the task of backing up a wide variety of services. This supplementary character leaves social work without distinct goals, theories, and interventions which it can call its own. We have seen that social services encompass a variety of fields. These, rather than specific activities, have become the means through which social work attempts to improve the quality of life. Social work is therefore not a discrete field, but a conglomerate of helping efforts carried out by various people in many different areas of practice.

Professional social work did not appear until well into the 20th century. Until then help was administered either by volunteers whose regular activity lay outside the field of social services, or by religious orders whose purpose was to assist others and who provided diverse training for their members. Volunteer work was (and is) considered the bulwark of social work because it builds on self-help, a principle greatly cherished by the Swiss people. A large part of the work performed by the associations mentioned earlier is still done by volunteers who also fill many of the executive positions of these organizations. Social services as they exist now would be impossible without the countless hours of selfless dedication with which religious personnel participate in the care of the needy, particularly in hospitals and institutional settings.

Professionals in the field are those persons who are paid for their work. They include not only social workers, but also all types of nursing and special education personnel (including physical and occupational therapists). Until recently, hospital and institutional housekeeping aides were also included. The duties, prerogatives, and goals of social workers have never been clearly defined or unified, and are generally determined by the milieu with which they interact.

Education

Several schools of social work throughout the country provide professional instruction. They are independent institutions without university affiliation, and graduates receive a diploma rather than an academic degree. Universities have only recently included lectures on social welfare problems as part of the curriculum of other disciplines. The course of study in social work is not at all comparable with that generally followed in the United States. It concentrates on practice settings (e.g., welfare, residential settings, industry), rather than on generic or methods principles. These schools are intended mostly for women. Male social workers usually come from a teaching or administrative background.

LOCAL SERVICES IN THE CANTON OF TICINO

To illustrate the spirit of independence which underlies the delivery of all services, the structure and nature of the local service network in one of the Swiss cantons, Ticino, will be described here in detail. As has been pointed out, services vary greatly from one area to another, and probably none of the cantons could be said to be typical of the others, least of all Ticino, which constitutes a cultural and linguistic minority. However, the essence of Ticino is representative of the unifying force which runs throughout the whole country and which manifests itself in the delivery of all services.

Ticino is the southernmost canton, occupying a wedge of just over 1,000 square miles, whose borders dip into northern Italy. It is known as Italian Switzerland, the vast majority of its 300,000 inhabitants being Italian speaking. The population is predominantly Catholic, and distributed among 247 communes, only three of which are considered to be "cities" of from 15 to 30 thousand inhabitants. Bellinzona, Lugano, and Locarno are Ticino's three largest cities. Although one of the main north-south transporation routes of Europe—the St. Gotthard line runs through the canton—all its contact points with the rest of the country are over arduous mountain passes, creating serious problems of isolation in the past. The internal geography poses similar problems on a smaller scale. Innumerable valleys and streams, along which villages and towns are scattered, intersect each other with access ways leading over or around the mountains which separate them. This complex layout, however, makes for the very picturesque geography which has been sought out by Swiss and foreigners alike since the late 1800s and which (in the Swiss tradition of turning adversity into advantage) has enhanced the canton's major industry: tourism. However, in comparison to the very high level of industrialization of most of the rest of the country, Italian Switzerland (which has no major production industries and also disposes of very limited cultivatable land) is in a relatively underpriviledged economic position. The emphasis here is on relationship, since even in this part of the country the living level can be considered high by Western standards. Who, then, are the recipients of the welfare provisions mentioned earlier?

Definition of Neighborhood

In most cases an entire village or town is the neighborhood. The size varies from a few hundred to a few thousand people. In the case of very small villages the neighborhood often transcends the physical boundaries of the village to include neighboring communities, not only in spirit but also politically. Two or more villages often have a communal government in common. The physical separation between these "neighborhoods" makes them into distinct political units; and their independence, as we have seen, is only in small part subject to the cantonal government, and is practically untouched by federal impositions. The neighborhood is where issues are ultimately resolved, and the heat of neighborhood political debates is rarely rivaled at the higher levels.

The economic picture is a different one. Self-sufficiency is practically unattainable except for a few urban neighborhoods. This feature reflects the country's dichotomy of political independence and reliance on the outside for economic stability. The general prosperity of the canton is the product of a complex pattern of interdependence. The alliance of small villages into political neighborhoods is determined by practical and economic factors. A village of a few hundred people or less is too small to provide employment to all of its workers, so they commute to a nearby community or to the city. Or a neighborhood may be too small to be able to furnish all the needed services on its own. It may have a doctor, a priest, and, in most cases, an elementary school but not its own dentist or enough people to support a hospital, a high school, or a supermarket. Specialized professionals, in many instances even the doctor and priest, are commonly shared not only by the villages within a commune, but also by politically independent communes. Several of the villages and/or communes will unite and attempt to pool their resources and will turn to the state only as a last resort. Neighborhood services, therefore, are not always located within the confines of the neighborhood as defined. On the surface this may look like a move toward centralization, but, in fact, it is the consequence and product of decentralization at work.

Informal Services

Private associations (such as "Pro-Juventute") began their formal and organized activity in Ticino during the first three decades of the century. Formally regulated public services did not appear until the mid 1940s. Until then, and long thereafter, the network of assistance available to the people was a largely informal although an often public one, concerned primarily with providing help in the form of financial or material aid. Anyone having witnessed poverty in other parts of the world would be hard pressed to use the same word for the conditions likely to arise in the communities in question. This is not to say that poverty did or does not exist in them, but it would be more fittingly described as a very modest standard of living.

Forty years ago the predominant social unit was still the extended family. A person experiencing financial difficulties would be most likely to turn to a family member for assistance. If this failed, a friend might help or recommend someone who could. If these were unsuccessful, the priest would certainly find a way out either from church funds, through a charitable organization, or by taking the person's plight to the municipal authority. Such transactions were handled with great discretion since no one wanted to publicize his distress. While help would always be forthcoming in the form of food, clothing, shelter, and/or money, the recipient would be frowned upon unless, through personal effort, he rapidly recovered from his state of need. To become temporarily indigent was a misfortune. To remain in this condition was a shame. For these reasons, services stressing self-help and rehabilitation were favored both privately and publicly. Problems of adjustment to stress situations were treated through the same channels; the priest was the main source of support outside the family.

The extended family dealt with marital disputes by mediation or threats, at times necessitating the intervention of the neighborhood authority. Children who could not be cared for by their families generally became a ward of the commune and were placed in foster homes or in private custodial institutions. What was then called "insanity" was not an uncommon occurrence and was attributed to alcoholism and inbreeding. Insane people were often kept in the family, hidden as much as possible from the outsiders' view. If the mentally ill became unmanageable, they could be taken to a public state mental hospital which had been in existence since 1898. Adults and children with debilitating mental or physical handicaps were also usually hidden away to vegitate. The resources of the ten budding "Pro Infermis" could not reach everyone, and families generally were not looking to be reached and expose their misfortune. This stigma of infirmity is one which persists into the present. The Italian language refers to handicapped persons as "disgraziati" (out of grace), an indication of deep-seated attitudes implying a certain culpability on the part of the afflicted. It is interesting to note that in a country which is built on the rights of the individual, one encounters considerable intolerance of deviations from the norm.

During this time of mostly informal service systems there was no such thing in Ticino as a professional social worker. They slowly began to appear as services became more formalized.

Formal Services

The Cantonal Neuropsychiatric Hospital was the only formalized service available at the turn of the century. Later a drug and alcohol abuse unit was added. Today it is still the only public psychiatric facility "for the treatment of all mental and nervous illnesses" (quoted from the Department of Social Service), and therefore serves all neighborhoods. The care of its 800 patients follows a strictly medical model, and no social workers are on the staff. A social worker recently deployed there by the canton was found not to be able to be "professionally useful" (observation by the Cantonal Social Service Agency) in this milieu. Mental patients are admitted by medical certificate. Substance abusers are committed by the authorities if they get involved with the law. Because conditions are good and treatment adequate, this facility is not considered a "snake pit," but the stigma of mental illness makes it a place of last resort and its occupants are not talked about. They continue to be "hidden."

The first voluntary associations to exercise organized activities were the nationally administered "Pro Infirmis," "Pro Juventute," "Pro Senectute," and "Caritas." Today because they offer specialized services, they are centrally located and remain outside the boundaries of most neighborhoods. Their outreach is done through publications to alert the public to their availability. The actual link-up, however, still takes place through informal contacts, due to the fact that the facilities are physically removed. All these agencies, with the exception of the one dealing with the aged, provide funds and equipment to persons in need primarily of special education, physical rehabilitation, vocational training, or any activity leading to the productive integration of the person into society. Only individuals totally incapable of functioning receive noncategorical assistance. The employment of social workers by these institutions has become customary in recent years.

In 1944, Ticino was the first canton to assume the financial responsibility for the welfare payments administered by the communes. This "depersonalization" of the service removed some of the stigma, and today welfare payments are routinely requested and granted. However, they are still considered a temporary measure, and habitual recipients are an exception. This is a purely financial transaction available in all neighborhoods with no social work intervention at all. The same is true of federal social insurance payments delivered by the communes.

Social Service Agency

The postwar years brought an increase in the use of available services and a beginning awareness of problems other than financial of physical. Major changes, however, did not begin to take place until the early 1960s when a survey by the cantonal Department of Social Services (an administrative body) revealed that more than 3,000 children under the age of 18 were being cared for outside their families. The extent of this condition caused considerable alarm, and a problem which had gone largely unnoticed became a public issue. Legislation with the purpose of protecting minors and regulating their care and placement soon was passed. It also became apparent at this time that administrative vigilance alone could not promote the changes needed, and a cantonal Social Service Agency was established in 1963 with the purpose of handling the social aspect of the problem. It was to focus on minors, but was expected to expand to include all groups. Later legislation created the addition of separate but coordinated services for the protection of mothers and infants and of the aged. These have offered nursing, home health, and home aide services, along with a variety of consultations of a preventive nature. They have built, sponsored, and regulated old age homes, and provided leisure time and vacation opportunities. Even though the auxiliary services have availed themselves of the assistance of social workers from the Social Service Agency, they have mostly provided concrete services.

The Social Service Agency was the only agency in which social work was the predominant profession. It employed about 40 workers and represented the first effort to transcend or complement purely material support. The agency did not reach the neighborhood level directly but operated out of three districts. Its efforts were directed mainly at providing emotional support and guidance (along with meditation, information, and referral) to families which found themselves dealing with a variety of authorities and institutions (e.g., police, guardianship, foster homes). Services centered around problems of care for their children. Existing needs of clients, combined with agency eagerness to intervene, produced a great amount of intake and counseling activity based upon the necessities of each individual case. While this may look like a perfect example of "individualization," it created a number of problems.

The first and foremost was one of breakdown in the system of task distribution. We have seen that the federal government delegates many responsibilities to the cantons and they, in turn, delegate to the communes, along with the authority to carry them out. In the case of the Social Service Agency, the canton delegated responsibility without executive authority or legal power. The result was that recommendations made by social workers could be accepted or rejected at will by the authorities handling the cases, often leading to decisions which were contrary to the principles of social work. Due to the positive or negative close interpersonal relationships which were likely to exist between the neighborhood authorities and the clients, these decisions were not always objective and impartial. The position of the social worker toward the client became an ambiguous one, not conducive to the establishment of a constructive relationship. The lack of clarity of the role of the social workers, which was not unique to this situation, created confusion for the workers, clients, and authorities alike.

A second major problem area concerned the emphasis on individual "cases" which often neglected the nature and influence of the environment while concentrating on its consequences. This often produced inaccurate diagnosis leading to inappropriate intervention. Furthermore, a personal relationship often took the place of a professional one when the focus was on the case rather than on planned action. It was also found that, in the pursuit of individuality, workers were not operating on a common theoretical base. The 40 social workers employed by the Cantonal Social Service Agency are graduates of 15 different schools.

All of the problems had practical repercussions which resulted, at best, in inefficiency. Yet when the shortcomings became apparent, and efforts were initiated to correct them, another obstacle appeared. The experimental nature of the agency had created a very cohesive group of workers on both a personal and professional basis. However, this cohesiveness showed a tendency of becoming part of a closed system, impervious to outside influence and reluctant to move to new types of activities. This, combined with the newness of the operation, accounted in large part for the complete lack of interventions at the group level and the total obscurity of community organization. On the other side was the reticence of the people to accept something new before they even had a chance to get accustomed to the still unfamiliar figure of the social worker.

The situation has continued to be complicated by the fact that recent years have witnessed a period of rapid social change, and new problems have arisen which are undermining the relative equilibrium not only of Ticino, but of the country in general. Swiss industry has traditionally depended on foreign labor, and unemployment has not been among Switzerland's problems. The rising economy at the start of the decade, however, began the demand for a heavy influx of outsiders. One-sixth of the total population and one-third of its labor force of three million is comprised of foreigners. Because these workers are often accompanied by their families and are granted the same privileges as indigenous people (save the right to vote), a very heavy stress has been placed on existing social resources such as schools, hospitals, police, fire, and sanitation services. The problem of economic assimilation has been additionally compounded by the cultural differences which have upset the traditional patterns of territoriality. Since most foreign workers come from Italy, Ticino has not had to contend with a language barrier. However, its position as a border canton has made it the target of most initial contacts and of a large number of workers from border towns who commute and eventually establish residence. These arriving foreign families are usually escaping from poverty in their own country and are likely to need assistance in establishing themselves.

Local residents have tended to resent the above situation, and there is a climate of general unrest, aggravated by the recent period of economic recession. Legislation was enacted to regulate immigration, but a popular initiative aimed at drastically limiting immigration has been repeatedly defeated due to the numerically stronger industrial vote. The latter have accused their opponents of xenophobia.

These difficulties have added to the problems of the Cantonal Social Service Agency, yet they have also signalled the beginning of a new awareness in a previously complacent population. Attitudes are changing, and people are starting to view services as part of their rights and themselves as potential consumers. The Social Service Agency, aware of internal and external problems, has begun an elaborate reorganization effort aimed at evolving a theoretically unified baseline service responsible to local demands. Unfortunately, there is no mention of consumer participation in the planning process. Progress has not yet reached this stage.

CONCLUSION

In Switzerland it is difficult to separate a description of the entire country's social service system from that of its neighborhoods because of the interrelationship of the two. The country's structure determines the working at the local level, and the communes carry the national spirit.

The services examined are intended for a relatively healthy society striving to preserve its integrity. The impact of the modern world has introduced factors which add universal problems to those endemic to the area. Both neighborhoods and services now are undergoing a period of transition which necessitates a careful reevaluation of needs and goals. Some of the problems are the consequence of no planning.

There is a general reluctance by the people to view the social component of problems. There is also a certain lack of therapeutic sophistication, especially in Ticino, which has resulted in a lag of the "social" element of services. Social work as a profession is in its infancy both in its utilization and in terms of development of skills, methodology, and goals.

REFERENCES

Repubblica e Cantone del Ticino (1971). Legge sull'assistenza sociale. Bellinzona.

Servizio Sociale Cantonale del Ticino (1972). Punti di reflessione sul cosiddetto laboratorio. Bellinzona.

——— (1974). Proposte operative per il servizio sociale cantonale. Bellinzona.

——— (1975). Seminario.

——— (1976). Seminario.

STEIGER, E. (1948). Handbuch der Sozialen Arbeit der Schweiz. Band I, vierte Auflage. Zurich: Art. Institut Orell Fussli AG.

Swiss National Conference on Social Welfare (1969). "Social Welfare in Switzerland." Zurich: Separatdruck aus Schweizerische Zeitschrift fur Gemeinnutzigkeit, 108. Jahrgang.

NOTES ON THE CONTRIBUTORS

JACQUELINE ANCELIN, after studying law at the University of Law in Paris, was trained as a nurse and then as a social worker. With a Rockefeller fellowship, Ms. Ancelin received special training in public and mental health both at Harvard School of Public Health and Simmon's School of Social Work in Paris. She has worked in the public health center in Soissous, France, and for the National Federation of Family Allowances Agencies in Paris. Since 1969, Ms. Ancelin has been Sous Directeur at the National Fund for Family Allowances.

MICHAEL J. AUSTIN is Professor and Director of the Center for Social Welfare Research, University of Washington School of Social Work, Seattle. He received his Ph.D. and MSPH at the University of Pittsburgh and his MSW in Community Organization at the University of California, Berkeley. Dr. Austin taught for six years at Florida State University School of Social Work and served for several years as a Regional Social Work Consultant (Denver) for the National Institute of Mental Health. He is the author of several books and numerous articles.

URI AVIRAM heads the Community Mental Health Program at the School of Social Work, Tel Aviv University, Tel Aviv, and holds a special appointment in health behavior and community medicine at the Department of Social Medicine of the Hebrew University, Hadassah Medical School in Jerusalem. Dr. Aviram obtained his doctorate in Social Welfare from the University of California at Berkeley. He is a member of the Advisory Committee on Mental Health to the Israeli Ministry of Health.

DANIEL BRACHOTT is currently Medical Adviser to the Israeli Ministry of Health. Dr. Brachott obtained his M.D. degree at Hambur University and his DPH at Liverpool University, School of Public Health. He is the former chairman (1964-1974) of the Department of Preventive and Social Medicine of the School of Medicine of Tel Aviv University, where he continues to serve on the faculty. Formerly (1965-1975), he served as the Deputy Director General of the Ministry of Health, and Director of Public Health Services.

ELIZABETH BROOKS received her MSW in advanced social work from Toronto University. She has held professional positions in Canada and Zambia before joining the teaching staff of the University of Zambia, where she has taught social work since 1971.

DORIS ENGELMANN, born and educated in Switzerland, where she earned her degree in Business Administration, has been living in the United States since 1962. Ms. Engelman received her B.A. and a Master of Social Work degree at Adelphi University. She is currently employed at Creedmore Psychiatric Center in New York, and her previous experience includes work with the developmentally disabled, psychiatric casework, and community outreach activities.

DONALD V. FANDETTI received his doctorate in social welfare from Columbia University in 1974. Currently, he holds the position of Associate Professor of Social Policy at the School of Social Work and Community Planning, University of Maryland. Before entering teaching and research, he held positions as a practitioner and administrator in public and voluntary service agencies in Rhode Island and New York State. Dr. Fandetti's main area of interest has been in the structure of organization of social services in our communities, with a long-standing interest in social class and ethnic factors in the delivery of social services.

CHESTER D. HASKELL is currently Associate Director of the Washington Public Affairs Center of the University of Southern California. Previously, Mr. Haskell served as Director of Public Management Training at the National Center for Urban Ethnic Affairs. He has worked closely with Arthur Naparstek over the past three years in developing policies and strategies supportive to the revitalization of communities. Mr. Haskell received his B.A. from Harvard University and his M.A. from the University of Virginia.

ALFRED J. KAHN is Professor of Social Policy and Social Planning at the Columbia University School of Social Work. He also is codirector, Cross-National Studies of Social Service Systems and Family Policy. Dr. Kahn has served as consultant to federal, state and local agencies, to voluntary organizations, and to foundations concerned with the planning of social services, income maintenance, child welfare and related programs, international collaboration, and social policy generally.

SHEILA B. KAMERMAN is Associate Professor, Social Policy, Hunter College School of Social Work, City University of New York Graduate Center, and codirector, Cross-National Studies of Social Services and Family Policy, Columbia University School of Social Work, She is a graduate of New York University. She has an MSW degree from the Hunter College of Social Work and received a doctorate in Social Welfare from Columbia University.

EUGENE LITWAK is currently a professor of sociology and social work at Columbia University. He received his Ph.D. from Columbia University Department of Sociology in 1958. Dr. Litwak has written many articles on the changing character and role of families in modern societies. He is currently doing a study on how families act as a natural support system which complements the role of large formal organizations in the field of aging.

DAVID MACAROV is a director of the Joseph J. Schwartz Graduate Program for training community center directors and senior personnel, which is jointly sponsored by the Schools of Social Work and Education at the Hebrew University of Jerusalem. He holds a B.S. from the University of Pittsburgh, a MSW from Western Reserve University, and a doctorate from Brandeis University. He is a member of the Editorial Board of the *International Journal of Social Economics* and is author of *Incentives to Work* and *The Short Course in Development Activities.*

ARTHUR J. NAPARSTEK is currently Director of the Washington Public Affairs Center of the University of Southern California. In addition, he serves as Principal Investigator on a four year research and demonstration project from the National Institute for Mental Health to provide more adequate and accessible mental health services to white, ethnic, working-class populations in urban environments. Previously, Dr. Naparstek was Director of Public Policy Research at the National Center for Urban Ethnic Affairs. He received his Ph.D. from the Florence Heller School of Social Work of Brandeis University.

VUKANI G. NYIRENDA received his DSW from the University of California at Los Angeles. He is currently the Registrar at the University of Zambia. He has taught social work at the same University. Dr. Nyirenda is author of a number of articles on social work, social work education, and social policy in African journals.

HOWARD A. PALLEY is Professor of Social Policy at the School of Social Work and Community Planning, University of Maryland. He has written widely on issues of health and social welfare. His articles have appeared in the *Social Service Review, Policy Studies Journal,* and the *American Behavioral Scientist.* Professor Palley has recently coauthored a book entitled *Urban American Public Policies.*

MEYER SCHWARTZ is the Dean of Simmons College School of Social Work in Boston. He has served as Community Development Advisor to the United Nations in Israel and the Republic of China. He received his MSW at Case Western Reserve University and his BSS at the City College of New York.

BRIAN SEGAL received his B.S. from McGill, his MSW from Yeshiva University, and his Ph.D. from Pittsburgh University. Currently, he is coordinator of the Social Administration and Policy Program in the School of Social Work at Carleton University. He is at present conducting extensive research and planning on correctional and social welfare manpower development as well as acting as a policy consultant to government.

DANIEL THURSZ is Dean and Professor of the School of Social Work and Community Planning of the University of Maryland at Baltimore. He has served in this capacity since 1967. Prior to that time he was the Associate Director of VISTA, the United States Domestic Peace Corps, established as part of the Office of Economic Opportunity. He has held a number of important positions in social welfare and has been a leader in the National Association of Social Workers in the United States. Born in Morocco, Dr. Thursz has maintained close links with several centers of social welfare development throughout the globe.

JOSEPH L. VIGILANTE is the Dean of the School of Social Work at Adelphi University in Garden City, New York, where he has served since 1962 in that capacity. Prior to joining the Adelphi University faculty in 1955, Dr. Vigilante was a caseworker and a child welfare worker in New York and Wisconsin. He has served as a consultant to a number of state and federal agencies. He has served on the national level with the National Association of Social Workers and is a member of the Board of Directors of the Council on Social Work Education.

STAN WEISNER is currently a lecturer in the School of Social Welfare University of California, Berkeley. Dr. Weisner has taught and conducted research in the United States and abroad. He has authored *Professional Social Work in Kenya–Training and Performance* (1972) and has recently coauthored studies on Title XX planning and *The Social Impact of Revenue Sharing* (1976) with Paul Terrell. Dr. Weisner received his MSW from the University of Minnesota (1969) and his DSW from the University of California, Berkeley (1976).

PETER WESTLAND graduated at Durham University and qualified as a social worker at the London School of Economics. He has worked as a Probation Officer and as an Inspector of Probation and After Care Services at the Home Office. In 1966, he became a Deputy Children's Officer in an Inner London Authority and, since 1971, has been Director of Social Services for the London Borough of Hammersmith. He is Social Services Advisor to the Association of Metropolitan Authorities.

SUBJECT INDEX